Roger Martin du Gard and Maumort

Roger Martin du Gard (1881–1958), De Agostini Picture Library, used with permission from Getty Images.

Roger Martin du Gard and Maumort

~

THE NOBEL LAUREATE AND HIS UNFINISHED CREATION

BENJAMIN FRANKLIN MARTIN

NIU Press / DeKalb IL

Northern Illinois University Press, DeKalb 60115
© 2017 by Northern Illinois University Press
Printed in the United States of America
26 25 24 23 22 21 20 19 18 17   1 2 3 4 5
978-0-87580-749-2 (cloth)
978-1-60909-208-5 (e-book)
Book and cover design by Yuni Dorr

Library of Congress Cataloging-in-Publication Data
Names: Martin, Benjamin Franklin, author.
Title: Roger Martin du Gard and Maumort / Benjamin Franklin
    Martin.
Description: DeKalb : Northern Illinois University Press, 2017 |
    Includes bibliographical references and index.
Identifiers: LCCN 2016015948 (print) | LCCN 2016031474
    (ebook) | ISBN 9780875807492 (cloth : alk. paper) | ISBN
    9781609092085 (ebook)
Subjects: LCSH: Martin Du Gard, Roger, 1881–1958.
Classification: LCC PQ2625.A823 Z716 2017 (print) | LCC
    PQ2625.A823 (ebook) | DDC 843/.912 [B] —dc23
LC record available at https://lccn.loc.gov/2016015948

Contents

Acknowledgments

Four of them there were, Roger Martin du Gard, the 1937 Nobel laureate for literature, Hélène, his wife, Christiane, his daughter, and Marcel de Coppet, his best friend and then his son-in-law. During the late 1930s and early 1940s, Martin du Gard was one of the most famous writers in the Western world. His works, especially *Les Thibault*, the two-thousand-page-long roman-fleuve that the Nobel Committee specifically mentioned, were translated into English and read widely. Today, he is almost unknown, to a great extent due to his leaving unfinished the long novel he began after winning the Nobel Prize, *Lieutenant-Colonel de Maumort*. *Maumort* initially seems to be an account of France's experience during World War II and the Occupation seen through the eyes of a retired army officer, but it becomes a morality tale, questioning, by Maumort's series of recollections, every received value of late nineteenth-century and early twentieth-century European civilization, however imbued by religion or by culture or by wealth. It was eventually published in fragmentary form in 1983 and translated into English in 2000. Even incomplete, *Maumort* is a work of surpassing brilliance, the pages haunting the reader long after they are turned, long after the book is set aside.

I have sought to recover the life of Martin du Gard, recover the lives of the three people closest to him, and so explain the genius of his literature and the cause of his decline. For that purpose, he left behind after his death thousands of pages of journals and even more thousands of pages of correspondence. To outsiders, these four were private, reserved, even secretive. They were so because by birth and formation they were very members incorporate of the French bourgeoisie. But with each other, behind this veil, they were passionate and combative. They tore each other apart with their words and their deeds. To the extent possible, I have let them tell their own stories. As a historian, I am traditional and old fashioned. The use of theory to explain the past and its literature holds no appeal for me. I believe that choice, or the refusal to choose, determines the fate of lives and the content of books. Certainly, Martin du Gard thought so as well.

My extraordinary and superb editor, Amy Elizabeth Farranto, strongly urged me to write this book and then cheered every chapter. No writer could ever have a greater blessing. As editor-in-chief at Northern Illinois University Press, she and her colleagues, Linda Manning, director, Nathan Holmes, managing editor, and Yuni Dorr, head of design and production, create worthy, fascinating, and beautiful books. Melissa Rebecca Wheeler assisted with the research, and Josie Abigail Stokes expertly compiled the index. My grand friends, Nicolas Kariouk Pecquet du Bellay de Verton, James Merlin Seidule, Norman McClure Johnson, Nancy Revelle Johnson, Vaughan Burdin Baker-Simpson, John Raymond Walser, Jane Catherine Overton Scanlan, Tyler Caitlin Lott LeBoeuf, and Paige Ivy Bowers, offered discerning, incisive comments. Throughout the writing, Janis Kilduff Martin and Pandora Vasell-Martin have been my dearest companions. Eugen Weber introduced me to Martin du Gard's books four decades ago through his fascination for the first of them, *Jean Barois*. I always expected that he would take on explaining *Les Thibault* and *Maumort*, but shortly before his death in 2007, he told me that I would have to do so. As I was carrying out that assignment, Jacqueline Weber died in 2015, having read drafts of all but the last two chapters. I believe that they would be pleased with how I have completed this book.

Roger Martin du Gard
and Maumort

Chapter 1

ILLUSIONS

WHEN THE SWEDISH ACADEMY awarded the Nobel Prize for Literature to Roger Martin du Gard on December 10, 1937, its permanent secretary, Per Hallström, singled out the laureate's "most perfected tool: the analysis of his heroes' thoughts, expressed beyond words, an insight into the darkness which engenders conscious actions." In his acceptance speech, Martin du Gard echoed, declaring, "The born novelist recognizes himself by his passion to penetrate ever more deeply into the knowledge of man and to lay bare in each of his characters that individual element of his life which makes each being unique."[1] Yet in his personal life, he was so often incapable of comprehending even the men and women closest to him, above all his wife, daughter, and closest friend. With him, they performed a decades-long pas de quatre that culminated with the dancers tangled in positions of estrangement and recrimination.

A hint of explanation comes when Martin du Gard's last creation, Lieutenant-Colonel Bertrand de Maumort, muses late in life, "My whole private existence was thus spent, with neither scruple nor remorse, in that 'no-man's land' which stretches beyond the written law into that free, airy, 'esoteric' zone (but also steep and sown with pitfalls), where the members of the secret aristocracy live, the men who are not of ordinary stature, who know it, feel it, and cultivate themselves as such; and who, for this reason, consider themselves alone authorized to define the scope and bounds of their freedoms; in other words, to observe a moral code of which they themselves have set the terms."[2] They were, these words, the novelist's own confession.

And why not? He spent the first years of his childhood at the large country house of his maternal grandparents, the Wimys, on the crown of a hill in Clermont, a brief train ride into the department of the Oise just north of Paris. He recalled "the dignity, the reserve, the fundamental nobility of this wholesome little society ... which took as its task bringing happiness to others, loving children, encouraging work, relieving misery, . . . remaining faithful to the principles of justice and to the rules of domestic honor, and seeing old age as autumn after the season of flowers."[3]

Roger Martin du Gard was born on March 23, 1881, to a well-established family of France's judicial *grande bourgeoisie*. They were not "noble": the addition of "du Gard" to the surname "Martin" was merely to differentiate this branch of a large family from the others—as in "Martin des Bouchets" or "Martin de la Gardette." His parents lived in Paris's tony eighth arrondissement, with his father's prosperous law office (*étude d'avoué*) on the ground floor of their house at 31 Rue de l'Arcade. Maître Paul Martin du Gard had his own country house in much closer Maisons-Laffitte, fifteen miles away. Roger and his younger brother Marcel passed their adolescent summers there, with hardly a glance from their mother, Madeleine. Their father was present only during the evenings, heading in to his office and the civil courts each morning on the train with other lawyers commuting from Maisons-Laffitte. Madeleine's trip to the train station in the family's phaeton to pick him up on his return became a kind of ceremony, after which they all dined outside beneath the trees.

The children in the neighboring country houses became Roger's companions, especially Antoinette Dufour, who would marry another friend, Pierre Quentin-Bauchart, Hélène Hoche, with whom he became hopelessly infatuated, and Jean Werlé, two years older, from whom Roger learned that "babies are not discovered in the cabbage patch and that Père Noël does not come down the chimney." This loss of innocence hit him hard. Curiosity about sex evoked both fascination and shame. Roger knew that at the end of the summer he would have to make his confession: "I thought about it with terror. I was certain that my guilty obsession was one of those sins for which God had lit the infernal boilers." The Abbé Bonnefoy, then his priest at the church in Neuilly but destined to become bishop of La Rochelle and eventually archbishop of Aix-en-Provence, showed no great concern at this transgression. Roger left the confessional "not only reassured but secretly emboldened: I would have to venture much farther into evil before scandalizing a confessor and meriting Hell."[4]

Roger's early education came at the hands of a tutor, Silvestre de Sacy, who had a title, viscount, but no fortune, manners but little learning, and in the end almost no influence on him. The priests in charge of Roger's religious training took their task more seriously, and his mother required him to recite the catechism from memory. In vain, it seems. The ceremony of First Communion did indeed fascinate him, but only because of the cream foulard robe, the many expensive gifts, and the sumptuous banquet. One of his catechists, the

Abbé Coqueret, arrived late for the celebration because he was caring for his aged mother. After surveying the room and its symbols of wealth, "he looked at me in silence, his expression pensive and indulgent mixed with melancholy and surprise." For Roger, "from this day on, I became as bad a Catholic as I had been a bad student: I feared God and did not love him ... God would not exist for me."[5]

In 1892, when Roger was eleven years old, his parents enrolled him as a day student at the Ecole Fénelon, a private Catholic academy in Paris on the nearby Rue du Général-Foy where priests oversaw the moral formation of their students even while sending them for classes to the highly regarded Lycée Condorcet, a few blocks away. Roger fell under the influence of Abbé Marcel Hébert, the headmaster, who was a Catholic "Modernist," seeking to reconcile the church's dogmas with the nineteenth-century's discoveries in physics and biology. Pope Pius X condemned this effort without reprieve as heresy in 1907. Scientists had always considered it futile nonsense, as did Roger, whose religious belief was scant. But Hébert's vibrant personality attracted him, with Roger coming to admire him as a guide, far more so than his parents or anyone his own age, offering consolation not as a priest but as a mentor and, over time, as a true friend. Unfortunately, neither admiration nor guidance improved his attention to schoolwork. Fearing that Roger was foundering, his father decreed that he spend the first half of 1897—he was then to turn sixteen—as a border under the supervision of Louis Mellerio, from the faculty at the Lycée Janson-de-Sailly, a school even more distinguished than the Lycée Condorcet. Now, for the first time in his life, Roger was in the hands of a master teacher who evoked hard work and dedication. From the outset, Mellerio placed his extensive library entirely at Roger's disposal, encouraging him to read voraciously but discriminately. Also from the outset, he established a schedule for Roger's studies and demanded such hard work that afterward his student would write, "I left his hands equipped for life with a stock of knowledge, admittedly elementary, but precise and solidly anchored."[6]

On a trip to the north coast of Brittany with Mellerio and his wife in April 1897, instruction continued on the beach. Roger had to rise at 7:30, spend 8 to 10 on Latin, 10:30 to 11:30 on Greek, and then whatever time was left before lunch on German. He had afternoons off to read on his own, but from 5 to 7 he had to study French literature, history, and geography. After a light dinner, bedtime came early at 8:30—perhaps mercifully. All the better to prepare for hiking on off days: nearly six miles along the coast to Tréguier, with a break for "two dozen oysters, a round of bread, a block of butter," and strong wine. Then further to the nearby rocks at Trégastel and the isolated lighthouse on the pink granite at Ploumanach, kept by a widow with three children who had to get up three times each night to replenish the oil powering the lamp and brave winter storm waves that broke over the base of the tower. Even in mid-spring the wind and rain and cold made the sea an appalling danger: debris from the recent wreck of a fishing boat littered the shore.[7]

Starched by Mellerio, Roger entered the Sorbonne in 1898, enrolling in the courses for the arts degree, the *licence ès lettres*, but without the constant presence of his tutor, he quickly fell back on his lackadaisical habits. He did not sit for any of the first-year examinations and when he did take them in July 1900, he failed badly. He had neglected his Greek and Latin for *War and Peace*, given him by Abbé Hébert. He began dreaming about a career in literature, dreamed about writing, like Leo Tolstoy, long-winded novels with many characters and episodes. Of course his parents were upset. As Roger wrote later to a then close friend, Gustave Valmont, "My father is seriously worried about my future. He finds me poorly prepared for life, to the point of saying that if he had a daughter, he would surely hesitate before entrusting her to a boy like me. He says that I am 'without maturity of spirit' and will 'see life only through novels and dramas.'" Did Roger grasp that the family of Hélène Hoche would judge him far more harshly? Wisely, Paul Martin du Gard offered his son a compromise: if Roger prepared a backup career, he would bless an attempt at writing. Essentially on a whim—he called it a "sudden temptation" (*tentation subite*), Roger decided to enroll at the Ecole des Chartes, which since its establishment in 1821 had been the premier institution for the training of paleographers. With incentive now, he worked determinedly the rest of the summer and qualified for admission in October. Once there, he attended diligently to his courses, passed his examinations, and in the spring of 1902 began a thesis on the Benedictine Abbey of Jumièges, founded in 654 by the Merovingian Saint Philibert. During the Middle Ages, it was a vibrant beating heart of civilization but since its last restoration in 1573 had slowly crumbled into ruin.[8]

Roger and Gustave Valmont were both born in 1881 and were classmates successively at the Ecole Fénelon, the Sorbonne, and the Ecole des Chartes. Then, they would perform their military service in the same unit at Rouen. Over the period of a decade and a half, they exchanged nearly six hundred letters, but their friendship was always edgy and eventually collapsed in recrimination. Roger wanted Gustave to be a confidant and sounding board, but over and over the reverberation was critical and cold. Early on, Gustave described him as an "intellectual aristocrat," which Roger immediately recognized as a pejorative synonym for "amateur." He admitted to Gustave, "the capital and incorrigible defect that shadows my entire temperament is sloth. ... During my saddest hours, when I doubt the future, I find there my absolute condemnation, my mediocrity in everything." Such self-condemnation merely emboldened Gustave to rejoin that Roger had "a deplorable tendency to triviality, even buffoonery."[9]

But when Roger turned to comments on religion and on the social order, he trespassed, at first unknowingly, onto a sacred realm for Gustave. Believing that every young man of his circle questioned faith and authority, Roger was capable of writing: "The god that I find in the Bible is egotistical, wrathful, intransigent, and speaks only to threaten. Jesus has clearly not inherited the character of his father, for his is the religion of goodness and peace instead of the religion of menace and reprisal." Or: "Useless to tell you that next Easter will not see me approach a sacrament *of which no one can find the slightest origin in the Gospels.* Everything in religion is the work of the Church, of the early Church already opposed to the work of Jesus." And especially revealing: "I am 'uprooted,' having *morally* abandoned, at least in part, my origins, my traditions, my beliefs. I no longer have the faith of my father and my grandfather, not their tranquil self-confidence, not their modest bourgeois ambitions, not their voluntary acquiescence to all sorts of principles and customs.... Yet I hold on to them with all my might, I am bound to this past that I have sought to escape ... here is the moral disarray and intellectual anarchy into which I have fallen."[10]

In the summer of 1902 a familiar element of the social order interrupted their work at the Ecole des Chartes: Roger and Gustave were summoned to the army base at Rouen for the military service required of all French males upon turning twenty-one. This training usually lasted three years, but for the tiny elite who were pursuing "higher education"—at the Sorbonne, the Ecole Normale Supérieure, the Ecole des Sciences Politiques, the Ecole des Mines, the Ecole des Chartes, and so on—it was only twelve months. These favored few, 150 in all, found themselves grouped into a single unit, the "platoon of the exempt" (*peloton des dispensés*). In the evenings, they were "intellectuals," imagining the books they would write, the careers they would make. In these discussions, Roger made a number of friends, Jean-Richard Bloch, Georges Klincksieck, and especially Marcel de Coppet, who would supplant Gustave as his confidant. During the day, they became soldiers, expected because of their intelligence to learn rapidly both procedures and weaponry, expected because of their background to adopt rapidly the discipline and verve. Certain dangers were inevitable: one of their platoon died from the typhoid fever that haunted the barracks. Roger proved to be a good soldier, well-liked by his fellow recruits, and even wrote his mother in August 1903 as his term ended, "I am surprised not to be overjoyed. I have great apprehension about returning to civilian life."[11]

This sensation arose from the knowledge that his suit for Hélène Hoche had reached its denouement and failure. In May 1902, not long before he reported for military training, Roger hinted at what might be their future, but she replied that the "little she had seen of the world displeased her and that happiness lay in withdrawing from it." When Roger asked, "You mean a convent?" she answered, mischievously, "Why not?" He did not take her seriously, and his parents were thrilled at the possibility of this match: the only daughter of a prominent and wealthy family. In July 1903, Madeleine Martin du Gard approached the Hoche family on behalf of her son and was humiliated to learn that they had never even considered the possibility that Hélène might marry Roger. Her mother even declared, "We all like Roger so much, but there can be no question of him for Hélène, who is destined for someone much grander." Indeed, before the year was out, she married a slightly older man, himself an alumnus of the Ecole Fénelon, handsome, accomplished, and possessed of a great fortune. Roger put up a good face, writing Gustave, "I am astonished at being calm; I should be raving mad." The reaction of his two friends defined their attitudes toward him. Gustave replied evoking "these equivocal, humiliating, dubious circumstances . . . you must be suffering at least as much from a draining of your spirit as from the breaking of your heart." Marcel wrote, "your letter distresses me and plunges me into great sadness. . . . I understand and appreciate all that you suffer."[12]

At the age of twenty-two, Roger was privileged, indulged, indolent, and above all passive. As if he were adrift in the sea, the waves of life broke over him. Sometimes he thrust his head back above the roiling water, as during his year of military service or since his enrollment at the Ecole des Chartes. Sometimes he seemed almost submerged, as in his pursuit of Hélène Hoche or in his failure to write something—anything—that might justify his literary dreams. He might claim to know what he wanted, but too often he had little sense of how to get it. Even dilettantism was out of reach. Yet criticism from his parents or his friends, or the parents of his friends, distressed him as unfair. The burden was on him to prove them wrong by pulling himself to shore.

At home he heard the voice of doom. "I have had several ever-more serious talks with Papa. You see, their extravagant worry about my future leads them to a perpetual hostility against everything that I am doing and planning, leading me to suffer more than ever." And so at the Ecole des Chartes, Roger redoubled his efforts. Half a year later, by mid-1904, he ranked tenth in his class, and when he received his diploma as an archivist and paleographer at the beginning of 1906, he had moved up four more places. His thesis on Jumièges elicited high praise from his advisors, whose recommendation for publication led to its appearance as a monograph in 1909. At least in part, he had answered his father's doubts. As for his personal life, the humiliation of the Hoche family rejection was a signal challenge. He feared that he was unattractive to women. Some six decades later, his brother recalled, "For any-one who knew his good heart, his intelligence, his intuition, [he] could never be unattractive. But in truth, he was no Adonis: he held himself badly, his shoulders round and his back hunched. He could dance, but awkwardly and out of step with both the music and his partner. He did not play tennis or ride horseback or drive an automobile, although our parents were among the first to have one; he could not swim, despite going to the beach almost every summer." Marcel de Coppet would change at least the dancing. For the Martin du Gard set, Marcel was exotic and not entirely proper: a Protestant, whose father had abandoned his family after squandering his fortune, preparing for a career in colonial administration of France's African possessions. Roger solid-ified their friendship after the military training at Rouen, and in August 1904 visited his home at Quiberville, on the Normandy coast. Marcel insisted that Roger learn to dance *properly* and accept every invitation possible in the hope of meeting someone, a lovely someone, to assuage his heartbreak over Hélène Hoche. Soon enough he did, another girl named Hélène.[13]

Roger met her at a ball in March 1905. She was Hélène Foucault, eighteen years old, daughter of a Parisian barrister—Paul Martin du Gard was a solic-itor—practicing before the Paris Court of Appeal. The family was profoundly and piously Catholic, far beyond Roger's ability to grasp: he thought them merely "devout." She was innocent, naive, utterly unworldly, never before attracting the serious attention of a young man, never herself feeling attracted to a young man. Now, she was. As for Roger, he was besotted—perhaps in rebound from his previous Hélène. Once they revealed their love to each other, they began to imagine a life as husband and wife. Roger proceeded cautiously, avowing to her his agnosticism but promising that he would never trespass on her beliefs, promising that any children would receive a religious education, promising even to accompany her on occasion to Mass. Later when he regret-ted these promises, he recognized that he had been sincere. Hélène certainly believed him so—and almost certainly believed that God had invested her with the holy mission of guiding him to share her faith. She regarded her life as a responsibility and welcomed the opportunity for service and sacrifice. Although her family was wealthy, she had little regard for possessions beyond the minimum required for security. When Roger broached his plans for a career of writing that might not bring prosperity, might not even come close to the upper bourgeois existence of her milieu, she did not flinch. Instead, a marriage of shared privations—understood that the privations would not be severe—would weld them together all the more tightly.

In Roger's words, "All these questions, grave, profound, and intimate, had their hour of frank discussion and conclusion. We have a perfect accord, even on the most delicate matters ... the regime of reciprocal concessions has begun ... what unforgettable hours of abnegation and tenderness. The idea that I am loved, me, and with such subtlety, such delicacy, such intensity, makes me cry like a baby." They agreed that they should marry, but what of their parents and their blessing? Hers, the Foucaults, had come to love Roger for the love he inspired in Hélène and embraced him entirely. His were divided. "My mother was not difficult to convert: she had confidence in me and in my choice, whatever it might be. . . . My father said, 'I will not refuse you my consent because this matter is yours and I do not want to be at odds with you. But I consider this marriage a folly, that it will have for you and for the one you wish to entrap in this straitened existence, regrettable consequences that will damage your future.'"[14]

They became engaged on December 12, 1905, and then married on February 19, 1906. The night before, Hélène made this unfinished entry to the last page of the diary she had kept since childhood: "Oh my God, my life as a young girl is finished according to Your Holy Will. You have granted that life so many blessings, the greatest of which is the strength to love You. You have called me now to another existence, to duties greater and more important, but You have called me with the same goodness and the same tenderness. O my God, I was not worthy of so many blessings, it seems to me that I have been a spoiled child who did not deserve them. You have prepared for me a source of great joy. You have granted me love! You are going to make me taste in an ideal fashion the most wonderful things of this earth. Lord, I do not deserve it, I am not worthy. O Holy Virgin I confide to you my joy, keep it safe and especially without. . . ."[15] Had Roger read these words, would he have pondered his father's warning?

The commencement of married life gave not a single hint of trouble. During their wedding trip to the North African coast, Roger wrote to Gustave, "We have the perfect tranquility of a sure and stable happiness," and, "On every question, I find from my wife perceptive support that I would never dreamed to have so soon." Hélène encouraged his writing, and in the first days of their marriage, he began a book about a country priest that he planned to call "Une vie de saint" ("A Holy Life"). He would work on this manuscript in a desultory manner for nearly a year and a half until a negative reading by Gustave convinced him—rightly—to discard it. On their return from honeymoon, Roger and Hélène rented a "large bright, cheerful apartment at the corner of the Rue Printemps and the Rue de Tocqueville" in Paris's seventh arrondissement, only a little descent in prestige from his parent's address. A few months later, Hélène was pregnant, "doing well but only on the condition that she see no one and sleeps, sleeps, sleeps. . . . This little being already absorbs her life."

Further on, "We wish for a little girl with such ardor ... Hélène is well, even *very well* at this moment. During the first months, she was so weak and tired, but now she has completely recovered." And close to the appointed time: "It is truly serious, an immense step. The responsibility of uniting lives with a consenting young girl is nothing compared to the responsibility I see dawning. This little being who must expect everything from me has the right to take possession of my entire life." After Hélène endured nearly eleven hours of labor, she gave birth to their daughter on the morning of July 22, 1907, and named her Christiane. "I will never forget Hélène's smile, a faint, lingering smile, such a wave of maternal love that passed over her contorted face, and in a moment, she seemed never to have suffered."[16]

Nearly seven months later on February 11, 1908, Roger and Hélène had Christiane baptized by the priest who had married them. They thought of their future, of the rituals that awaited the three of them next, First Communion and then marriage—"the years rose up before our eyes so much, so much that twenty years would pass as nothing and that our happiness might be so fragile and brief." During the service, Roger had a sense of anxiety, "to see this little soul confided, arbitrarily, to the Catholic religion by the will of her mother and the consent of her father. But I thought of Hélène, who has drawn from this faith so many pure, exalted joys, so many compensations for the annoyances in the life of a young girl, which is only a painful waiting, and I would have been wrong to express any regret whatsoever. By her generous and intelligent manner of reconciling her religious sentiments and her new conjugal life, Hélène has left me no right to mistrust or to worry about the future. May she do with Christiane what she has done with herself. In good conscience, I should abdicate and confide to her the responsibility of educating our daughter."[17]

They had been married almost exactly two years. Their families had footed all their bills. During much of the summer and fall, Roger and Hélène lived at Le Tertre, the Foucault country home in rural Normandy near Bellême and so about a hundred miles west of Paris. Everything about it enchanted Roger: a true seventeenth-century palace from the reign of Louis XIII, a long, magnificent brick building with a slate mansard roof, two smaller wings, an exquisite French garden, tree-covered walks, all with "incomparable purity of proportions" and set on a knoll that sloped to forested grounds. The very name "Tertre" meant "hillock" or "mound." Here was the proper setting for Roger finally to take up the literary career he claimed to want but had set aside—for courtship, for marriage, for fatherhood. After Christiane's birth, he began to work seriously, reading and taking notes, but he could not escape the fear that he might turn out a failure (*un raté*): "this specter haunts me, as it has haunted me before." By May 1908, he had a plan for a novel that mirrored this anxiety of having ambitions beyond talent. He gave it the title *Devenir!* (To Become!).[18]

Roger described his protagonist to Marcel, now far away in Madagascar serving as attaché to the governor-general: "André Mazerelles is a young twenty-one, full of plans, hopes, dreams, and irremediably vacuous, a disappointment, a misfit, of a special kind. The kind who, born to be a merchant or notary, is infected by the virus of literature, that epidemic that has ravaged so many, believes in his talent but merely reflects the people he has met and has no creative impulse. ... He exhausts himself in plans and dreams, who, pitifully, desperately, comes to nothing, who can only imitate because he has nothing of his own. More dead than alive, he struggles dreadfully before foundering, capitulating with all his hopes, frittering away the little energy he has in hopeless mediocrity." The specter of winding up a *raté* certainly was haunting Roger: Mazerelles represented his fears about himself. Because Gustave Valmont had adopted the monarchist and integral nationalist ideas of the right-wing Action Française movement, and thereby strained his relations with Roger, Marcel was the sounding board for this confidence. Writing from Tananarive (now known as Antananarivo), he proved his worth as a friend: "Aren't you sensing how stupid your fear is of becoming a failure, a weakling, a poor being doomed to eternal sterility by a heredity in contradiction with your nature!"[19]

Roger wrote rapidly and his book appeared in print on June 4, 1909, after he paid a substantial subsidy to Paul Ollendorff whose La Librairie Ollendorff was the publisher of Guy de Maupassant, Paul Adam, Jules Renard, and Willy (Henri Gauthier-Villars). Both the public and the literary world ignored *Devenir!* despite Roger's having sent sixty carefully chosen recipients inscribed copies. To his parents, who had given him the money for the subsidy, he wrote, "I am astonished ... to receive *about eight* replies." To Marcel, he was blunt—and more exact: "I have got back six letters of acknowledgment. ... It's a complete fiasco." And one of these six was from Edith de Coppet, née Olivié, whom Marcel had married in November 1905, and who took the time to write after reading Marcel's copy.[20] The author had the unenviable privilege of emulating his protagonist.

Even so, from writing *Devenir!* Roger had learned a great deal about the framing and composing of a novel. He was already thinking of a new project, the account of a woman, Marise, who would be the feminine counterpart of Mazerelles. He quickly set it aside as a misstep, though once again, he paid a subsidy, this time to Bernard Grasset, whose Editions Nouvelles published a fragment of the manuscript as *L'une de nous*. Now, a new idea possessed him, once again personal but this time not solipsistic. He turned to the question of religion and its solace in the modern secular world, the problem that had troubled him since his adolescent confessions and First Communion and that was now much on his mind, especially since the baptism of Christiane. Through a letter to Coppet in March 1910, he set this question in terms of "moral anguish": "What is life and why death, and why suffering, and why our complete futility before such terrible and inexplicable matters? And duty, and conscience? The emptiness that is in me is exactly the place where religion is lacking. Nevertheless, I have beliefs and suspicions of certitude. My sincere, irrevocable *irreligion* is a component of the well-ordered whole I seek for myself but is thus far utterly lacking." He had already sent Coppet the plan for this novel. As an adolescent, excited by new ideas, his protagonist turns away from religion through the study of philosophy and science. As a grown man, robust in his material and intellectual success, believing only in himself and in his own creative force, he rejects religion altogether. As an old man in decline, his powers spent, he feels decrepit and alone. "He perceives death, the black emptiness lining the horizon, and he shivers. All the illusions of his youth as a believer little by little return to him, warm his numb heart, and offer him this marvelous alleviation of death, to consider life as a passage from God to God. He has a vague memory of the strength he felt in himself for not believing, but now he has so much need to believe!"[21]

Death was a new preoccupation for Roger. When the wife of the painter Maurice Ray, a friend of his parents, died in April 1910 following surgery for a tumor beneath her tongue, he could not turn away from Ray's grief: "It is ghastly to see this man whom we have known smiling and voluble utterly prostrated, tears on his face and sobs in his throat, fighting desperately against despair without any success. His presence is the death's-head, the incessant warning, *Tu pulvere reverteris* [You will return to dust]." Belief was an ongoing conundrum, increasingly anguished because Hélène became the focus. Her religion, he realized, "was a 'passion.' She has never seriously examined her faith and even, through her natural good sense and moderate opinions, constantly expresses opinions absolutely, diametrically opposed to what a Catholic would say in her place. And because she does not truly accept all the rules of her church, she has her own personal religion. Not to be discussed, not to be judged—simply a fact. God has appeared to Hélène *a thousand times*. She has entered into communion with supernatural forces, she has had *intimate contact with God*. Losing her faith would be like losing a vital organ: the equilibrium of her life would be disturbed, and she would surely die."[22]

Roger understood Hélène's dilemma. By the time she realized his rejection of belief, she already loved him: "She suffered, pondered at length, but then

did not have the courage to sacrifice this love for her faith." With the keen
regret of hindsight, he knew that he should never have married her. "I was
ignorant of the true Catholic mentality. . . . I considered religion a collection
of beliefs held by a certain social level, the stuff of reactionary ideas, a vague,
good-natured *modus vivendi*. I was even agreeably surprised to discover the
profound religiosity of my wife. Tolerant! Yes, I was, but slowly, surely, by daily
irritation, I became the stereotypical anticlerical. . . . In a household like ours,
the ferment of dissension *may destroy our happiness!* . . . Hélène already tells
me that she has reproached her parents for consenting to her marriage and
swears that she will never, never permit Christiane to marry a man whose
religious convictions differ from hers." And now Roger was preparing a novel
that might "cause her suffering, even irreparable harm."[23]

The writing took place amid a series of upsets. First came the crisis with
Germany over Morocco called the "Agadir crisis" from mid-summer to late
fall in 1911. Roger noted that in the face of German threats, "all of France
awakened . . . in a spirit ready *to accept war*. . . . France dons her armor, her
attitude incontestably worthy. However much I withdraw by nature from this
defensive nationalism, I cannot fail to praise it. France has superb bearing,
not at all arrogant. The sensation we had of powerlessness, of dependence,
was *dreadful*." In February 1912, to be precise about some details, Roger made
his first visit to the Bibliothèque nationale (National Library), where his bourgeois sensibilities came under assault. He noted "the odor of poverty, the odor
of misery, and what idleness! The wretched patrons are some grimy unshaven
priests with dirty fingernails who look at *art*, some faded women with fetid
underwear still trying to pass as coquettes who copy documents for a little
money and so think themselves intellectuals, and a few snobs at loose ends
who play at being the erudite elite because in some journal they have published the costs of a queen's lingerie or the rectification for the attribution
of a reredos from some part of the fifteenth century. Everything is hideous,
foul-smelling, and pretentious." But he stayed long enough to get his facts
straight. In early April 1912, Hélène underwent an appendectomy after suffering for some time with chronic abdominal pain, and by the end of the month
was "almost completely well."[24]

Far more telling on Roger were moments that could have been taken from
the pages he was writing. About the time of Hélène's operation, he found—
probably because she meant him to find it—the rough draft of a letter to her
spiritual advisor, Abbé Julien Marchand: "I did not write you on the usual
date because I wanted to spare you my jeremiads. . . . *The past leaves me only
regret, and I expect nothing more from the future. That's why I sometimes have
no courage.*" She was twenty-five years old, married for six years, her daughter

not yet five years old. Roger's reaction was not dejection, because his wife was in profound disarray—perhaps partly from her physical ills—but annoyance, even anger, that she had been hiding such feelings from him. "We are tied for life, outside of my affection and hers, by the existence of Christiane. Religion is the cause of all this. . . . She does not have a sufficiently physical nature to love me in spite of her moral aversions—and besides, the physical, for her, does not exist: flesh is sin. What would give her joy is more children, but can I accept them, serenely, knowing that they will escape from me, that she will do everything possible to transfix their young brains with religious exaltation, without the least critical spirit." Eleven months later in March 1913, he considered his mother's latest endeavor, luring his father back to the church after Roger's great-uncle, Lucien Desboudets, had died abruptly of a heart attack—and long without sacraments. Roger estimated that the campaign would take only a matter of months because his father would not, "to cross this threshold, have to abandon much." For after all, Madeleine did not have the fervor of Hélène. Finally, in June 1913, Roger had a warning about the stability of marriage from a trusted source. Marcel revealed that he and his wife Edith were separating. They had married on November 23, 1906, just three months before Roger and Hélène, but of course, they were Protestants, not Catholics.[25]

Meanwhile, Roger had completed his novel and given it the title *S'Affranchir* (To Free Oneself). He sent the manuscript to Grasset, who had published the Prix Goncourt winners in both 1911 and 1912, and who replied on June 17, 1913, "*S'Affranchir* is not a novel but a dossier. . . . My opinion is clear: your book is an absolute failure. You are going to think me severe, but I am absolutely fair, and render you a service, in saying that you are deceiving yourself." Undeterred, Roger took it immediately to Gaston Gallimard, his classmate from the Lycée Condorcet, who published more daring novels as well as the *Nouvelle Revue française*, which since its founding in 1909 had been recognized as a leading literary journal. Gallimard, his chief editor, Jean Schlumberger, and André Gide, the very definition of a daring novelist, read the manuscript. They were all ecstatic at the chance to publish it, with Gide writing to Schlumberger, "But who is this Martin du Gard, of whom I have heard nothing? How is it possible for him, in a first work, to have given us a book so wise, so mature, so intelligently clear? . . . I have nothing to criticize, and I approve without restriction." Ultimately, though, they did prevail upon Roger to change the title. When the book appeared in November 1913, it was *Jean Barois*, after its protagonist, and was a surprise best seller—far surpassing Marcel Proust's *Du côté de chez Swann* (*Swann's Way*) from Grasset. At the offices of Editions Gallimard, the writers and editors greeted him as one of their own. Roger Martin du Gard was launched.[26]

The original title came from Michelangelo's "Captive Slave," the figure only half emerged from the marble, struggling to escape the stone from which he is born. As Roger had proposed when he first imagined the story, Jean Barois struggles to escape the family, the religion, the society, the very mentality from which he is born. At one point, he does believe that he has liberated himself, but as his life ebbs, he is drawn back into his past, his freedom becoming an illusion:

The novel opens in the small town of Buis-la-Dame, about fifty miles north of Paris in the Oise. The mother of Jean Barois has died of tuberculosis, and he has inherited a disposition to the disease. His father, a physician with a practice in Paris, orders a program of food, fresh air, and rest while warning, "All existence is a struggle; life is simply winning through." The local priest, Abbé Joziers, counsels, "The suffering of every creature is willed by God ... He made it a condition, indeed the prime condition, of life." As devout as he is obedient, young Jean strengthens as he prays. A few years pass, he is healthy and wins admission to the Sorbonne, where he studies both medicine and natural science. Although what he is learning shakes his faith, he finds a temporary refuge in Modernism, but only temporary—like Martin du Gard himself. A critical moment comes when his father, ill and failing fast, returns both to Buis-la-Dame and to the religious belief he had long discarded. On his deathbed, he first adjures Jean to marry Cécile Pasquelin, his childhood sweetheart and daughter of his godmother, then explains his conversion, "that unknown quantity—it's a terrible thing to face." No longer devout but still obedient, Jean marries Cécile. He accepts a position teaching science at a Catholic school, Wenceslas College, but to expiate his father's weakness, adopts an ever more strident materialist philosophy before his students. When Cécile, whose simple faith seems a rebuke, begins a novena in hope of becoming pregnant, he ridicules her. The rector of the College admonishes him and Cécile weeps hysterically, but Jean coldly replies that suppressing his views would mean "abandoning all my human dignity, all decency of mind." He resigns his post and agrees to a separation from Cécile. Months later, he learns that she has given birth to their daughter. In a poignant scene, once more in Buis-la-Dame, he holds the baby she has named Marie and remembers "how naively he had dreamt of giving and receiving perfect happiness."

A few years pass and Barois, now in his middle thirties, is living alone in Paris. He has gathered in his apartment a group of high-minded friends who are determined, like him, to parade their idealism before the world. They decide to found a journal, *The Sower*, and to take as their motto, "Something we know not is stirring in the world today." The words are from Félicité de Lam-menais, the French priest whose support for political and religious freedom in the 1820s and 1830s led to his censure by the Vatican. Although *The Sower* starts with only thirty-eight subscriptions, they gain prominence through an early and passionate stand in the Dreyfus Affair. By disputing the evidence used to convict Captain Alfred Dreyfus of treason, by questioning the resistance of the army and the government to an open examination, they make themselves targets of a public opinion fiercely convinced otherwise. When public opinion begins to shift, when the number of "Dreyfusards" begins to match the number of "anti-Dreyfusards," they ride the wave of change. The culmination of the Dreyfus Affair means not only the pardon and eventual exoneration of Alfred Dreyfus but the political victory of the Radicals and Socialists who take up his cause—significantly later than *The Sower*. For the men closest to Barois, this triumph has the ugly sensation of a Roman circus. Marc-Elie Luce is suspicious, "*We* were a handful of 'Dreyfusistes'; they are an army of Dreyfusards." When the Radicals prove to be as "political," as prone to corruption as their predecessors, as likely to act not for the interest of ideals but for "the interest of state," François Cresteil d'Allize reacts with disgust, "We lanced the abscess, we counted on a cure—and now gangrene's set in."

Not long after, Cresteil kills himself. He had given up his commission in the cavalry and estranged himself from his aristocratic family to take a stand for "truth." But "duty, virtue, goodness—they're all just make-believe, ... fine-sounding names to cover up selfish instincts ... all roads lead to the same place, the same dark hole." Barois himself nearly dies in a carriage accident, and when he regains consciousness recalls that just before the impact he began to recite, "Hail, Mary, full of grace." Fearing the example of his father, he writes a testament to his belief in science and to his rejection of religion because "I know nothing more harrowing than to see an old man, whose whole life has been devoted to the furtherance of some noble idea, go back in his declining years on the principles that inspired his life's work and play traitor to his past." Yet something has broken within him: he cannot regain his health, and he no longer has the same spirit of combat. To his surprise, Marie, whom he has seen only a single time, appears at his door. She wishes to spend her eighteenth year with her father, to fulfill a provision in his separation agreement with Cécile that he had long ago dismissed as ridiculous. In her face, he has a "vision of Cécile as a girl, of the unrecoverable past," and he agrees. Only after she spends the year reading everything he has ever written, only then she tells him of her decision to take the veil. To his protests, she replies, "But don't you see, Father, that if my faith could be shaken by arguments it wouldn't be faith?"

At *The Sower*, the most dogmatic of his colleagues, L. Breil-Zoeger, preaches a militant atheism that might once have attracted Barois. Now, he asks, "What's the obscure force that urges me toward right conduct if not a deep-seated religious feeling that has survived my loss of faith?" Yet the revived mysticism of nation and Catholicism that he discovers in the new generation entering their twenties and thirties frightens him as much. He meets two of them in his office and hears them denounce "that sterile navel-gazing contemplation; ... the France that has been through the Agadir crisis and lives under German threat has no use for it!" They tell him, "What's indispensable to us, if we are to keep our will to action vital and alert, is a moral discipline behind it." Barois comprehends the power of these convictions and would rather stand with these young men than with Breil-Zoeger, but he recognizes full well that they regard him as the enemy. He decides to resign as editor, telling Luce, "I'm not sure of having sowed the good seed." When he explains himself, Luce says only, "I can do nothing to help you—now." He finds his direction when he and Cécile meet for the first time in almost twenty years, at the ceremony in which their daughter formally joins her convent in Belgium after a year's novitiate. Marie tells him, "Father, in every line you wrote, I realize that you are seeking God." She embraces them as she begs, "Please stay together now."

Barois joins Cécile in Buis-la-Dame. As the tuberculosis he held at bay now savages his lungs, he is desperate and afraid. He turns to the new young priest, Abbé Lévys, and sobs, "So now I know my quest is ended, ... and I shall joyfully obey; yes, all now is clear, crystal-clear. At last everything has a meaning." When Luce visits, Barois tells him, "Only see for yourself how calmly I can face death, now I know I shall live again beside Him. ... You and I were sowers of doubt, my friend. May God forgive us." Later when Lévys walks him to the railroad station, Luce complains that Barois has returned "to those consoling fairy-tales." Lévys responds, "Were you capable of consoling him? No. Whereas I brought him peace." A few days later, a dying Barois receives extreme unction and dies, like his father, grasping a crucifix. As Lévys and Cécile go through his papers, they discover the testament he drew up after the carriage accident. From the opening sentences they recognize the voice of the materialist editor and intellectual. Lévys watches as Cécile casts the pages into the fire.[27]

So much of *Jean Barois* exemplified the "moral anguish" Roger wished to convey. What is the source of ultimate principles? Are the latest discoveries of science merely a conceit compared to the eternal verities of religion? The recognition of ambiguities, the rejection of cant, the balance of antipathies, the very depth of the prose proved that he had long since left behind the callow youth he had been. Just as *Jean Barois* was going to press, Roger added a dedication to Abbé Marcel Hébert, his former spiritual advisor and now older friend, the mentor who had first introduced him to the problem of religion in a secular world. His words were delicate: "Your religious feelings can but be wounded by some of the tendencies of this book. Aware of this, I am all the more grateful to you for permitting me to dedicate it to you." Roger expected misunderstanding, warning his mother, "I have written a philosophical novel, not an autobiography." He was not prepared for the onslaught from the revived political right that he had so accurately described. Now clearly in the camp of the Action Française, Gustave Valmont wrote him: "I have been gripped from the opening pages by the beauty and the gravity of the subject, by the talent of the author, but of your philosophy, it is, to my mind, detestable. . . . I do not think myself wrong in identifying your own ideas with those of your hero, because I have only too often had evidence of how much you resemble each other." Roger replied carefully, tactfully, thanking Gustave for "the affectionate and open tenor of your letter, . . . and regarding your reservations, they were exactly what I expected." But the following day, he sent a copy of Valmont's letter to Marcel de Coppet with this comment: "He is severe, especially between the lines, perfidious and wounding. I am disappointed, I admit it."[28]

An attack on *Jean Barois* by a journal closely linked to the Action Française reopened the wound. Writing in *La Revue des idées et des livres* on January 25, 1914, Henri Clouard argued that the novel was monotonous and unconvincing by citing lengthy transitional excerpts out of context. When Roger complained to Gustave that the company he kept had published a review that was "underhanded and in bad faith," Gustave's only response was, "Yes, I found Clouard's review summary, offhand, and boring." Now angry and hurt, Roger wrote back, "All my long-held affection bristles with rancor against our divergence of thought. Once we were two brothers, almost twins, marching in the same rank, at the same pace. Now, we are old childhood friends whom life has led to opposite poles, who still have between them memories and habits but nothing living and real." Gustave might have tried to retrieve something of their friendship, but instead answered stiffly, "It is not admiration I desire but courtesy and scrupulous discretion toward my person, respect for the whole order of grand values and grand ideas to which I have sworn my life, guided by my reason at least as much as by my heart." Yet almost four months later, Gustave wrote to Marcel in faraway Tananarive, expecting him to be a go-between. As Marcel explained in a letter to Roger, "Gustave hangs on to me, hopelessly, a little through affection but mostly from his sense that you have turned your back on him, or rather that life has separated you in an irreparable manner. Your literary success has wounded his pride because he has nothing to match it." Roger replied to Marcel, "Gustave thinks the opposite of me *on everything*, and I have no desire to see him."

In mid-July, Roger and Gustave did exchange letters that are best described as recriminations extinguishing their longtime friendship.[29]

And so it was the quartet alone that remained: Roger, Hélène, Christiane, and Marcel. Roger and Hélène, thirty-three and twenty-seven, married for eight years, trying to understand each other and their marriage; Roger and Hélène, parents for nearly seven years, divided over the care of Christiane; Roger and Marcel, exchanging through correspondence intimate details of their lives and families while separated by nearly 5,500 miles. The formula for possible misunderstandings was not arithmetical but geometrical.

Christiane was no puzzle. In Roger's eyes: "She has the kind of mind I had at her age, a little lazy and sleepy but reflective. She has a dreaminess that can make her seem silly, but I distinguish, with certainty, solid elements of thought and especially observation. . . . In her manner, however, she can be calculating, egotistical, capricious, stubborn, and willful, the essence of a spoiled bourgeois child." For some of these faults, he blamed his mother's influence, but he saw the root of the problem in the household he and Hélène had created, "divided, hostile, each of us following our own way, colliding with each other, wounding each other without cease." He feared that Christiane would always be "torn between two contradictions and so come to nothing."[30]

The contradictory nature of their marriage was on display as they toured Italy for a month in the late spring of 1914 to celebrate the success of *Jean Barois*. At first, Roger was testy and petulant: "This trip disappoints me so profoundly, so bitterly. . . . Imagine, the uninterrupted presence of Hélène, tender and enchanting, taking me by the arm, asking only to sit with me on the sand or to stare with me up at the stars. I am *like one possessed*, I am smothered, I cry alone—from desire, from malice, from boredom, *from the need of something I do not know*. . . . Hélène's tenderness wraps me more tightly than a shroud. And I think myself a monster. I took this trip *only for Hélène*, to make her believe that I still love her. . . . She is like a poor wounded bird. She was a young girl who would surely have been happy if I had not seduced her with my promises and my lies. She has made her life with me, she has sacrificed everything she can, and she gives me proof each day of an all-consuming love. And me? I permit her to feel that her presence is a hindrance to me, that this trip would be a new world for me if only she were not here. . . . And yet I love her, incontestably. What a deception marriage is—and when I think of Hélène's fate, what a monstrosity. I consider myself an *absolute bastard*, but I cannot do better." A few weeks later, he was calling Hélène "truly intelligent and indeed clairvoyant. . . . She has the courage to be lucid. She loves me ardently, profoundly, and I believe, for always, but tranquil, certain love will not enhance her life or give her the moral calm she needs. .... I wound her over and over. .... With greater physical and moral freedom, I would have less trouble remaining the sure and faithful husband that I must be to assure our conjugal future." Once they were home, Roger wrote in his journal, "Resolve to lie.... Otherwise, marriage is a hell."[31]

His own marriage a failure and without children, Marcel de Coppet read Roger's accounts with interest and dismay. Were Roger and Hélène careering toward a separation of their own—separation, because Hélène would never agree to a divorce? Or would their life together become an endless battle, with Christiane the prize? What might be the definition of fidelity—to all three? In the summer of 1914, any decisions were suddenly stayed by the cataclysm of war that would engulf them all.

Chapter 2

~

REALITIES

BETWEEN THE ASSASSINATION OF Austrian Archduke Franz Ferdinand at Sarajevo on June 28, 1914, and the mobilization of the Russian and German armies on July 30, the potential for general war in Europe went from possible to inevitable. Roger Martin du Gard wrote in his journal: "Anguish. Impossible to think of anything else. . . . Day of frenzy. No longer any hope." The French government ordered its own general mobilization on August 1. Within two days, Roger and his brother Marcel were to join a logistics unit at Fontainebleau as non-commissioned officers. Their mother was in tears, telling them, "Remember that I taught you your prayers." They had a piece of luck when the unit commander assigned them to the same section, overseeing trucks transporting supplies to second echelon troops. A few days later, on August 10, they moved into the Marne region, northeast of Paris, to Montmirail, where Roger wrote to Hélène trying for reassurance: "This letter is for you alone. Marcel and I are doing important work, but we are not in any real danger. When you consider what others are facing, those under fire and those awaiting battle, you will, like me, agree that our separation is a minor thing indeed. . . . I beg you to take care of your health, and I think also of Christiane with such anxiety." On August 13, at nearby Reims, having seen the effects of the first battles, he was no longer so strong: "I have your photographs in my pocket, but I have not wanted to look at them. I have so little time to myself, so little time alone except in the evenings, and then because I want to sleep I avoid emotional upset with a fierce egotism. The letter from Christiane, which I received at Fontainebleau a week ago, shook me terribly. I would prefer that you do not send along any others. The thought of our little girl breaks my heart. I cannot look at her picture without crying like a baby."[1]

The first month of fighting produced staggering casualties for France. From August 5 to September 5, the French army suffered more than 329,000 casualties—the combined killed, wounded, and missing. On a single day,

August 22, it lost nearly 27,000 men dead at the battles of Charleroi and Ardennes. Although the French forces withdrew in good order, the German army was advancing rapidly through northern France and descending upon Paris. "Widespread anxiety with the enemy so close, only six miles away," Roger wrote in his journal, "I look all around me for *the spirit of patriotism,* but it does not exist. We are two hundred soldiers and their officers, retreating from the invasion. Most of us think France is fucked (*foutue*)." So did France's leaders, who moved from Paris to Bordeaux. All of them were wrong. The commander-in-chief of the French army, General Joseph Joffre, saw the moment to counterattack along the Marne River and did so on September 5, with the assistance of the small British Expeditionary Force. After seven days of extraordinary fighting, Joffre stopped the German advance. Both the French and German armies had casualties of some 250,000 men each, the British about 13,000; the French dead were about 80,000. On September 7, two days into the battle, Roger encountered "dreadful, unforgettable sights. We pass through villages entirely abandoned, the doors hardly closed." But by September 9, "The Germans retreat." Although not far: when the supply unit moved west into French Flanders, at Bailleul: "German infantry is only 500 yards away." With the battlefront in stalemate, both sides dug elaborate defensive works and settled into trench warfare, this Western Front ultimately reaching 434 miles in length from the North Sea to the border with Switzerland.[2]

Writing Marcel de Coppet, now transferred to Zinguinchor in France's Senegal colony, where he served as administrative chief (*commandant de cercle*), Roger confided: "I do not want to exaggerate the risks we run. *They do not exist,* compared to those of the infantry. But we are exposed to fire on certain days because we are the only automobile convoy attached to the cavalry. This is between us: *Hélène knows nothing of these risks.* . . . She is with my parents at Vichy, which has become an important staging center for the wounded. She works as a nurse, her time taken up from morning to night. My father helps direct operations of the Red Cross. For seven weeks, I had no news from them at all, not even knowing where Hélène was." In December, he learned of Gustave Valmont's death on September 6, in the first fighting along the Marne. Although estranged, they had been friends since adolescence. He had a despairing letter from Henry Foucault, Hélène's brother, whose infantry unit had been in the trenches for seven weeks. To Abbé Hébert, he wrote, "I see daily the savagery of all. . . . It is not civilization against barbarism, it is the same vileness, the same cruelty, instincts awakened, two barbarisms grappling."[3]

When Roger's captain dispatched him to Paris on a special mission, he telegraphed Vichy and had "the impression of going with a vertiginous rapidity towards Hélène, who herself rushes madly toward me in the night." They had two days together with Christiane, long talks which revealed to him how much they both missed him, Hélène especially: "She suffers terribly from my absence ... she cannot endure this separation morally or physically. I realize that, despite all, I am *the sole axis of her life*." He urged her not to worry about money: his family had "great reserves, and this if ever is the moment to share them." He urged her to worry less about him: "I am like a dog that has been thrown into the water, swims as well as it can, and once back on the bank, shakes itself violently, then goes back home." He also asked a favor now that his unit had moved into the soggy ground of northwest France, at Hesdin, south of Lille: "For a long time I have hesitated to spend anything much, but every day, my feet are soaked, and that leads to painful congestion in my head. I have tried everything. Nothing works. I spend hours in the mud, and because no regular leather is watertight, the only alternative is marshland hunting boots. Coppet is sending a money order to repay an old debt, and when it arrives, please go the Saint-Etienne shop on the Rue du Louvre and buy me a pair of mid-calf-length lace-up boots. They are made of waterproof leather, a layer of rubber between two layers of leather. They will cost forty or forty-five francs [$165–$185 in 2015]. Some others in the unit already have them, and they are truly the only *impermeable* ones." Hélène's package with these special boots arrived on New Year's Day, 1915, and Roger was gleeful: "It's raining buckets, so I immediately put on my swamp boots, which fit marvelously well, are supple, light, and above all, absolutely waterproof. This evening is the first in a long time that my feet are not wet." For her New Year's gift, he had his friend Maurice Ray deliver the traditional bouquet of violets. Such are the consolations of wartime and marriage.[4]

However long it seemed, Roger had been a soldier only five months, and he was to be an extraordinarily fortunate one, escaping with hardly a scratch after four and a half years of war. Instead, four of his longtime friends died in battle: Valmont (September 6, 1914), Michel Fleury (May 1, 1916), André Fernet (June 1, 1916), and Pierre Quentin-Bauchart (October 8, 1916); his cousin, Pierre Margaritis (May 30, 1915), and his brother-in-law, Henry Foucault (end of March 1915), were wounded, Foucault grievously. Once near Auxi, Roger came upon the 39th Infantry regiment with which he had trained at Rouen a dozen years before and thought, as he wrote his father, "I would have been killed or maimed long ago if I had been mobilized with them." For most of the time, he was far enough behind lines not to worry about enemy fire: "Imagine eighty trucks along the road. One of them is mine." Weather was the great concern, especially in French Flanders, where conditions were miserable. "If I go outside, the wind scatters my papers and covers me with dust, or drizzle forces me back into my shell. I rarely have a tranquil hour. In the truck, I have a bench and table where I can work." And at Abbeville, along the Somme River: "for five days dreadful storms, a tempest that uproots trees, shakes our vehicles, deafens us night and day, while torrential rains drench us completely."[5]

Still, moments of peril tore at Roger's resolve to spare Hélène the reality he faced. Ordered to the dangers of the Verdun sector, he revealed his fear even as he tried to hide it: "Since my arrival, I am literally penetrated by the horror of all that happens here each day. . . . Human life counts for nothing, it's blood, blood everywhere. . . . I see it all, but without running *any risk*." The following day, he dropped any pretense. Convinced that his death might be imminent, he wrote letters "in case of accident" to his wife, his father-in-law, and his own parents. For Hélène, he bared his emotions: "I was almost killed last night by a German shell. That could happen to me this evening or tomorrow, and if so, I want you to have this farewell from me. . . . I have nothing to tell you that you do not know already. I confide Christiane to you with confidence and absolute security. Teach her to love all that is unselfish and fine, elevate her above the stupidities of our milieu, give her no other guide than her intelligence and her heart. I shall be so proud to watch her grow up if I see you again." For Albert Foucault, he expressed his gratitude: "With my whole heart, I thank you for what you have done for us and for welcoming me into your family. . . . I sincerely hope that we all see one another again." For his mother and father, he confessed his failings: "Our clashes may have hidden my affection for you and my gratitude for all that you have done for me. I regret the troubles I have caused." In his journal he added: "Almost killed twice. I do not accept this war. I do not accept this death." When the danger had lessened, he explained to his mother-in-law, "We just passed three truly difficult weeks. Our section was attached to the artillery and engineers at Verdun to resupply the advanced trenches during the fighting near Eparges. We endured fifteen nights under German artillery bombardment."[6]

For Ernest Hemingway, courage—"guts"—was "grace under pressure." Every soldier under fire experiences fear; the test is how he deals with that fear. Roger Martin du Gard had that grace under pressure. In June 1916, his commanding officers recommended him for the Croix de Guerre, the decoration created the previous year to honor individuals who distinguished themselves through acts of heroism. Typically, he insisted that he did not deserve it, just as he insisted that he did not deserve promotion to head of section, then later to warrant officer. And perhaps rightly, because after the Verdun experience he declared to Hélène, "I would like to give you greater confidence, but I have completely lost mine. *I have seen* firsthand the German defensive works, and I no longer believe that we can chase them out of France by going on the offensive." Both were sick at heart over the news that her brother, Henry, had suffered a severe head wound on the Belgian front. Transported to Bordeaux, he survived cranial surgery but was subject to epileptic seizures and had little sensation on his right side. A few weeks later in the same region, Roger's cousin, Pierre Margaritis, had a less serious wound, a rifle bullet easily removed from his back. But then, "within five or six weeks he will be sent back into battle, perhaps to die." As he wrote to Coppet, "Everything is disrupted, all values overturned, all of France, thoughts, feelings, instincts, institutions, and individuals seem hurled pell-mell into a crucible and melted together." He reminded Coppet that their friend Quentin-Bauchart, an infantry captain who because of heavy losses among the officer corps was now commanding a battalion, had spent the last thirteen months at the front and was "thin, pale, heavily bearded, and forever marked by this war."[7]

Then came the sorrowful news that Abbé Hébert had died on February 12, 1916, from complications after prostate surgery. To Margaritis, Roger wrote, "I loved him for his pure heart." His captain granted him forty-eight hours leave to attend the funeral in Paris, and there he shared a cab with André Fernet, a friend from the Ecole Fénelon who had already made a reputation as a magistrate, playwright, and poet. When the war began, he volunteered to be an aviator—and would have chosen the infantry if turned down. Roger found his strident nationalism and assertion that victory was worth whatever the cost appalling. Three and a half months later on June 1, Fernet himself became an addition to that cost when his plane crashed in Lorraine. A little beforehand, he had written to Roger, "I could not live with the secret shame of not having done everything I can. . . . Whatever happens, I am ready with the sacrifice of my life . . . because it is necessary." The Battle of Verdun from February to June left more than 337,000 French casualties, the Battle of the Somme from July to November another 204,000 more. In a letter to Maurice Ray, Roger called the Somme "a massacre *without precedent*. . . . What horror, what depths of horror!" In his journal, he wrote, "It is slow, hesitant, indecisive, not at all the hoped-for *liberating* offensive." And in the midst, the death of Quentin-Bauchart on October 8: "I am shattered. Another death that grieves me, wounds me most deeply. Valmont, Fernet, Fleury, all gone."[8]

Roger's morale was profoundly damaged. "Lousy day," he wrote Hélène at the beginning of November, "like all those when we are sending up to the trenches wretched poilus ["dirty, hairy ones," slang for French enlisted men], knowing that half or more will never return." During the third week of the month, he had the great luxury of a long leave to see her and Christiane in Paris. Midway through, he ran into the noted artist Frédéric Montenard, then in his late sixties, who took note of Roger's uniform and exclaimed, "Is it not grand? Is it not fine? Are we not fortunate to live at such a moment, to witness the heroic resurrection of France!" Roger replied quietly, "Perhaps you see these frightful years of war as a noble moment for us, but I find all that dreadful and disgraceful." Indignant, Montenard spat out, "You should be shot, you hear me! I ask you never to speak to me again! Never offer me your hand! Never!" Roger sounded like the characters in Henri Barbusse's *Le Feu: Journal d'une escouade* (*Under Fire: The Story of a Squad*), which won the Prix Goncourt in 1916 and was purportedly an authentic account of life and death in the trenches. In fact, he would recommend it to Margaritis as "the only book on the war that *exists*." Heavy on his mind were a series of letters from Quentin-Bauchart's widow, Antoinette, whose anguish threatened "the balance of her mind, her very equilibrium."[9]

What of Roger's equilibrium? Throughout the Great War, he had far more time with Hélène than most soldiers could dream of having with their wives or girlfriends. His responsibilities, logistical and resupply operations, kept him mostly in the rear of the fighting, from which leaves were more common. His demonstrated competence—two promotions and decoration—combined with his social graces to make him ideal for administrative missions to Paris. Family money on both sides made traveling to meet each other far easier. But when together, they were an established married couple: instead of passionate embraces, discussions about their future and their child. After six days with Hélène in August 1915, Roger noted in his journal only "complete accord on plans, family relations, life after Christiane's marriage." After another in February 1916, he wrote to Marcel, "these renewals confirm for me the solidity of our bonds." In the brief space between the success of *Jean Barois* and the outbreak of the war, they had agreed that Roger should make his career in literature despite the likely privations—compared to their own upbringing. He kept asking her, "Are you still preparing yourself for the 'leap into misery'?" On her own, Hélène rented an apartment for them at 9 Rue du Cherche-Midi, in the sixth arrondissement of Paris. They would be just around the corner from Jacques Copeau's Théâtre du Vieux-Colombier, for which Roger wrote a broad peasant farce, *Le Testament du Père Leleu* (The Last Will of Old Man Leleu), as a diversion while waiting for the publication of *Jean Barois* in 1913. The neighborhood was hardly a bad address but it was across the Seine River and across social boundaries from the lives of their parents. When he saw the apartment in May 1916, Roger's reaction was "first impression, 'unexpected.' Second impression, 'impossible.' Yet something tells me that we will live there." To his cousin Margaritis, Roger wrote, "People will say of us, 'They have taken a little place near the Montparnasse train station; they have sold almost all their furniture; they live in tiny rooms; their families are distressed. Hélène has no evening dresses and never crosses the Seine. The poor grandmothers never see Christiane because Roger does not want her growing up in their milieu. She goes to a school on the left bank and has a lot of impossible friends. They've cut her hair, and she looks like a boy."[10]

In Roger's absence, Christiane was literally Hélène's to nurture. Roger could complain, as he did to Marcel, "Christiane is growing fast. I have the feeling, inevitable and egotistical, that she is beyond my control. ... She is indefinable, changing from week to week." Yet, he sometimes had to admire the result: "It's a surprise to learn that you have finished first in French [at your school]—a wonderful surprise." And, he had to admit that through the very force of circumstances Hélène had become—different: "I believe that you have, during this war, during this solitude, acquired the power to evolve more rapidly, to reach the depths when formerly you remained on the surface. ... for the past two years I have had the impression that you were *more alive*." He encouraged her to dare, to seek "intellectual liberty," because "you are called to live alone between a husband who is busy, preoccupied, crotchety, possessed by his irresistible demons, and an only daughter who will be gone from us quickly." She agreed with cheer, "Certainly, solitude has driven me to work on myself, facilitating an interior life that for me has always been intense." In another letter, she was blunt: "I believe that on his return Coppet will find me changed and that our friendship will be altered, that is, capable of existing apart from you."[11]

Just as Hélène was asserting her independence from Roger, Antoinette was declaring her dependence on him. She was one of his childhood country house friends from Maisons-Laffite. Her late husband, Pierre Quentin-Bauchart, another friend, had made the army his career. As Roger put it, his values were "*fine* and *noble*, ... self-denial, courage, sacrifice of himself for his country. ... Quentin was one of the grand souls, simple and pure; he marched straight ahead." In the presence of Quentin-Bauchart's death, even as during his life, Roger could not but feel the lesser man. Antoinette's grief took on "a grandeur, a clarity, a sharpness, and a radiance absolutely extraordinary. ... The poor little one wants to see no one but me, and I have spent hours with her every day during this leave. ... Hélène does not accompany me." Roger did not think he was deceiving his wife in any fashion, for he sent on to her every letter he received from Antoinette, even as he declared, "I have always had for her a special sympathy, I am with her as with a child I have known and loved since small, as Coppet will be able to experience for Christiane. Her suffering is so solitary, so abandoned. . . . I would like to devote several months to her rescue." Was he truly so innocent that he could not recognize the danger in his words—the danger in the attraction? Coppet certainly did and wrote him sternly: "I must say frankly what I think of your relations with Antoinette. I condemn them absolutely because, *inevitably*, they will end badly for her. Unbalanced as she is, she will believe that she has the choice between death or passion. You must not, whatever the price, become that passion. . . . I have always had the impression that there were not in the whole world two beings more made one for one another than her and you."[12]

Roger replied carefully, defending himself and his motives. "At the heart of this matter are a frightfully unhappy victim who must not be rejected and a tender, reserved friend who has done nothing worthy of reproach. In her absolute solitude, Antoinette has hardly anyone but me who can relate to her, because I am of her background and because I understand her grief and her longing as none of her own family can. For her, I am more than a brother because I am at the same time a brother, a brother from childhood, and a friend at a higher level than her brothers. . . . I have the proof, the proof of what I say and not what you suspect, in her correspondence, regular, copious, full of confidences, but supremely reserved. . . . I have sent your letter to Hélène, and I wait to hear what she thinks of it. I send her, one by one, the letters from Antoinette. She is thus able to judge." Then to Hélène, he wrote, "You almost never speak to me of Antoinette's letters that I send you regularly. . . . Coppet's suspicion not only is painful but obliges me to question the affection Antoinette offers me. . . . I sense a caution that I cannot forget and that will damage my friendship with her—perhaps mortally."[13]

Hélène's response was reassurance combined with a distinct warning: "Your letter this morning has moved me greatly by the confidence and the candor you offer! It is indeed the greatest proof of love you can give me—and you will never know how I am touched by seeing you judging me capable of comprehending all you feel, all you fear . . . I am persuaded, and I speak as a woman, that in the state of distraction in which Antoinette finds herself, your sympathetic affection produces in her something other than feelings of gratitude. You excite a fondness for which there is no possible outcome, and what she loves in your letter is not the advice you give her but the way you give it. *All without her realizing it.* The excitement of a nature such as hers can make her prey to the most illogical and incomprehensible passion. . . . Do not worry about what you have done so far, but consider how you can modify your relationship while recalling that last sentence from Coppet: 'I have always had the impression that there were not in the whole world two beings more made one for one another than her and you.' Think about those words when you write to her." Roger backed down: "Truly, I cannot see even the shadow of danger from her, but I am less assured than I was."[14]

Quickly, Roger discovered that Antoinette needed his attentions less and that Hélène needed them more. A coincidence? In mid-July, feeling run down and anxious, her heart racing, she consulted a physician who frightened her with his warning that the tachycardia risked causing a heart lesion. She took to her bed at Le Tertre immediately and for weeks did little but stare out the open window. Roger described her condition as "a breakdown" (détraquée). Outwardly, he blamed the war, of course, and how the war imposed a provisional quality on their lives. But to Marcel, he complained that Hélène had taken on "a kind of disordered activity, always running, scurrying, never able to sit down, *no longer able to sleep*, as if possessed by some sort of crazed agitation, without reprieve, without rest." Did Roger recognize that he may have played a part in Hélène's collapse? After four months, he obtained a ten-day leave to spend the beginning of December with her and left chastened. He wrote to her from his dugout, "I have just put your photographs safely away and closed my locket because otherwise, I cannot prevent myself from crying."[15]

Antoinette's anguish and Hélène's breakdown were the personal parallel to France's anguish and breakdown. The hecatombs of Verdun and the Somme had cost more than half a million casualties in 1916. Revolution in Petrograd forced the abdication of Tsar Nicholas II on March 15, 1917, and raised the fear that Russia might withdraw from the war. The failure of an offensive under General Robert Nivelle along the Aisne River in April brought 134,000 more casualties. At the beginning of May, the French 2nd Division refused orders to mount a new attack, and mutiny spread among other frontline units. Wild rumors had some French soldiers electing their own officers and marching on Paris. Although a new high command under Generals Philippe Pétain and Ferdinand Foch rapidly restored order by adopting an entirely defensive strategy and by executing mutiny leaders, profound pessimism gripped the nation. In midsummer 1917, this despair acquired a name, defeatism (défaitisme), and a proposal, peace at almost any price. By the late fall, the options for France were clear. The return to office of former prime minister Joseph Caillaux, who before the war had advocated Franco-German economic cooperation and was now the nexus for defeatism, would mean the opening of peace negotiations. The return to office of former prime minister Georges Clemenceau, who before the war had repeatedly warned of German intentions and his determination to stop them, would mean a fight to the death (guerre à outrance). On November 20, 1917, the French legislature invested the nation's future in Clemenceau. Rarely have the returns been greater: in less than a year, he led France to victory.[16]

But beforehand, what terrors. In December 1916, Roger was writing friends, "Peace made today would be bad but worse tomorrow," and, "At heart, I have no hope, and I am absolutely convinced that this war is vain, that the outcome will be as disastrous for us as possible and that nothing can change this fate." In the aftermath of the mutinies, he wrote to Maurice Ray, "You will see, you will see. I hold for certain that *no further offensive will be possible* on the French front. No leader will risk it. You have to hear the officers talking of their men. You have to see their anguished faces, their great fear of imminent storms! You will see. It's high time that this war be over." And he went further, revealing how much his experience had eroded the certainties of his youth: "This atrocious war has not even served to open our eyes to the bankruptcy of moral standards, of religious verbiage, of grand words devoid of sense and reality: Universal Justice, Human Dignity, Law, Civilization." To Margaritis in September, after meeting with Jean Fernet, brother of André, who had died three months earlier, he wrote, "Like us, he believes this war to be a vast rejection, a vast upheaval, *a reversal of all values*." He had no faith in Clemenceau, writing again to Margaritis, "When you tell me that you expect a great deal from him because for three years he has been denouncing the errors that we have all seen for ourselves, I cannot agree. I expect nothing, only the worst." He even denied that Clemenceau had the trust of the poilus: "His energy does not make him sympathetic because he has too much taste for seeing armies fight each other." When Clemenceau charged Caillaux with treason, Roger called it "dancing around the scalp." And when German agent Paul Bolo Pasha was executed with much fanfare on April 17, 1918, he commented disgustedly, "We now have Bolo's hide! France is saved!"[17]

Yet Roger was not simpleminded in his attitudes. He could lob condemnations at France and its conduct of the war because he was French. He understood keenly the difference between France and Germany—and never more so than when Bolshevik Russia sought a separate peace with Germany in negotiations at Brest-Litovsk in February 1918. "I have just read the conditions that Germany imposes on the defeated Russia. I read them with tears. Russia is reduced to the frontiers of what was once called 'Muscovy,' before Peter the Great ... Russia has forty-eight hours to accept, three days to sign. Russia is finished.... Germany triumphs insolently. Not only by its arms but *through its doctrine*. I wonder whether the democratic expansion has not met its end, its interment for generations." He did not like Clemenceau and was surprised by his success, but he had great hopes for what victory might mean. "The crushing of Germany does not make me leap for joy, but the crushing of German militarism, yes, because the best means of defeating our own is to destroy any pretext for it: that is a *war aim*!" And considering Roger's attitudes during the war, this single anecdote is worth recalling, from a letter to Hélène on Christmas Eve, 1917: "The cold is truly terrible. This morning, at my door, 12 degrees below zero [10.4°F]. The wine freezes, the eggs freeze. Life is unbearable. One detail among a hundred: to go to the latrine, I have to walk two hundred meters in the snow, across icy ground with the wind as sharp as a needle. Alas, these necessary trips are painful."[18]

Some two months earlier at the beginning of October 1917, as Hélène kept to her bed at Le Tertre and Roger sought leave to visit her, the first wave of what became the 1918 influenza pandemic laid him low. For seventeen days, he struggled with fever, respiratory difficulty, and gastric distress that left him barely able to stand—"I who am never sick." Over the next year, he came to regard his illness as the dark augury of future profound tragedy. On November 6, Gervaise, the young daughter of Pierre Margaritis and his wife, Noël, died after suffering for ten days with a virulent urinary tract infection. Army bungling prevented Pierre from arriving in time to see Gervaise take her last breath in Noël's arms, to see Noël close her eyes. The old priest who had performed their marriage came to the house offering consolation, and Noël sent him away. When he returned the following day, Pierre was there. They greeted him stone-faced, and after five minutes of "glacial silence," the priest accepted their rejection but left saying, "I know of nothing in the world more awful than losing a child." Unable to leave his post, Roger could offer him only the counsel "to shut your heart against this horrible sorrow, bind your wounds, and wait." What else was there to say?[19]

They were cousins, Roger and Pierre, who had discovered each other as young men and were now increasingly confidants. For Roger, Marcel de Coppet was far away both in distance and in comprehension of the war experience. For Pierre, a bitter childhood during which his father once confined him in a reform school had left him with few other friends. In early October 1918, with victory over Germany increasingly certain, they were exchanging letters about the shape of the future. Suddenly, Roger had a cryptic note from Noël, "Pierre is saved!" Eventually, he learned that Pierre had come down with influenza on October 15, and was evacuated to a hospital at Buffon, about 150 miles southwest of Paris, because he had a dangerously high temperature, 104.5°F, and elevated albumin in his urine, a sign of kidney failure. Over the next week, his temperature went down to 99.1°F, and his spirits climbed: "That's nothing. I'm getting well." But he also admitted, "*I am weak*" and worried that the albumin level did not improve. For inexplicable reasons, the authorities permitted Pierre's father but not his mother or his wife to visit him. Stuck at their home in Versailles, Noël could only judge by his letters to her, and it was after this first week that she wrote Roger the exclamation of joy. In fact, Pierre's condition rapidly worsened as his kidneys deteriorated. By October 28, his temperature was back to 104.3°F. The following morning, the physicians treating him confirmed that he had pulmonary edema, and he knew then that he was lost. He asked for paper and pencil and scribbled notes. The one to Roger read: "Dear Old Friend, I am wiped out. I ask that you burn all my writings. I give you my ring. What rotten luck! I embrace you." When his father came to visit in the afternoon, he confided the notes to him and said, "I know that I am going to die this night, stay with me." His father did not believe that Pierre was so sick or perhaps he was unwilling to make the effort and instead returned to Versailles. A few hours later, Pierre refused the offer of sacraments from a priest. Sometime after midnight, he dictated a note to the nun who was nursing him: "Tell Roger Martin du Gard how I died. Embrace him for me." Then, all alone, he joined his daughter in death just before dawn on the morning of October 30.[20]

Sensing the worst even from Noël's note, Roger had immediately asked for leave and was granted a three-day pass on October 31. Going directly to the hospital in Buffon, he found Pierre's body covered by a sheet amid others in the basement. The head nurse cut a lock of hair that Roger could give to Noël. The following afternoon, he went to the Margaritis house in Versailles. Pierre's parents "were loudly proclaiming their son's merits as if to compose a legend for the future." But Roger had already learned the details of Pierre's last hours and wondered, "He died alone, excruciatingly, feeling death creep on him hour by hour, writing his farewell to each of us, begging his father not to leave him without anyone on this last night. How could his father not have stayed with him? How abominable." Noël was lying down, "immobile, overcome, defeated, yet in her despair, a quality of resignation." He gave her the lock of hair, and she showed him the note Pierre had dictated as almost his last conscious act. He died, Roger concluded, "with a simple grandeur."[21]

Ten days later on November 11, as he awaited the official word of the Armistice ending the war, Roger wrote Hélène, "The memory of Pierre weighs heavily on me, at this moment more than ever." The next day, he clarified, "Pierre's death touches me as I have never been touched before. No one can know, and I do not know myself, how much I leaned on him." And two weeks more, "Coppet is far away. I miss Pierre's letters more than ever. I feel all alone." In his journal, Roger labeled an entry "Anniversaries" and wrote, "I bear the weight of all the war's bereavements." Then, he made a list:

+Valmont, September 6, 1914; +Hébert, February 13, 1915; +Fleury, May 1, 1916; +Fernet, June 1, 1916; +Quentin-Bauchart, October 8, 1916; +Grandmother, February 20, 1916; +Gervaise, November 6, 1917; +Pierre, October 29, 1918."[22]

Roger's preoccupation with dying and death, and with the attendant question of accepting or not the consolations offered by the Christian religion, dated at least from the death of Maurice Ray's wife in 1910. These issues were the essence of *Jean Barois*, with its extended descriptions of both father and son first contemplating their mortality then succumbing to the final agony but only after grasping a crucifix. And these issues arose in the death and funeral of Félix Le Dantec, a prominent scientist and professor of embryology at the Sorbonne, who died on June 6, 1917, at the early age of forty-eight. Working with Louis Pasteur, he had studied endemic yellow fever in South America and had undertaken ground-breaking research on the intracellular digestion of protozoa. During a protracted stay at the Hauteville sanatorium after contracting tuberculosis in 1900, he began writing about the conflict of religion and science, especially *Le Conflit* (1901), *L'Athéisme* (1907), and just before his death, *Le Problème de la mort et la conscience universelle* (1917). No one was less likely to embrace a crucifix at the moment of his death, and he did not do so. Yet a priest officiated at his funeral.[23]

Writing to Hélène about Le Dantec, Roger picked a fight by turning the issue into a personal one: "I cannot understand this petty posthumous betrayal. His wife, no doubt. But who did she think she was deceiving? The Good Lord? I confess that the idea of being buried in the church after the blessing of a priest is much less painful to me since I have said openly what I avow and because my *Barois* is present to witness my unbelief. I have left behind no document asking to be buried as I have lived, outside the church, fighting against it. I leave to those who survive me the freedom to respect or not respect my life and my memory. I hope that you will not have to take a side, not have to choose between the logic of things and your own preferences—because I believe that you will have much trouble deciding." And after this shot across the bow of his wife's religious sensibilities, he wrote to Pierre, "If I die, I place Hélène *entirely* in charge of my funeral, leaving her *free* to *betray* or *not betray* my beliefs. Because I attach no importance at all to receiving holy water from an obsequious curate on my old unrepentant carcass if a civil burial would inordinately and forever increase Hélène's suffering."[24]

Behind this religious baiting was a looming battle between husband and wife over the future of their daughter. When their marriage was new and Christiane an infant, Roger resolved to entrust Hélène with her education, recognizing that doing so meant, as he wrote to Marcel, confiding her "to the Catholic religion by the will of her mother and the consent of her father." Soon enough, however, he finally comprehended the fervor of Hélène's faith, her mysticism seemingly unbounded. He grew anxious at the state of their marriage, anxious for a daughter driven from pillar to post. And then the war

separated him from them, forcing Roger and Hélène to find within themselves new sources of strength to survive alone and to seek from each other
the support to do so. Roger saw Hélène on leave and sometimes Christiane,
but for the most part they were on their own or under the care of his or her
parents. For most of the war, Roger made not the slightest complaint about
Christiane's upbringing, while the place—the problem—of religion in their
marriage was temporarily ignored. But not forgotten, as Roger's letter about
Le Dantec revealed.[25]

For Hélène, the war years brought the disintegration of her family. In June
1915, her brother, Henry, suffered a severe head wound on the Belgian front.
After surgeons trepanned him four times, he was left much diminished, his
recurrent epilepsy provoking profound depression. In late May 1917, her
mother, Marie, was diagnosed with cancer of the breast. An ablation in early
June postponed her death nearly two years but left her with extraordinary
pain. In November 1917, her sister, Suzon (for Suzanne) announced her intention to enter a strict Dominican convent. Fearful every day for her husband's
safety, responsible entirely alone for her child, grieving for her brother and her
mother, Hélène coped as well as she could until she collapsed in the summer
of 1917. Her reward for recovery in late fall was to learn that Suzon, to whom
she was especially close, was abandoning her family for life as a nun.[26]

Roger was, of course, concerned above all with his own survival, but also
with his discomforts and discontents, as his letters to Hélène made clear.
And the war years brought destruction to his version of family, his closest
male friends, all of whom died except Marcel. He made plenty of time for
Antoinette Quentin-Bauchart until Marcel and Hélène warned him off. His
letters to Hélène were often excessively sentimental, as if tainted by feelings of
guilt. Despite his repeated assurances to her, he could not shake the fear that
in *Jean Barois* he had sketched his own like, Jean Barois estranging his pious
wife Cécile with his rejection of religion and their daughter, Marie, becoming
a nun. And why not that apprehension after Suzon made her declaration? Yes,
the news came to the Foucault family, as Hélène wrote him, "like a clap of
thunder," but, as Suzon explained, the decision came after "long preparation
and reflection." With her mother a mystic and her aunt soon undertaking a
novitiate, what was the influence on Christiane, who was now ten? Roger was
unsure. As he explained to Marcel, Hélène had "guided Christiane's spirit and
sensibilities exactly as I would have wanted. Except on one point: the religious.
Now is not the moment to act, but I shall do so through my daily presence,
later." He wrote this letter because Marcel was about to return to France for
the first time in five years. Roger could not obtain leave during what was the
final, and unsuccessful, German offensive, but Marcel met with Hélène and

Christiane over several days at the end of May 1918. Hélène's report to Roger was gushing: "Once an initial awkwardness was over, we chatted away like old friends, leading to sublime moments in my otherwise monotonous and constrained life." And Marcel praised Christiane highly: "I can hardly tell you how much she pleases me and how happy I am to see her. She is so composed and so confident, so self-assured."[27]

How annoying: his oldest and best friend was charming Hélène and finding Christiane without fault at the very moment Roger was anxious to impose his will upon them. Almost immediately, his letters turned petulant. Christiane, he complained, "*completely lacks imagination*; she does not know how to invent games; she has none of the poetry of childhood. She plays at arranging her things or at leading her doll around as if she is the head of the household—*no fantasy* in that." Hélène replied with dexterity by agreeing, "I am aware that Christiane has hardly any qualities of intelligence, of reflection, and none of imagination. I am distressed by this deficiency in a mind so well organized." But after Roger did have a leave with them in mid-July—because the Germans were now in retreat—she abandoned any tact and outmaneuvered him: "Your stay here produced on Christiane the same effect as always: excessive self-confidence, a rude manner, a haughty voice. Although her attitude shocks me, I can deal with her when we are alone, but her scornful tone toward your mother and your father shocks me profoundly." This last news forced Roger to write a stiff letter to Christiane. "Since I left, you have several times displeased your grandparents by acting like a spoiled child. I wonder whether this behavior is a little my fault, whether I was right to treat like you a grown up. You are too sure of yourself for a girl of your age who does not know much about anything; you do only what you want, and I never see you resist temptation. You take advantage of your mother's affection and of your grandparents' frailty to get everything you desire, to question the rules they make, and to reply disrespectfully."[28]

Not making much headway, Roger shifted to a new tack a couple of weeks later. He wrote Hélène how glad he was that Christiane had a horror of sewing and how he would prefer to see her lounging on a divan smoking cigarettes. Then, he complained that at Le Tertre, Hélène spent "enormous parts of the day" mending, ironing, washing, lengthening, and shortening. "The truth is that *you have a taste for manual tasks* which has become a kind of mania. You are an old ant, unrepentant and stubborn, and I will be obliged to live in the attic to escape your feather duster." Hélène's reply began ominously, "I wanted to wait until the end of the day in order to reply with the greatest calm possible. Your comments are based on complete blindness despite your having known me for a dozen years. . . . When you are sorry to see me occupied with a thousand details of housework, you fail to see that I do so to augment your comfort and your well-being. I do have a great taste for order, but for a simple order. I will always suffer from dust, and I will always want my house to be clean and well-kept. . . . *When I appear to have a taste for manual tasks, it is because I am your maid—or that I do not have the money to have someone do it in my place!*" The new tack was clearly a failure.[29]

Yet having insulted his wife, Roger now insulted her sister. Alone among her family, Hélène agreed to accompany Suzon to the Dominican convent at Montrouge in September 1918. From that moment on, Suzon, to whom she was so devoted, would be lost to her. Roger's reaction was to write Hélène, "Nothing can prevent my regarding a convent as a shelter for the weak because they find it easier to accept this serene existence free from earthly trials than to accept daily life with its pains, ugliness, and obstacles." And to Suzon, he wrote, "I see you leave with much sorrow. Beyond sharing Hélène's pain, I am personally saddened by the irreparable void that your withdrawal leaves in this family." No wonder that Hélène described his "support" as "more a thorny barrier."[30]

When Roger was finished with insults, he still had fights to pick. Since the middle of the war, he and Hélène had been preparing for the "leap into misery" that they would endure as Roger sought to establish his literary career. The symbol was securing the apartment on the Rue du Cherche-Midi. His parents especially were discouraging, and as German defeat appeared inevitable, Roger wrote a brave letter to his father: "I do share your apprehensions for things once the war is over. . . . We will do our best to reduce our needs to the level of our meager conditions, without that being a detriment to my work. You have handed down to me an honorable and highly esteemed name. I hope that I may add some luster of celebrity in passing it to Christiane." These words of determination aside, what Roger wanted, and what he believed he deserved, was further monetary support from his parents. His parents believed otherwise.[31]

In January 1919, not yet demobilized and assigned to the troops occupying Rhineland Germany at Kircheimbolanden, Roger laid bare to Hélène the reality of their situation. "The secret, fundamental, essential hostility toward our plans by my parents has survived the war. They do not say: 'Roger leads a respectable life. He has a wife and daughter who is our only grandchild. They do not have great needs. Without depriving ourselves, let us help them live simply in order for him to work at his desk without worrying about money.' Instead, they say, 'Our parents never gave us money, though providentially they died early and left us with a substantial inheritance. We have already given the succeeding generation more than we were ever given. Let them manage on their own.' So much for family!" He went on with the details: "We need eighteen thousand francs a year [$37,600 in 2015]. Our income from investments is, in lean years, nine thousand francs, in better ones, twelve thousand francs, and at best, fifteen thousand francs. We will have to nibble at our capital, nine, six, or three thousand, depending on the year. We should get through about eight years, but at that point we will have to seek a loan to go on. I am repelled by the thought that inheritance after the death of my parents might be the essential factor. . . . Yet Papa said of me to my brother, 'Too bad for him. You should not take on a wife and child unless you have decided *to earn your own way*.'"[32]

Before Roger could put the war years behind him, he had one last fight to lose, though fatuously, he would think he had won. Christiane had been preparing for her First Communion, one of the holiest moments in the religious life of a Roman Catholic. Roger had promised Hélène many times that he would accompany her to church on that day and that he would stand at her side as their daughter received the sacrament of the Holy Eucharist. Christiane made her First Communion on May 25, 1919, but Roger was not present. If he had still been a soldier, he could have used failure to receive leave as an excuse. In fact, he was demobilized in February, and the three of them had moved to the Rue du Cherche-Midi apartment in early March. On that May Sunday, he was in Barbizon, just outside Paris near Fontaine-bleau. He explained to his brother, "I have decided, in accord with Hélène, that I should disappear. Doing so is the only appropriate act. I am not able to participate at this ceremony of which I disapprove even as I accept it. And I believe that my presence in Paris, in the apartment, during this celebration would be absolutely out of place, painful for me, of course, and painful for Hélène and Christiane, obliged as they would be to adopt a certain constraint in my presence. My absence is especially hard on Christiane, but the hurt is necessary, and in my view, desirable. She finds herself placed between her father and her mother in a difficult situation, and, however distressing, she needs to recognize this fact without delay."[33]

Roger seemed proud of himself in this declaration, but his brother reported that after the First Communion service, emotions ran high in the apartment. Years later, Christiane recalled that she and her mother sobbed uncontrolla-bly. And from Conakry, in the French colony of Guinea, Marcel de Coppet brought Roger up short: "Without doubt you believe that this agonizing epi-sode in Christiane's life will have an influence on her way of thinking. I share this conviction, but I am not certain of how it will affect her. Suppose that she reacts in a manner opposite to what you expect, that she reads *Jean Barois* and becomes a second Marie. I do not think it likely, but who knows! And for Hélène, this abstention had to have been horrible. Perhaps I am exaggerating her feelings, but she must have felt utterly alone. Incidentally, I have written her and would have done more if I had dared. I am older and now far from my earlier sectarian attitude. I am less sure, not of my negative beliefs, but of the necessity to share them. I am now convinced that in these matters, each is better off keeping to himself."[34]

Roger Martin du Gard had survived the war without. Could he survive the war within?

Chapter 3

~

HUBRIS

SOPHOCLES WARNED, "NO PRIDE on earth is free from the curse of heaven," in his *Antigone*, which Roger Martin du Gard studied as a young man and apparently paid little mind. The analogous "pride *goeth* before destruction, and an haughty spirit before a fall" appears in Proverbs, but Roger never bothered much about scripture. Too late, he would come to realize their truth with a great suddenness and extraordinary finality.[1]

Immediately following the Great War, Roger gloried in a sense of mastery. Rather than confront him over his absence from Christiane's First Communion, Hélène submitted completely to his domination. Overwhelmed by successive blows—her sister's entering a convent, her mother's agonizing death from breast cancer, her "leap into misery with Roger," his betrayal of the promise to support a Catholic upbringing for Christiane—she handed him a letter that began, "My Roger," asked plaintively "whether you believe yourself capable of supporting me such as I am at this moment, with all my faults," and concluded, "better and more than ever I embrace you." Roger wrote triumphantly in his journal, "She cannot live without me." Late in the fall when Hélène dared to complain that his "ironic tone toward everything I say or do" had encouraged an attitude of defiance toward her by Christiane, he replied, "I have seldom received from you such an unjust reproach. . . . I deny it absolutely."[2]

Roger had another letter, this one eight pages long from Marcel de Coppet in Guinea, who sounded even more defeated than Hélène. "I am staggered by the void within myself. I am nothing. I am death. The meaning of life escapes me completely, any meaning of life in general, and mine especially, no longer exists. I have no ambitions, no desires. I have neither wife nor children, and I do not even want to have them." Of his closest friend, Roger wrote in his journal, not triumphantly but with superiority, "He suffers because he has removed every constraint from his life. Limits are what give life structure, and in eliminating them, he reduces his own to an empty husk while searching for a freedom that vanishes the closer it seems to attainment."[3]

For Christmas and New Year's, Hélène was once again claiming exhaustion, and Christiane was confined to bed with scarlet fever. But Roger—Roger was exalting over the steps he had taken to secure his place in the literary world. The war had almost completely destroyed his circle of male friends. Now he made new ones well suited to his new life, some already celebrated, the others soon to be: novelists André Gide, Georges Duhamel, and Ferdinand Verdier, classicist and archeologist Félix Sartiaux, and Gallimard editor Jean Schlumberger. He had a project, one he believed would occupy him for at least two decades, a roman-fleuve, the extended account of a family, the Thibaults: "My book will cover forty years, divided into thirteen periods, each of which will constitute a book; with more than twenty-five characters, you can imagine the intersecting plots of all these jumbled lives." He had a sense of the broad sweep, though the details would change: "There is the Thibault family, father and two sons, Antoine and Jacques. There is the Fontanin family, the mother and two children, Elie and Jenny. Jacques marries Jenny and is killed in the war. Antoine then marries Jenny, his sister-in-law. He becomes a celebrated physician, but as he dies from cancer, he realizes that his life has been that of a poseur." Roger began filling dossiers with notes, observations, and rough drafts of important scenes. He wrote in his journal on July 18, 1920, "Today I start writing *Les Thibault*. . . . I have this book before me as a long future to live day by day. I experience simultaneously dread and a sense of security." By late September, he was complaining about his lack of progress even though he had completed more than eighty pages.[4]

As Roger began his *Thibault*, he altered his living arrangements. Over lunch in March, Gide complained to him how constant interruption made the work of writing difficult in Paris and how "isolation" was necessary for serious thought. Roger agreed: the "leap into misery" had been easier to imagine than to live. He quickly decided to acquire a writing studio outside Paris, in Clermont, about fifty miles north. He would take the train there Monday morning and return to the Rue du Cherche-Midi Friday evening, leaving Hélène and Christiane to fend for themselves through the week. Hélène made a weak and pathetic protest: "All I ask is to rest silently in your shadow. I have always loved being next to you while you work. I recall good times when you were in the midst of *Barois*, when I had the joy of watching you write and the pride that I was not in the way, as I have always feared." Roger refused to change his plans—even when Hélène took to her bed again, this time with a worrisome combination of anemia, elevated blood pressure, and congestion in her left lung; even when Christiane had a tonsillectomy. He wrote Marcel about his daughter in most unflattering terms. "You would hardly recognize this big slovenly girl who is ruggedly built, dresses like a boy, has brusque manners, a broad face, enormous hips, the breasts of a wet nurse, a loud, sharp voice, firm opinions about everything, desires of irresistible intensity, going from one extreme to the other, burning tomorrow what she adored yesterday, determined, boisterous, apathetic, and obstinate."[5]

This disregard of his wife and daughter was callous. Did he mean it? He certainly acted in a contradictory manner that could only have heightened their sense of ambiguity around him. When his new friend Félix Sartiaux announced plans to marry at the age of forty-five, Roger cautioned, "The wedding is only the point of departure, and you cannot rest a single second because the conjugal future is inherently unstable. I have had so many ideas about it that seemed good to me: I bought and paid for them, one after another." Yet to Georges Duhamel, he crowed, "my wife and my daughter fill my lungs with good air." Roger revealed one clue to the puzzle when he mused, "I think the sentiment that flourishes naturally in me is not *love* but *friendship*. From schooldays on, I have been an exceptional friend. I have the gift of friendship. I am sympathetic, sincere, loyal. With Hélène, my love quickly became friendship. With Christiane, my paternal fondness inclines in the same fashion. My dearest ambition would be eventually to have with her an ease, an openness, a complete understanding between us." Six weeks after denigrating Christiane to Marcel, Roger had changed his mind, "I see developing in her *values* that are beyond price in my eyes: a subtle sensitivity, a sound balance to her judgments, reliable, straightforward, nuanced, a fundamental candor, a natural seriousness, a lively intelligence, . . . an instinctive understanding of what is essential in life. All that prevents me from regretting that she is ridiculously egotistical, concerned above all with her own well-being, abrupt and ungainly in her movements, and often vulgar in her behavior." Christiane could surprise him—favorably. When he went over with her the assignment for her history class about the Reformation and insisted on the necessity to be "tolerant and broad-minded," she replied, "Oh, yes, of course." He could charm Hélène. In early January 1921, she left Christiane in the care of his parents and joined him at Clermont. "She sobbed one evening in my arms. As if by magic, the following morning she awoke, her nerves calm, her face relaxed, animated and full of good cheer. Here is the proof that everything can be made right, that in fleeing Paris and everyone else, in living simply with me, away from all responsibilities, Hélène rediscovers her youth—rediscovers herself."[6]

Yet the great issue of contention remained: would Roger or would Hélène be dominant over Christiane's upbringing. In the middle of her thirteenth year, Christiane was precocious. To her father, she declared that she would "marry late, after having tested her inclinations" and would choose "a man at least thirty years old in order to be certain of his worth . . . preferably an artist, a true artist, who had ideals but was also 'comme il faut.'" And in the middle of her thirteenth year, Christiane was insolent. To her mother, she replied, "You think me always in the wrong, but I see, day by day, that you are the sole cause of all the trouble between us." Hélène confronted Roger: "I love Christiane for herself. I think of her future. I know by experience that for a woman, happiness is possible only through submission, sacrifice, perpetual restraint. I have a single goal, to develop in Christiane these qualities, without which she will be unhappy and will create unhappiness around her. You, on the contrary, love Christiane for yourself. For your selfish pleasure, you seek to develop the qualities and even the failings that are your own, and you are glad to find them in her. . . . I cannot endure watching you, with my own eyes, ruin Christiane's character, encourage in her vanity, egotism, independence, undermine my influence, make of her a spoiled child, without character, without moral strength, incapable of yielding to the requirements of life, of submitting to a husband, of raising children, someone capricious and reckless, overly confident of her intelligence and judgment, everything contrary to what a wife and mother should be. Let me tell you: for fifteen years I have hated certain failings in you, and the thought that you want, consciously or not, to mold Christiane in your image is odious to me. *I have many times been glad not to have had more children, for fear that they might resemble you. Having a single daughter is perhaps already too much!* I have only one hope, that Christiane grows up quickly, marries, and goes away, away from you. But until then, I have before me eight or ten years of martyrdom, and when I anticipate all the suffering you will cause me, my courage fails."[7]

And Hélène was not finished with her indictment, after all, she had the vocation of a Catholic mother to fulfill, to guarantee Christiane's moral education and spiritual formation. When Roger criticized Hélène for constantly scolding Christiane, "Always this conception of life as duty, imposition, and constraint, never joyful, carefree, effusive," she exploded, "All that is your fault! If I can no longer put up with Christiane, it's your doing! If you had not come back from the war, it would never have happened! She was calm, obedient, thoughtful, confident, affectionate. I had the trust and regard of my daughter! You arrived, and everything changed in a few days! You criticized me in front of her. You never treated me with respect. You spoke to me as if our child were not present between us. You deprived me of my daughter, you tore her away from me. You represented fantasy and liberty. . . . Christiane has become the arrogant, irritable child that she is because you have encouraged in her a resemblance to you. . . . *I am dying from it. You are making me a corpse.* I have nothing left to expect in this world. You took my youth, my joy in living, and now you take my daughter, but my life within I can preserve from your destruction! You have slowly poisoned all the wellsprings of my life! But God remains to me, and my death, of which I think more and more each day, will be my liberation! Do not believe that I love you less. I love you passionately, more and more—the war proved that I cannot live without your love, that I cannot be separated from you. So it is my fate, my misfortune, that this love has brought me only suffering! I am like a garden through which a fire has passed. Only cinders are left. You have been my torturer—without wanting to be."[8]

The following day, Roger wrote, "Hélène says that I have made of her a corpse. To the extent that she is right, I must humble myself, must never neglect her, make an ever larger place for her in my life. It's all I can do to make amends." He had a letter from Marcel, now at Fort Lamy (N'Djamena) in Chad, who corresponded with both of them and though 2,600 miles distant comprehended Hélène's dilemma exactly: "Between you two, she is the victim, and this perpetual sacrifice seems to me all the more excruciating because it is absolutely in vain. Her sacrifice has prevented nothing and will never prevent anything, for Hélène will always be vanquished in this struggle that she leads against life. All things considered, she is indeed fighting against life. Ah, how I curse the odious principles of the Christian religion, of Christian education, the single cause of Hélène's unhealthy sensitivity, of all her present sorrows and all that perhaps await her still." In reply, Roger noted his distress that Christiane continued to attend early morning Mass several times a week and described Hélène's "excessive taste (and increasing, alas) for self-sacrifice . . . relentless, without a smile, without spontaneous joy." Even Suzon wrote from her convent. "Will we ever get back the Hélène we once knew? Sometimes, I tell myself that she is dead. Life has been too harsh for her. . . . I wonder whether the little wick that still smokes will ever flare up into the beautiful, cheerful flame of before?" Roger wanted to blame Hélène's emotional outbursts and saturnine moods on something exterior to himself and their marriage. He settled on the death of her longtime confessor, Abbé Julien Marchand, in June after a painful illness. Roger described Hélène's "unremitting grief. . . . She placed her faith not only in God but in God as taught by Abbé Marchand. His death deprived her of the only true friend she had and took from her a vital sense of security and refuge that she could not find on her own." Maybe Roger was right, because by late fall Hélène slowly grew less morose, and they rode out this marital storm. At the end of December 1921, he could write, "I finish the year with a sense of complete happiness."[9]

Despite this turmoil, perhaps even because of it, Roger worked rapidly and well on his *Les Thibault*, completing the first two parts by January 1922. Three months later, and almost exactly two years after he began the manuscript, Gallimard published his *Le Cahier gris* (The Gray Notebook) on April 15, and then *Le Pénitencier* (The Penitentiary) on May 15. Roger's intimates could not but be aware that he borrowed from them for the principal characters: Antoine Thibault was a version of Roger himself, Jacques Thibault of Pierre Margaritis, their father Oscar Thibault of Pierre's father, and Daniel de Fontanin of Marcel. The detail and realism about them were a legacy of the training in research Roger had received at the Ecole des Chartes. The fluency and facility of his writing were the result of tirelessly drafting the various scenes, occasionally as many as eight times, until they met the high standard of refinement he had established with *Jean Barois*. To Roger's delight, Romain Rolland, the 1915 Nobel laureate for literature and author of the ten-volume roman-fleuve *Jean Christophe* (1903–1912), was impressed enough to write that this beginning to *Les Thibault* was "true, alive, original, brave and sound." Roger himself had grandiose expectations: "I already imagine my grand work finished, not just *Le Cahier gris* or *Le Pénitencier*, stupid titles and divided arbitrarily, but *Les Thibault*, complete in its thirteen parts, published in five or six volumes. I nourish the illusion that the current readers of these first volumes will be only a small fraction of the ones I hope to have later." The dedication page read, "To the dear memory of Pierre Margaritis, whose death in a military hospital on October 30, 1918, obliterated the powerful creative work ripening in his pure and anguished heart." This declaration portended—and rightly—a return to the moral anguish in *Jean Barois*, because for Roger, the questions he had posed before weighed even more heavily on his mind now.[10]

Antoine and Jacques Thibault are scions of economic privilege, born into France's upper middle class. Their father, Oscar Thibault, has made a fortune in business and regards this success as a tribute to his own shrewd capacity and as the blessing of God upon his righteousness. He is ostentatiously Catholic, proud of his position as a lay personage in the church and always consulting his confessor, Abbé Vécard, before taking any important decision. The time is June 1904—Antoine is twenty-three and a medical student, Jacques is fourteen, attending a Catholic school. As the novel opens, Jacques has run away from home, but worse, absconded with Daniel de Fontanin, not merely studying at a lycée, one of the elite state secondary schools, but a Protestant. Oscar Thibault calls him "that wretched little heretic." Abbé Binot, the rector at Jacques's school, has found a grey notebook that the boys used to exchange

letters, and the tone of fervid emotion raises suspicions about their relationship. After presenting this evidence, he adds primly, "Yes, we know only
too well what lies beneath the sanctimonious airs of Protestants." Antoine
thinks Jacques will return on his own, and unafraid of sullying his hands
or endangering his soul through consort with Protestants, he dares go to
the Fontanin home, where he meets Daniel's mother, Thérèse, and younger
sister, Jenny. The households are mirror images: Oscar Thibault's wife, Lucie,
died giving birth to Jacques while Thérèse de Fontanin's husband, Jérôme,
has largely abandoned her to pursue affairs with other women. Jacques and
Daniel have taken a train to Marseille and plan to find passage to the French
colony of Tunisia. For Jacques, rejecting his birthright and making a new life
far away is the ultimate rebellion against his father's strictures. For Daniel,
the escapade is an adventure, not much more than a caprice. Gendarmes
pick them up on the road from Marseille to Toulon and bring them back to
Paris. Thérèse de Fontanin embraces Daniel with joy and relief. Oscar Thibault barely acknowledges Jacques as he excoriates, "He's a young scoundrel,
with a heart of stone. Was he worth all the anxiety we've gone through on
his account?"

In retribution for his sins, Jacques is confined at his father's monument to
right-minded virtue, the Oscar Thibault Foundation at Crouy. Some fifty miles
north of Paris, it is a reformatory for hooligan youth that relies upon stern discipline, manual labor, and daily Mass to eliminate delinquent habits—and for
additional persuasion, a diet of bread and water. Jacques is spared the worst of
this regime, but his father demands, "The young ruffian! We've got to break his
will." Although forbidden to inquire after his brother's welfare, Antoine goes
to Crouy after ten months and finds it "reeks of the prison-house." He offers
to take charge of Jacques himself and enlists Vécard on his side by insinuating
that the guards engage in sexual abuse. When his father objects and insists on
the right to mete out discipline in his own fashion, the priest compares him to
a Pharisee. The accusation stings Oscar Thibault: "His shoulders sagged and
he dropped back into his chair. He was picturing himself on his deathbed,
and a dread came over him that he might have to face his last hour emp-
ty-handed. He tried to reassure himself by recalling the high esteem in which
the world held him." Then, he relents. The arrangement brings a chastened
and more composed Jacques back, not to his father's house but to a separate
apartment he shares with Antoine. He spends his days and nights preparing
for the competitive examination that determined admission to the summit of
universities and liberal arts in France, the Ecole Normale Supérieure. His only
recalcitrance is a secret and sporadic correspondence with Daniel against his
father's specific edict.

Antoine continues his medical studies and makes hospital rounds with the attending physicians who are his mentors. Increasingly self-satisfied, he regards himself "as a fine figure of a man, built on exemplary lines. What particularly pleased him was the look of grim determination on his face." He shares this trait with his father and insists that "pride comes in very useful as a driving force." Aside from passing liaisons with young women well below his social station, he avoids romantic entanglements. But like Jacques, he is drawn to the Fontanins, who are so different from the Thibaults, easy, informal, pardoning. In Antoine's case, the draw is Thérèse, whose mature sexuality is a perfume he inhales deeply as he tells her, "Your Reformation was a revolution on the religious plane, for it opened the door to ideas of spiritual freedom." His mere presence in her house, a Protestant, a married woman estranged from her husband, would have scandalized Oscar Thibault. And if he could overhear their conversation, the praise of heresy would not be the worst of his worries. For Antoine was dismissing any requirement for ultimate truth: "I don't claim . . . that science explains everything, but it tells me what things are, and that's enough for me. I find the *how* of things sufficiently interesting for me to dispense with the vain quest of the *why*."[11]

Roger was about half a year late with the third part of *Les Thibault*, which appeared as a two-volume set in October 1923 under the title *La Belle Saison* (The Summer Months). He could blame part of the delay on an unreasonable fear that Germany planned a new war, writing to Marcel, "the menace is imminent and grave. . . . Everyone is against us," and predicting to Verdier, "a new war with Germany, this time with France fatally alone, our rapid defeat, and our subjection to a pan-Germanism blended with Bolshevism that will be far worse than our shameful, rickety, nationalist Republic."[12] He could blame more on realistic fears about the health of his parents. His mother suffered from unexplained uterine bleeding, his father from arteriosclerosis and perhaps dementia. In December 1921, Roger himself experienced what may have been a transient ischemic attack, a mini-stroke. Afterward, he recalled, "I had such a dizzy spell that I lay down on the sofa, and then, feeling worse and worse, took off my clothes and went to bed. Truly, I had the intuition that I was going to die. *Not be ill but die* from a blood clot to the brain. I felt a strange sensation below my left eye. I lay quietly, utterly lucid. . . . I was astonished that my distress was not greater. I noted how rapidly I became acclimated to the idea of death."[13] But the true cause of the delay was his developing friendship with André Gide.

Near the end of 1920, Gide visited Roger at his writing studio in Clermont. After they discussed the progress of *Les Thibault*, Gide revealed his extravagant life as a bisexual. To Marcel, Roger exclaimed, "In comparison, all the works of Dostoevsky seem children's books." Then, in March 1922, Gide declared to Roger the intention to flaunt his unbridled sensuality through the publication of two books, *Corydon* and *Si le grain ne meurt* (*Unless the Seed Dies*). *Corydon* consisted of four Socratic dialogues arguing that homosexuality was not unnatural and should be accepted as an accompaniment to heterosexuality; Gide had privately printed some portions of it between 1911 and 1920 and had distributed them discreetly. *Si le grain ne meurt* was Gide's confession of his introduction to homosexuality during his youth while on a trip to Algeria with Oscar Wilde and his subsequent engagement to his cousin, Madeleine Rondeaux; their marriage in 1895 was never consummated. Roger argued strenuously against publication, warning that Gide would create around himself "an atmosphere of mistrust, indignation, and contemptuous calumnies." Gide responded that he had "a duty" to reveal himself as "the being that he was," that he could not be like "most people who rather than exalt what makes them exceptional and unique instead muffle their true selves." He insisted that the novels of Marcel Proust, the theories of Sigmund Freud, and the proponents of free love in Italy and Germany made the moment propitious. Roger could not convince him otherwise, and both books appeared in 1924.[14]

During the summer of 1922, Roger and Hélène anticipated the royalties from the initial volumes of *Les Thibault*, which by December were approximately 10,000 francs ($14,000 in 2015), by celebrating with a long vacation on Porquerolles, a resort island just off the French Mediterranean coast. In the midst of their stay, Gide arrived with two trunks of clothes, took the room next to theirs, and announced that his friends Mme Maria van Rysselberghe, wife of the Belgian neo-impressionist painter Théo van Rysselberghe and known as "the Lady in White" (*la Dame Blanche*) from his portrait of her, and their daughter, Elisabeth, would soon join him. The following year in 1923, Gide would have an affair with Elisabeth, who was then thirty-three years old to his fifty-four, as well as the daughter of a good friend. The sexual component of the relationship was brief—and likely the only liaison of his life with a woman—but it resulted in the birth of a daughter, Catherine. Because at this moment in 1922 Gide was a celebrated novelist, not yet a notorious celebrated novelist denounced for debauchery, Hélène did not object to the presence of Roger's friend. Soon enough she did have an objection, Gide's inviting Roger—the invitation pointedly not including Hélène—to the ten-day retreat, the *décade*, established by Paul Desjardins, Hellenist scholar and columnist for Parisian newspaper *Le Figaro*, at the abbey of Pontigny in Yonne, near Auxerre. Desjardins had organized retreats from 1910 to 1913 before he had to cancel them because of the war and planned to start anew with one near the end of the summer in 1922. His approach was to invite a core group of French literary and academic figures to whom he added special guests chosen because of their expertise in the several interrelated topics under discussion that year. After the 1922 retreat, Roger became one of the core group, and his annual sojourns to Pontigny would lead to angry recriminations from Hélène.[15]

Six months earlier at the end of 1921, Roger convinced himself that he and his wife and his daughter had reached at least a temporary calm. If so, by early spring he realized his misimpression. "Hélène," he wrote in his journal, "is nervous, irritable, and exhausted. Her relations with Christiane are deplorable: Christiane, annoying and insolent, Hélène, wounded and severe." For Easter, he took Christiane with him to Clermont and left Hélène alone with her religious obligations. There, he decided that his daughter's true need was "not freedom but *complete freedom*. . . . She is no longer a child. She is a grown-up"—Christiane was then still three months from her fifteenth birthday. And in a prediction that he would recall with bitterness, "I believe that her dominant trait is sensuality, and by that I mean, notably, a taste for living, for dominating, for imposing her will. . . . The life of an ordinary woman, husband, home, children, will not suffice to make her happy."[16]

That summer, Roger and Hélène vacationed together at Porquerolles without Christiane. After Gide and his friends arrived, she reproached him. "I am aware that we no longer have the same need for each other. I love you too much still. I am never as happy as when I have you to myself." About the forthcoming retreat at Pontigny, she was resigned: "I predict that on coming back from such a learned and exalted gathering, the return to our home will be a kind of dive into shabbiness. Once more our reunion will be distressing, once more the year 1922 will have added to the distance between us, once more we shall have to admit it, cold-bloodedly. . . . With tenderness for you, Your Stranger." She was right. Roger filled pages of his journal with enthusiasm for the retreat, where he found Gide, Maria and Elisabeth van Rysselberghe, Schlumberger, novelist and biographer André Marois, celebrated French critic Charles du Bos, equally celebrated German critic Ernst Robert Curtius, Robert de Traz, editor of the *Revue de Genève*, Jacques Rivière, editor of the *Nouvelle Revue française*, and of course, Paul Desjardins and several of his students. Roger concluded triumphantly, "Visibly, I won the *sympathy* of everyone." To Marcel, he boasted that the retreats were "*meetings* of 'superior people.'" Back in Paris, "Hélène believes that life separates us more and more and says so as a fact, not an accusation. She feels estranged from my new acquaintances, by which she means everyone who thinks differently from her. . . . I cannot renounce living, meeting people, making new friends. I cannot renounce advancing. By the fact that she is tied to an immutable religion that gives her a fixed, solid, permanent attitude toward life, she seems left behind. . . . My dreams of the future are the opposite of hers. I imagine establishing myself somewhere, far from Paris, in worthy surroundings with everything I hold dear, organizing my work there, taking in friends, . . . while she dreams of having only a pied-à-terre in Paris and roaming the world, looking at the scenery and countryside, contemplating without end the sky and the sea." No wonder that later, when Roger read to Hélène some passages from the next section of *Les Thibault*, she exclaimed, "How strange that you are able to analyze your characters so brilliantly but you are never able to understand me!"[17]

More and more, they thought about each other with such regret. Roger wondered, "Does Hélène hate me without yet realizing it?" When she left him a note about her visit to Issy-les-Moulineaux, the Parisian suburb where the Abbé Marchand had been vicar, and her conviction that she was *awaited in the next world*," she was certainly not referring to him. Remembering how often Hélène had sought out Marchand and that he was buried at Issy, Roger supposed that he "must have been the great love of her life, whom she wishes to be her eternal companion in the life to come. Her feelings inspire in me such a gentle melancholy. If only the Abbé Marchand had not been a man in a cassock and that Hélène could have loved him 'in this world.' I would have accepted it. . . . Could Hélène find happiness outside of me, I would almost be relieved." Her thoughts were not dissimilar; on March 7, 1923, the anniversary of their introduction, she wrote him: "Eighteen years ago today, we saw each other for the first time, and fate bound our lives. We would have trouble recognizing each other." And some two months later, she added: "Not a single time this winter have you noticed the great efforts of tenderness, sacrifice, and kindness I have made for you. . . . Let us admit that 'the good times' are over for our marriage and that since last year we have entered a new phase in our conjugal life. We should put up a good face and do our best to adapt. . . . I remain without fear for the future because I am certain that you will arrange everything for the best. When Christiane is married and I have more freedom, I shall travel so often that you won't get tired of me." Roger retorted, "Why do you think I have been hard to live with this winter? *I believe exactly the opposite.* . . . I truly believe that this winter we have rediscovered equilibrium and peace." Not long after, he gave the lie to his protest and proved her right: for her sixteenth birthday, Christiane was to have a trip to Great Britain in July but vehemently resisted having her mother as a chaperone. Roger had her go with Antoinette Quentin-Bauchart instead.[18]

These domestic alarms, the interplay of emotions, and the subtle, even insidious, influence of Gide's deeds and disclosures had an influence on the third part of *Les Thibault, La Belle Saison*. For the first time, Roger dwelt on carnal morality.

Five years pass. Jacques has prepared so diligently that he obtains the third-highest score on the examination to enter the Ecole Normale Supérieure. Antoine has specialized as a pediatric physician and is increasingly recognized as the most talented of his generation. Seeing only the externals, Oscar Thibault proudly assumes credit for the achievements of his sons and takes the legal steps necessary for them to inherit his full name, as in Antoine Oscar-Thibault, to distinguish themselves from Thibaults who have accomplished less. He knows nothing of how far they diverge from his ideals. Within Jacques, the old resentments still rage. Sometimes, he contemplates submitting to his father's conventional bourgeois patterns, "get his degree, become a cogwheel in the machine." More often, he imagines giving "full rein to the destructive forces that surged within him ... against morality, the cut and dried life, the family, society." Within Antoine, the rebellion is insidious. Called to treat a young girl hit by a delivery van, he discovers that she is hemorrhaging severely and will die before she can be taken to a hospital. He has to carry out an emergency operation in the family's dining room and saves her life by suturing a ruptured femoral artery. Afterward, he is attracted to one of the neighbors who assists him. This Rachel Goepfert would excite his father's disapproval in every way. She is half-Jewish and has been a ballerina, a circus horse rider, and the mistress of a scoundrel, Hirsch, who has fled to the African Sudan to avoid arrest. She seduces Antoine immediately, telling him, "A night like that works you up!" Gazing at her the next morning, he feels "like a starved jungle creature whose raging hunger nothing, nothing could ever quiet."

Among the Fontanins, Jérôme's profligate affairs excite his son Daniel to emulation, his daughter Jenny to revulsion. Daniel has become a successful painter whose association with the prominent art dealer and publisher Ludwigson has brought him the sales and the flamboyant notability that assure sexual conquests. Jenny thinks her brother is sullied by "impurity" and worries that he "may end up losing ... the sense of sin." Perhaps from his experiences at the reformatory but more because he sees himself as a rebel who holds himself to a higher standard, Jacques has a similar sense of abstention. During brief furtive moments, they confess to each other their fears and believe they share a profound, and utterly chaste, love. For Antoine and Rachel, confession provokes a crisis. Her sensuality enraptures him—"Rachel's nakedness in all its splendor"—her salacious comments arouse him—"My dream for when I am old is to ... run a brothel. ... I'd like to be sure of having young folk around me, fine young bodies." But further revelations unnerve him. By her first lover, she had a daughter who died as an infant. And Hirsch, though an arms smuggler, murderer, and sexual pervert, is the only man she will ever love. Trepidation twists his heart, and Antoine senses in himself "the antipathy of a domesticated animal for the prowling denizens of the wild that are a menace to the home." When Rachel announces that she must leave for the Congo to look after her investments there, Antoine is relieved.[19]

Roger's protagonist and sometime alter ego might have assuaged his troubles, but Roger himself was entering a period of emotional turmoil. The first episode was a cryptic encounter on October 3, 1923, with Robert Honnert, a young student at the Ecole Normale Supérieure who had written him a series of fawning letters. Their meeting had a preface: about a month earlier, Roger had attended his second retreat at Pontigny where he found Gide "literally *possessed* by his *obsession* with homosexuality." When Roger met Honnert in Paris, he found him effeminate, loud, and poorly mannered, despite his education at the renowned Lycée Louis-le-Grand—yet also alluring. After dinner, they continued their conversation in Honnert's room at a student hotel. Did Honnert try to seduce Roger? In his journal, Roger wrote, "Nothing happened. I would say, indeed, *the contrary.*" But perhaps Roger was tempted. Nearly two months later, he pondered: "I familiarize myself more and more with the idea of suicide. I think of it with a shiver of anguish but also a sense of security. If ever I succumbed to evil that could not be pardoned, I would kill myself."[20] Throughout the rest of his life, Roger had close friends and associates who were thought to be, and sometimes were, homosexual or bisexual. Based upon his journal, where he revealed his most profound emotions and fears and where he never hesitated to portray himself at his worst, Roger was neither.

On April 3, 1924, Roger's father suffered a massive stroke. With his wife and two sons gathered in grief around him, he lay unconscious for two days before he died. A single day later, in the midst of the planning for the funeral, his mother's surgeon informed Roger that she suffered from advanced uterine cancer. In keeping with the custom of the time, she was never told of this diagnosis, but she must have known because her physicians began radium treatment at the end of the month. By August, they no longer held out hope for remission. She was now in constant pain, alleviated only through injections of morphine. Without being asked, Hélène assumed control of her care, keeping watch at her bedside, sleeping in the same room. Finally, she won praise for her compulsion to duty and self-sacrifice, Roger writing: "The odor of decomposition is unbreathable. Hélène lives within it, calm and methodical, courageous and skilled. . . . I shall never forget what she has done and how she has eased my mother's end." He revealed to friends, "My mother is spared nothing, the most hideous and degrading physical miseries"; "purulent ulcers, we live in horror." And so Roger himself just hoped for an end to the torment: "I do not want my mother's death. I want that I did not have to wait for this death." On December 31, his mother's physicians gave up all hope, and she died two weeks later on January 13, 1925. Roger confronted eternity: "Before this casket, distraught to my depths yet brutally sincere, I find in myself not the slightest impulse of spiritual illusion, and the *materialist notion of death* imposes itself upon me with evidence more *overwhelming* than ever. We found in my mother's drawer a note in her hand, written since my father's death, with these final wishes. Here is the first sentence: 'I ask God's forgiveness for not having known how to make of my two sons good Christians.' The second: 'I ask Roger to do for me what he refused to do for his father, a last sign of the cross with holy water on my tomb.' I experienced nothing so profound at the death of my father." For her funeral on January 16, "The whole morning, I was not able to hold back my tears."[21]

But with the tears came the knowledge of a large inheritance: how much unclear, but sufficient, Roger believed, for his new ambition. Since mid-1922, he and Hélène had been spending more and more time at Le Tertre—so much for the "leap into misery" now that he was a best-selling author. Hélène's father, a widower since 1919, contemplated selling the estate and moving to an apartment in Paris. Of his children, Henry was disabled from the head wound, Suzon was a nun, and Manon had no interest in country living. That left Hélène and Roger. They were indeed interested. In the Norman countryside, he could "live like a nobleman" (*vivre noblement*), a *literary* nobleman. She could revive her childhood memories and exercise her compulsion to order a household. Christiane had fallen in love with everything about Le Tertre from her first moments there. In September 1924, just as the possibility of his mother's recovery vanished and the certainty of financial legacy loomed, Roger began serious talks with his father-in-law. A month later, they agreed on a price of 200,000 francs ($230,000 in 2015) for the buildings, grounds, and furnishings, with 50,000 francs ($57,500 in 2015) due immediately in cash. On February 7, 1925, three weeks after his mother's funeral, Roger took possession and began plans for extensive renovations.[22]

Christiane accompanied Roger on this inspection tour, but Hélène remained in Paris. Ten months of caring for Roger's mother had come close to breaking her own health. But more important, because emotionally exhausting, was the incessant wear on her psyche of such a contentious marriage. She sometimes blamed herself, "Why am I so incapable of showing them warmth?

I love both of them passionately, but my love is trapped inside me," and sometimes blamed Roger, "Our differing tastes and ideas oblige me to make so many concessions. . . . The good equilibrium of our life together requires that I do not 'displease' Roger." One evening she shouted at him in tears, "What do we have in common? There's nothing to be done. We would do better, I believe, each to resume our individual liberty. Marriage is a tar pit." In 1914, Roger had written, "marriage is a hell." Now they each had a metaphor, but no escape because between them was their daughter, and both of them were determined to control her destiny.[23]

Neither could see Christiane clearly. For Hélène, she was the child led astray from her Catholic formation who might still be recalled to her proper role in life and faith. For Roger, she was the budding young woman freed from childhood shackles asserting her independence. They did, both of them, recognize her disposition to resist but failed to realize how dangerous defiance could be when combined with a lack of maturity. Clarity of vision about Christiane belonged only to Marcel de Coppet, who was in France on assignment for a year from mid-1923 to mid-1924. He spent some time with Christiane and came away worried. At the end of February 1924, he wrote to Roger warning that she was "not their little girl" anymore and was about to escape their influence. During a long conversation a month later, he was blunt: if Roger and Hélène went ahead with their plan for sending Christiane to study in England that winter, she would surely "fall prey to who knows what adventures" because she was already "troubled morally." Roger acknowledged that she acted as if she were twenty-five even though she was not yet seventeen but declared, naively, "She always has the brake of religion." Marcel shrugged his shoulders and replied, "If you understood her better, you would see that's zero." He added his opinion that she would never pass the baccalaureate examination, which she had already failed once, because she was only pretending to study for it. Fathers believe what they will about the daughters they adore. Roger did delay for a year Christiane's study in England. He accepted as expected failure in her second attempt at the baccalaureate that fall. Most of all, he regretted that Marcel's departure meant that Christiane would not have his "decisive influence."[24]

Roger's own "decisive influence" was reserved for something else. He boasted to Marcel, "In 1925, I will install myself at Le Tertre. And I believe that this date will separate my life in two parts, more so even than the war. At forty-five, fully mature, in the midst of a literary enterprise fully sketched out, when I see clearly what my life has been and what it must be in the future, I have this possibility to create a fortress around my work." He hired architects and workers, took inventories, moved forty cases of books, and discovered that everything took longer and cost more than he expected. Some two years later, he had learned hard lessons: "Before having taken on the job of construction chief, I had thought with some confusion about my easy life, about my work as an 'intellectual.' But in watching them on the job, I realized that I had the right to hold my head high, that beside me, not one of them had the right to speak of making an effort, taking pains. . . . These laborers work like soldiers, singing, watching the clock, rolling a cigarette, stealing time in order to do no more than the construction chief, myself, can require of them. Then, they deride my 'fine château,' treating me like some idle bourgeois who knows nothing of construction or of the exhausting proletarian life. Yes, I live off my investments, and yes, I inherited money, but though I have no working-class consciousness, I am conscious of being a worker whom they have no right to ridicule." In between, when he complained to Hélène about "the small errors, the poor workmanship, the difficulties to resolve from morning to night," she replied, "The undertaking was too heavy for a single pair of shoulders, but you wanted to assume it, you wanted to be the one to direct it, and so you alone have to bear the burden." Or when he insisted to Marcel, returned to Fort Lamy, how Le Tertre would be "an exceptional refuge against all that makes my life unpleasant," Marcel answered, sharply, "You are deceiving yourself to justify a costly extravagance."[25]

"Extravagance": finally, the truth was spoken (*voilà le grand mot lâché*)—for Roger was spending money as if his royalties and inheritance were limitless. From late February until early June 1925, he, Hélène, and Christiane spent nearly four months at Hyères, the oldest resort on the French Riviera. Roger's intention was rewarding Hélène for her selfless devotion to his mother and seeking yet another accommodation among the three of them in an atmosphere where the only injunction was to rest and restore themselves. The first weeks went well, as Hélène recovered from her exhaustion and Christiane studied for her third try at the baccalaureate. Then, because Roger had learned that Gide and Elisabeth van Rysselberghe were nearby in Brignoles, he invited Gide for a visit. Hélène was prepared to welcome him for a day or so, but he developed a painful ear infection and wound up staying for two weeks, by the end of which she was angry and resentful.[26]

Afterward, Roger returned to Le Tertre, Hélène and Christiane to the apartment in Paris. He passed time by finding fault with renovations, Hélène by finding fault with Christiane and then complaining about her to Roger, and Christiane by celebrating her eighteenth birthday, finally passing the baccalaureate, and complaining to her father about her mother. When Roger recounted these griefs to Marcel, he received a response that tested their long friendship. Of Christiane, he wrote: "I know her better than you do, or, rather, she has permitted me to see of herself more than she has shown you," and, "You are aware of the affection I have for Christiane, the impulse that drives me toward her." Of Hélène, he wrote: "she and you have lived a life side-by-side, full of love, while understanding nothing of each other; Hélène has suffered terribly from this lack of comprehension on your part, you but little from hers." Because Roger had always encouraged closeness between Christiane and Marcel, he could hardly complain that he had been successful, but about Hélène, he knew how to upbraid his friend: "The essence of your argument is, 'I would have loved her differently.' If you had 'loved' Edith as I have loved, and as I love, Hélène, you would never have lost the bewitchment." To attenuate this reproach, he explained Hélène's "incredible attachment" to Abbé Marchand: his was the only photograph she carried with her to Hyères, and since his death, "despite the love she undoubtedly has for me, she has become a kind of inconsolable widow—to the point that when she thinks of eternity, it is with the thought of rejoining him for an eternal union, while I will have been only an earthly and incomplete attachment." While at Hyères, he had written in his journal that the Abbé Marchand always acted as if "he had God in his pocket."[27]

Roger was claiming to Marcel and, more important, to himself that he comprehended his wife and daughter, that he could guide his family through its emotional storms. The next months should have warned him that the course was taking them perilously close to dangerous shoals. After one outburst from Christiane, shouting, slamming doors, and sobbing in her room, she exclaimed, "Don't you know that it's all because I love you. I don't love you like a father, but like a friend. Oh, it's too much." But after another one, she told him, "Let me get married as soon as possible to get out of here at last and be free!" Although she offered him a glimpse into her interior confusion and contradiction, he stared instead at her exterior. When he took her with him to the Pontigny retreat in 1926—he had, of course, never taken Hélène—he complained that she was without grace: "She is incontestably intelligent and sensible, but she dresses badly, has no sense of color, sings off-key, cannot tie a bow, cannot arrange flowers." More disappointing to him: "She has a secret horror of Gide, just like Hélène."[28]

The scenes with Hélène were quieter but treacherous. In August 1926, Edouard Herriot, then France's prime minister, offered Roger appointment to the Legion of Honor (*Légion d'honneur*), a distinction of considerable national significance but having nothing to do with literature. Roger had little regard for such awards, but because Gide had put Herriot up to it, he accepted, even as he declared that he would never publicly wear the rosette, the symbol of membership. Once she knew of Gide's role, Hélène wrote him scornfully, "I continue to be astonished—even more than astonished—by your acceptance of the rosette. Once again, you will say, with pity, 'She does not understand me.' So I won't even try." Instead, she applied the words "scorn," "arrogance," and "wickedness." When Roger invited Théo and Maria van Rysselberghe to Le Tertre for a week about two months later, Hélène did not disguise her antipathy to friends of Gide. By the end of the year, she openly wished to "live alone, in two rooms, with a maid, and no encumbrances." Roger referred to her as "a capricious and difficult invalid who must be treated carefully." Why should she complain when she was now "mistress of Le Tertre, having every-thing *material* that she could desire."[29]

Hélène made her complaint explicit in a letter to Roger dated June 9, 1927, that she left on his dresser before heading out to morning Mass. Two weeks earlier, she endured another visit by friends of Gide, again includ-ing Maria van Rysselberghe, now alone because her husband had died in December. Hélène denounced what she called "an atmosphere of lies, heavy and unclean." She claimed that since May 1922, Roger had used her as part of the camouflage several of his friends adopted to conceal "the vulnerable points of their lives." "Now, I am always suspicious of you. . . . Not one of your assertions, your actions, your decisions seems authentic to me. I no longer believe anything you tell me, whether about yourself or about your friends. You appear incapable of telling me the truth. . . . You are two peo-ple, the one that you are and the one that other influences have made you. I am forever wondering which of the two is speaking to me, judging me, and seeming to love me still." Roger replied by trying to shift the blame: "What you call 'an atmosphere of lies' is simply an atmosphere of '*caution*.' Every-one is cautious around you, beginning with me. We have to be. Everyone senses that you are unwell, unhappy, weak, and all who approach you do so with caution." He promised that if she wanted to leave their marriage, he would not stop her, would pay her expenses, and would welcome her back "at the inevitable hour of regret and return" because "I love you as much as I am able and forever."[30] With these words, he believed that he had parried her accusation. He was wrong.

Roger's sense of confidence was high because he was well on his way to more volumes of *Les Thibault*. He had set writing aside to oversee the reno-vations on Le Tertre, telling his publisher in May 1925 that twenty years later when the novel was complete, "no one will be looking up the dates when each volume appeared." By early 1926, he was making up lost time, by early 1927 contemplating twenty volumes instead of ten, and by that fall, promising three new volumes for early 1928. He would keep that pledge, but by then, the world he thought he had constructed securely around him was disintegrating.[31]

Chapter 4

~

RETRIBUTION

IN CLASSICAL GREEK MYTHOLOGY, the Erinyes (the Furies) were three, Tisiphone, Megaera, and Alecto. Terrible to behold and implacable, they chastised sinners by visiting upon them suffering and affliction. The pre-Socratic philosopher Heraclitus wrote, "Not even the sun will transgress his orbit but the Erinyes, the ministers of justice, overtake him." How could Roger have believed that he would escape their vengeance?[1]

In early July 1927, the Martin du Gard brothers met in Paris to discuss the estate of their parents. To his shock, Roger learned that while the total represented a considerable inheritance, it was less than they had anticipated and had been reduced by taxes and court costs and by declines in the value of various stocks and bonds. For Marcel, who had spent nothing of his share, the revelation was disappointment. For Roger, who had spent lavishly, the revelation was devastating. Of the fortune he had anticipated, about half was gone. He returned to Le Tertre, his so costly retreat, bowed from worry and shame. "Work, work," he told himself, "my books will be all I leave behind for Christiane." The following weeks, he woke repeatedly from sleep drenched in perspiration, imagining himself ruined, the whole world accusing him of having left his wife and daughter bankrupt. He delayed almost a month confessing all to Hélène. The impact on their current budget could be borne because they had, for the most part, been living on the income from their own property and investments and because the royalties from *Les Thibault* would increase as he completed more volumes. The problem would arise, and perhaps soon, when Christiane married. They would have difficulty providing her with a proper dowry, meaning an annuity. Of the losses, "nothing in the world will permit us to reconstitute them. *Nothing can be done!*" And plaintively, "I have kept this news from you because you warned me, and I did not take heed."[2]

Yet almost immediately, Roger was off to Pontigny for the 1927 *décade*—on "Romanticism in Depth"—and then prepared Christiane to leave for Great

Britain, where she was to study at Bedford College in the University of London. Hélène's reaction to the revelation about their financial condition and Roger's dispositions for himself and their daughter was "glacial silence." The hurt was worst about Christiane, and she wrote in her diary, "I have the frightful impression of being superfluous *between* them, superfluous *among* them. I feel as if Christiane were Roger's daughter by a first marriage and that I am only a stepmother or an aunt. By himself, he has planned every aspect of her life in London." As if to prove Hélène correct, Roger sent Christiane a long letter about marriage: "When I think of your marital happiness, I believe that it will depend in great part on the worth of your husband. . . . I mean that you must have a husband capable of giving you more than a heart of gold or the sweet joys of daily life. I believe that one of your most powerful instincts is *a taste for dominating*, to be among the first (in the best sense of the term, not for reasons of vanity or conceit but of nobility). Alone, you cannot fulfill this desire. To do so, you must have a husband who is a master of his times, who can satisfy your ambitions as well as his own. . . . The husband I imagine bringing you happiness must be a man already accomplished, a man with a remarkable personality. . . . I am absolutely certain that you will not find happiness in marriage unless the man whose name you bear is of great stock, *a true force.*"[3]

Christmas Day 1927 gave proof of the estrangement. Despite Christiane's absence for three months and her having been slightly injured when bumped by an automobile as she crossed a London street, despite Hélène's discovery of a rectal cyst and having to undergo a painful procedure for its removal, Roger and Christiane were at Le Tertre, Hélène in Paris. To her husband and daughter, she preferred midnight Mass celebrated by her new confessor, Abbé Maurice-Antoine Sudour, the headmaster of the Catholic academy Ecole Bossuet. After Christiane returned to London, relations between Roger and Hélène improved, and she spent more and more time with him at Le Tertre. Soon, he wrote in his journal of "*great happiness* after twenty-one years of marriage and so many discords. What a mystery." And she wrote in her diary about "the sweetness of life that I offer Roger by my submission and my tenderness." She had a point to make, telling him: "What I want for the time that remains to us is for you to recognize that, in spite of all, *I have never prevented you from realizing yourself*, whether in your literary work, the organization of your life, the choice of your residence—not even in this survival of yourself that you seek through your daughter." But the troubles resumed as soon as Christiane returned home at the end of June, Hélène adopting "forced smiles and false gaiety."[4]

In the middle of August, Roger took Christiane with him to the 1928 Pontigny retreat, this one on "the Postwar Generation." Not long afterward, he boasted in his journal of "her ripening intelligence. . . . I am happy with her, with what she is becoming, with what she promises. . . . I even have the impression that I have given Christiane all that I can give her and that now what follows, the completion, the crowning of the work, no longer depends on me. . . . My attitude toward her marriage proves how much I have changed. . . . Certainly, I am not indifferent to her choice of a son-in-law, but I am ready to accept him and let him continue my role." That very night, Hélène confronted him, sobbing: "I cannot live with you, with your egotism and haughtiness, without feeling suffocated, without feeling gnawed away, without feeling harrowed. . . . Perhaps if we separated radically and totally for always, I might be saved and revived. But I have lived through so many years of suffering and despair that I might well die before being cured. Because I love you terribly." Although Roger tried to comfort her, his vanity intruded. He thought that his never having had an affair, never having had the least flirtation, that he had led "an honorable life" was an answer to her desperation. Later, writing in his journal, he realized that Christiane was the source of her lamentation but comforted himself with the thought that he had saved his daughter from "domestic qualities" to imbue her with "true values."[5]

A week later, Hélène renewed her attack and this time without quarter. "Thief! You tore my child from me! She was mine, mine alone, she had been my daughter until you returned from the war. And from the moment you arrived, you shamefully *ripped her away*. . . . I should never, never have had a child with you! When a woman has the misfortune to love a man like you, she should refuse, whatever the cost, to have a child! But from the moment that I had this weakness, that I had a daughter of yours, I should have had others, five or six others, and that way I would have had something that was mine. . . . If I had money, I would already have gone! I know what I would do. I would begin my life over, adopting a child, a boy, a child who would be mine, who would love me, and who would not love you and who would be the opposite of what you are!" In her diary, she wrote of feeling "like a stranger in the midst of my own family, not speaking their language, having absolutely nothing in common with them." Roger rejected her accusation entirely as "truly monstrous," "an indisputable lie."[6]

Roger had against Hélène Christiane's declaration of devotion: "I want you to know that whatever happens to me, I will never be able to live for long away from you." With extraordinary presumption, he wrote to Marcel, "If she marries a man who tries to distance her from me, it will not last ten years, and if she marries a man who is close to me, Hélène's torture will increase tenfold." Of Hélène, he added, "She cannot live without me and will never seek a divorce or a separation because either would be a hundred times worse than her daily martyrdom." This quantitative arrogance upset Marcel, especially because he had a letter from Hélène making her own case. Now Marcel replied to his longtime friend, "In this three-sided drama that is your family I would not hesitate to condemn you if your cause was not at the same time Christiane's. . . . Perhaps I love Christiane more than you do, and I tell you so without hesitation." At the turn of the year, Roger wrote that "because of Hélène, I have had numerous, painful trials." At the turn of the year, Hélène wrote: "My duties as a mother, I do not know them anymore. They are completely gone from my life. The maternal sentiment has been systematically wrenched from my heart."[7]

Reading these last journal entries and letters evokes foreboding—and more than a hint of the cataclysm that would soon envelop all four of them. Yet through this personal turmoil, Roger never sensed the looming crisis. Instead, he focused on the characters of *Les Thibault* with great constancy of purpose. He needed the money, and, more important still, they dominated his imagination. The deaths of his parents and the renovation of Le Tertre had put him far behind the schedule Editions Gallimard hoped to maintain for the appearance of volumes. Over nearly three years, he made excuses to his publisher and to his friends, even admitting, "I am in a period of eclipse," though he never wavered in his insistence that this roman-fleuve would be not just his great work but a great work, period. To attain that height, he had to "push further, . . . taking my characters to a precise psychological point in life and *then go beyond*! Not just to *continue* but to *advance*, to gain ground on the unknowable, to mine the depths." By the summer of 1927, he was back to writing ten hours a day, making up for lost time, turning Le Tertre in "a true literary factory, a Thibauderie." Less than a year later in the spring of 1928, he had a thick manuscript, which Editions Gallimard published as the next two volumes of *Les Thibault*: part 4, *La Consultation* (The Consultation) and part 5, *La Sorellina* (The Little Sister). At the end of 1928, he had another, thinner, manuscript, which appeared in 1929 as part 6, *La Mort du père* (The Death of the Father).[8]

These second three volumes continued the moral quandaries of the first three, now heightened through acute physical and spiritual suffering. For death and dying, Roger had the aching personal experience of how his father had died suddenly, but his mother only after lengthy and excruciating pain. For faith and disbelief, he had his recurrent conflict with Hélène, and, because he was unwilling to ask a priest, the advice of devout novelist and playwright Henri Ghéon.[9]

Martin du Gard has advanced the plot from 1910 to 1913. The focus shifts decisively to the meaning of disease and death, with Antoine the principal character. Jacques is absent until near the end of *La Sorellina*, having disappeared just as he is to enter the Ecole Normale Supérieure. During a heated confrontation with his father, Jacques declares his love for Jenny, his father forbids any relationship with a Protestant, especially a member of the Fontanin family, and Jacques threatens to kill himself. Because he has left no trace for three years, Oscar Thibault fears he has driven his son to suicide. That guilt burdens him all the more grievously because he recognizes the approach of his own end from kidney failure. Antoine oversees his father's treatment but his practice is pediatrics. He has an excellent reputation, and his appointment hours are busy, filled with the children of the prominent—to his father's great satisfaction.

Would the so-Catholic Oscar Thibault comprehend the casuistry his elder son has to apply? A friend brings his frail stepdaughter for an examination. Antoine diagnoses advanced tuberculosis, a hopeless case. Because she has a few months of normal life left, he does not blight them by delivering a sentence of death. A German teacher at the Lycée Charlemagne recounts how he and his wife married in their early middle age, and because he never expected that they might have a child, he did not tell her of having syphilis when he was younger. They do have a child, a son who is mentally deficient. He wants to know whether he is responsible. Antoine wonders what can be gained from assigning blame. Again, he chooses to mislead, assuring him that the boy's condition is not his fault. The infant daughter of two friends is in great pain from an ear infection that has penetrated to the brain. When they call in Antoine for a consultation, the attending physician explains that the child will certainly die within a few days and suggests ending her misery through an overdose of barbiturate. Antoine refuses and to make certain that his colleague will not do so, administers the proper amount himself. Afterward, he wonders: "The laws of nature are the only laws that count; they, I admit, are ineluctable. But all those so-called moral laws, what are they really? A complex of habits, foisted upon us by the past."

The casuistry extends to home. Antoine believes that the strategic use of morphine to relieve his father's pain prevents him from realizing the nearness of death. He is wrong: Oscar Thibault bravely insists to his longtime secretary, "there comes an hour when rest is all one yearns for. Death should have no terrors for a Christian." He is not too weak for bombast, giving Antoine one more lecture on bourgeois morality: "I have always been proud of belonging to that prosperous middle class that in all ages has been the mainstay of my country and my Church. But, my boy, that relative affluence imposes certain duties.... Ah, the Family! I ask you, are we not the pivot on which turn the middle-class democracies of today?" Yet in the opiate haze, he turns maudlin. He recollects his wife, Lucie, their courtship and early marriage, then her death twenty-three years ago giving birth to Jacques. And of Jacques, what torment he now feels for the way he treated his younger son. Has he always blamed him for Lucie's death? What retribution is he to face in the life to come for this sin? Aware that his father is failing rapidly, Antoine revives the efforts made earlier to discover his brother's fate. The search then had been in Great Britain, but he turns to Switzerland after reading a long story, "La Sorellina," in the Geneva-based magazine *Calliope*. Although the plot is set in Italy, he recognizes immediately the resemblance to his brother's brief life. The author is Jack Baulthy, a pseudonym transparent to anyone looking for Jacques Thibault. Antoine travels to Switzerland and locates him in Lausanne, sharing a rooming house with sundry socialists and anarchists. At first Jacques is unwilling to return but finally relents before Antoine's insistence that he make a final peace with his father.

The brothers arrive just in time as Oscar Thibault suffers extreme pain from kidney blockage. He calls for Abbé Vécard to make a final confession, but the words of absolution do not comfort. With dread he considers his life: "Selfishness and vanity. A thirst for riches, for ordering others about. A display of generosity, to win honors, to play a specious part.... That 'life of an upright man'—he was heartily ashamed of it. He saw it now as it had really been. Too late. The day of reckoning has come." He is in true agony, spiritual as well as physical. Antoine draws morphine into a syringe, an amount well beyond the usual dose, an amount certain to provoke death. He injects it, persuaded that he grants mercy not only to his father but to everyone around the deathbed witnessing this anguish, this disintegration of a human being. Afterward, "the thought came to him, stark, clean-cut: 'And it was I who killed him.'" To one mourner he replies, "Your sympathy is wasted, Madame. I did not love my father." The last will and testament directs the funeral Mass to be celebrated at the Oscar Thibault Foundation that is the reformatory at Crouy. Sharing a compartment with Antoine as they return to Paris by train, Vécard offers this didactic summation: "Can you imagine what it's like ... coming to the brink of eternity without faith in God, without discerning, on the further shore, an almighty, merciful Father stretching out His arms in welcome? Do you realize what it means, dying in utter darkness, without a single gleam of hope?" Antoine replies with fervor, "I, perhaps, have seen more unbelievers die than you have.... And quite sincerely, I wish for myself that, at that moment, I may be open to all the consolations faith can give. I dread a death without hope as much as a death-agony without morphine."[10]

Roger had cast his characters adrift in a world where rules were defended in theory but abandoned in practice, where faith had its consolations but no longer its primacy, where meaning was the ultimate ambiguity because established by each individual. And now he was about to have a special private lesson about the implications of such a world. He was to discover how difficult it was to be Antoine, the character he had modeled on himself, detached, objective, and agnostic, in the presence of Daniel, the character he had modeled on Marcel de Coppet, charming, gifted, and amoral.

At the beginning of May 1929, Roger met Marcel at Bordeaux as he arrived from Chad for eight months of home leave. Their relationship had frayed over the last two years. Marcel's career had stalled—his last assignment was chief of staff to the governor of Chad—and he blamed Roger for not intervening in his behalf with Edouard Herriot, who was no longer prime minister but was indeed a member of the cabinet. Marcel thought that the Legion of Honor rosette might well have carried some weight. Roger disagreed and anyway had come to resent Marcel's claim to have a superior understanding of Hélène and Christiane. Irritated, he wrote in his journal, "For some years, my attachment to Coppet has been a cause of torment, anxiety, disappointed hopes. . . . I owe to him infinitely more sorrows than joys." Now, they hoped to bind up their long friendship through visits and talks, and especially by a trip during the fall to the French colony of Tunisia.[11]

The man who stepped onto the quay at dawn after a journey of some five thousand miles—by rail from Fort Lamy to Dakar, and then by ship to Bordeaux—looked like a prisoner released after many years of confinement in the tropics. His jacket was shabby and missing a button, his shoes worn, his face brown and dry from the sun. His squinting eyes gave the impression of a hunted animal. At the hotel, he spoke timidly when requesting a room. Then, he trudged up the stairs carrying a large bundle of clothing and an umbrella. By noon, he had transformed himself into a high colonial official, washed, shaved, "impeccable and solemn in a somber suit." Roger and Marcel had a long luncheon, trying to recapture their closeness of the past, and afterward took the train to Paris. Marcel was anxious to begin his campaign at the Ministry of the Colonies for the governorship he believed he had earned. Roger was meeting his brother, the other Marcel, who in his mid-forties was finally taking a wife, Marie-Louise Verdé-Delisle. She was twenty-five, only three years older than Christiane, and they were marrying in some haste, their engagement announced in late April with the ceremony planned for early June. Roger suspected that she was chasing the Martin du Gard inheritance and privately called her family "canaille." He offered an oblique warning to his brother, who ignored it completely.[12]

Throughout the summer, Marcel de Coppet visited Le Tertre frequently, and Roger came to believe that they had overcome their differences: "I have the feeling, and I believe Coppet shares it, that if instead of our having a friendship that has lasted a quarter century we were only to meet today, we would, approaching our fifties, find the same reasons to be friends as in 1903." More often, Marcel pursued love affairs, to his current mistress adding the seduction of women far younger than he was, including the daughter of a cousin. In late August, he attended the Pontigny retreat with Roger and Christiane and then took Christiane to visit his parents at their home in Quiberville, on the Normandy coast. From there in early September, Roger received from his daughter two disturbing letters. In the first, she wrote, "I am learning to know and love Marcel more each day . . . He is one of those rare men one can respect without the slightest reservation, the only one I have ever met who inspires in me such admiration. He is the sort of man I would like to marry." In the second, she warned, "I have changed greatly in the last few weeks. Many good things have come into my life, much happiness and much hope concerning the future. I am no longer a scatterbrained kid. I am a young woman who has considered her destiny seriously and with her whole heart."[13]

Roger was in shock and dismay, writing on September 11: "Coppet is *smitten* with Christiane, and he has *let* Christiane become *smitten* with him. . . . I never suspected for an instant that such a folly was possible. . . . They act as if they are drunk. Marcel is odious to regard. . . . He has forgotten everything. Not just his age, his health, his character, but twenty-eight years of confidence and friendship. . . . I can see how Christiane could be attracted to this handsome older man, gallant, considerate, whom she already knows well. . . . But for Coppet, a man nearly fifty does not embark on such an insane passion without recognizing that he is twenty-five [sic] years older than Christiane, that he was infected with tuberculosis, that he has a serious heart condition, that he has an independent character and is incapable of fidelity and constancy in love. . . . In her inexperience, Christiane no doubt sees herself married to Coppet, carried off to the colonies, happy with the man she loves, seeing no further. . . . What can he offer her: Perhaps ten years to live! An incompatibility of age which, once the first months of passion pass, will leave them strangers." When Roger tried to reason with Christiane, she took the initiative: "I understand that you are overwhelmed, but once the moment passes, you will agree that our decision is natural and excellent not only for us but for you and for mama. I am twenty-two years old. I have had enough of discovering young men who do not deserve me. I have now an admirable man, a man of immense worth, who has loved me since I was born and whom I have loved since I knew him. For the past few years, he has been my one great friend. . . . . . What weighs against our marriage? The fact that he is twenty-six years older than me? His health? ... He is astonishingly young still, and solid. You say he can have only feeble children, but nothing is certain. I have health enough for us both, and it's the mother who counts. Besides, children or no children, when you can be the wife of someone so exceptional, you renounce everything else. ... I have even thought of you. I would marry the only one in the world who instead of taking me away from you would bring me closer. The accord among us three, even among us four, is unhoped for. Coppet is the only man whom mama could love as well."[14]

After this soliloquy from Christiane, Roger went to Hélène. They cried in each other's arms, but she offered him no solace. She blamed his influence for turning Christiane away from the conventional life for a woman. Her voice calm, she told him: "I feared the worst. ... You played a criminal game with your daughter. You threw her into the worst society without a moral background. She could have done anything she wanted. Everything was possible. I do not approve of what has happened, but I was prepared for much worse." Discouraged, Roger sought out Marcel, who claimed that he had wanted to break the news during their trip to Tunisia but that Christiane was unwilling to wait. To Roger's objections, he replied, "You speak of my age. I can't do anything about it, but I sense myself young at heart. You speak of my health, harshly, even. *I am aware of it*, but I believe you exaggerate the dangers. *There is no question of having children. That, never.* For two reasons, among which the question of health is second. My principal reason is that I do not want such a tie between Christiane and me. ... Before too long, I will have aged, and the love passion of this child for this ripe man will have evolved, and between us only affection will be left. At that moment, *I will step aside.* I will say to Christiane, *take back your liberty.* She will be twenty-five, twenty-eight, thirty years old. Too late to love again? Too late to remake her life with a man of her own age? The experience she will have had with me, will it have diminished her, harmed her? Sincerely, I believe not."[15]

Roger returned to his study, shaken, his steps slow. He took out his journal and wrote an account of his rounds. What had he learned? He thought of "*Christiane's calm passion,* her expression serene and happy." He thought of "*Hélène's calm,* her half-acceptance forcefully affecting me." Most of all, he thought of Marcel's categorical insistence, "*the certitude that there would not be children* and thus his idea of their marriage as short-term, with the possibility that Christiane might reorient her life in her thirties." But Roger did not agree with Marcel. Christiane, he believed, would stay with Marcel until his death. He also noted how his emotions had shifted. "It's strange and perhaps monstrous, but for the last two days all the tenderness of my heart has been for Hélène, whom I sense is *my companion*. In Christiane, I sense, above all, a stranger." A few days more, on September 15, having cleared the initial disarray from his mind, Roger began examining the calendar of events. Hardly a month earlier, on August 12, Marcel had been torn between attending the Pontigny retreat and spending a week or so with his mistress, while Christiane was mulling an offer of marriage from a serious suitor. Clearly, what happened next could only be described as a "moment of madness" (*coup de folie*). To Roger's mind, as soon as Marcel felt the slightest infatuation for Christiane, he should have admitted it and then gone far away. If, some three months later, he then proposed to marry her, Roger and Hélène might well have raised objections but not about the taint of deception.[16]

For this taint of deception had filled Le Tertre with recriminations. Roger already prefaced any comment about—or to—Marcel with the phrase, "if a man were loyal and of good sense," and he had no confidence in Marcel's characterization of what his marriage to Christiane might be. Marcel assumed that Hélène would approve of him as a husband for Christiane, but she had begun "to speak of him with physical repulsion." As for Christiane, because Roger opposed her plans, "*she detests me.*" She enters my study "only *to insult me*, her eyes black, her teeth showing, ferociously." Roger believed "their double treason—in deceiving me—is a *grave* matter, an act which cannot but leave a lasting break." Marcel reproached Roger for his failure to welcome the marriage proposal, "not understanding," as Roger put it, "how I have been sickened by the way he and Christiane have treated me, deceived daily by the two people in the world about whom I was most certain that whatever happened, I would be the first to be consulted and warned." As for Hélène, she handed Roger a long letter, sorrowful, accusatory, yet pardoning, that laid bare the state of their marriage. Roger called it her "indictment" (*réquisitoire*): "The very bourgeois nature of your daughter demanded a methodical, disciplined upbringing that would have taken account of her intelligence without leading it astray.... You believed it your duty to replace all that by making her breathe an atmosphere full of intellectual exaltation, charged with higher ambitions. ... This training destroyed in your daughter all discipline in life, all control of herself, delivering her to the pursuit of pleasure, of the 'available,' which is not, I believe, a reassuring guarantee for the start of life and which has left her prey to temptations of all sorts. ... I say to myself often that if Christiane had remained my daughter, as should have been my right, she would already have made an intelligent marriage with every hope of happiness, and we would have around us a happy household and grandchildren. ... You were not created to form a woman on your own. You do not love them, you do not know them, they are strangers to you. They have complexities that escape you. All the serious moments in your daughter's life have passed by without your noticing. . . . You still have something: I, your wife, your companion for a long time, who loves you passionately, enough to have accepted everything, to have forgiven everything without reserve, and who has for you a limitless wealth of tenderness and devotion." Finally, as for Roger, recognizing his only salvation, he replied to Hélène, "Of your letter I want to retain only the hope of rapprochement between us."[17]

Four days later on September 25, Roger and Marcel departed for Tunisia as if they had not been openly antagonistic to each other during the preceding two weeks. Roger and Hélène hoped that separating Marcel and Christiane for months might cool their infatuation. Conversely, Marcel hoped to use his time alone with Roger to invoke their long friendship, while Christiane hoped to use hers with Hélène to invoke maternal bonds. To no avail for any of them. After a month of trying not to offend each other, Roger and Marcel cut the trip short. They landed at Marseille and parted stiffly. Marcel took the first train to Paris, where he continued his campaign for promotion—and successfully so, winning appointment as interim governor of Chad, with the likelihood of a rapid end to the provisional status. Roger took his regrets to Hyères, where, out of season, the hotel had only a skeleton staff, no heat, and no hot water. He remembered a conversation with Edith, Marcel's first wife, who had said, "He is entirely capable of dishonesty," and that Gustave Valmont had thought him "perfidious." His friend was, Roger concluded, *infinitely more proud than straightforward.* And then realized: "I sound like some retrograde bourgeois who spouts advanced theories but wants the most banal and conformist marriage for his daughter." The following day he resolved to accept what he could not change, "to keep my feelings to myself and from now on *to show Marcel and Christiane nothing but happy consent.*" He then wrote both of them letters expressing his good will for their marriage.[18]

To this attempt at conciliation, Marcel replied icily, "You are wise to lay down your weapons. The ones you are using are neither attractive nor even decent." Christiane did not reply at all, but in a letter sent to him during the Tunisia trip, she wrote, "You understand nothing of what is noble, exalted, and pure." Perhaps she had a point, for her father and mother were dwelling indelicately on their daughter's sexual morality. Roger knew of Marcel's many love affairs and decided that he would have had no objection to Christiane's having a liaison "provided the man was worthy of such a gift. I care nothing about Christiane's virginity, and when Coppet found the occasion to assure me that he had taken no liberties with her, I doubt he realized that I am so 'advanced.'" Hélène had a similar opinion for an entirely different reason: "I don't see why

Coppet does not simply carry Christiane off to Chad for a while—but without tying her to him legally. That would spare our announcing her engagement and marriage and leave them to decide on the length of their union. . . . For me, because this marriage cannot be recognized by religion [because Marcel was both Protestant and divorced], there is no difference between the formalities they accept and the ones they decline."[19]

By mid-December, final plans were underway. The wedding was to take place on December 31, in Paris, at the mayor's office in the seventeenth arrondissement on the Rue Batignolles. Immediately afterward, husband and wife would take the train from the Gare d'Orsay to Bordeaux and then board ship for West Africa. At Dakar, they would begin a triumphal trip by rail to Fort Lamy in Chad, where Marcel would assume the powers of governor, his new *young* wife by his side, together the embodiments of French colonial authority. Christiane had busily announced everything to everybody and was then surprised when Le Tertre filled with family and friends offering Hélène their sympathy. Roger remarked wryly, "Around me are priests, nuns, the Foucault family, and all manner of conventional people. I look at them in horror, and their disapproval makes me bristle, but through the force of circumstances, I am *on their side*." Christiane's temper flared over a letter from Hélène's younger sister, Manon: "If I have delayed in writing, it is because I feared that I would say irreparable things. I do not have the courage to congratulate you or to rejoice with you in what you call happiness but which is really only a fragile illusion. How can you call yourself joyful when you have broken the hearts of your parents? . . . Seeing you assume so many formidable responsibilities, I am afraid, because I do love you. Yes, I am afraid, because these moments of folly will no doubt be paid for by terrible suffering." In a frenzy, Christiane denounced what she termed her aunt's "ignoble letter," her "stupidity and, maliciousness." When Roger defended Manon: "I find this letter perfectly measured and dignified in its severity," Marcel took revenge for her by demanding the return of all the letters he had written Roger since their friendship formed in 1903. Roger's direct refusal widened the rift.[20]

The last week of December gave proof of the sundering. Christiane had an emergency extraction of an impacted wisdom tooth. Hélène slipped on a patch of ice, gashing her forehead and deeply bruising her cheekbone. Roger was bedridden with lumbago. All three were in significant pain, but Roger's ailment alone threatened the marriage because by French law, the father of the bride had to give his consent in person. Marcel had already determined that arranging for written consent would require more time than they had. Christiane insisted that he get out of bed no matter what. That moment permitted Roger "to measure Christiane's ferocity. . . . I am not a sick father. I am only a possible obstacle." And she was not through with the infliction of suffering. She chose the night before the wedding to reveal that she intended to have children by Marcel. So they had lied about that plan as well. She finished by shouting at both her mother and her father, "*We are finished!* Finished! *To hell with you!* It's what you wanted!" After the civil ceremony the following day, Roger wrote, "the abduction is consummated. . . . For a second time I have been present for Coppet's civil marriage." With profound emotion, he added: "I shall never forget what Hélène has been throughout this month. Perfectly *good.* A true *companion.* Gentle, sensible, steady, sensitive, understanding, and devoted. *That has helped me so much.* The thought that she is with me means everything. Truly, some ties never break."[21]

When announcing to friends the engagement and forthcoming marriage of Christiane, Roger began by concealing his hurt, writing of "reciprocal passion before which we must give way" and that "Coppet has been my best friend for twenty-five years. I am sure that Christiane will be happy." But quickly, he admitted, "My feelings are infinitely complex, especially the grieving. I must keep silent. And go on. I shall do so, keep on living once they are married and departed. Until then, I have to remain calm, remain courageous, and wait as the days pass." And: "I watch my only child depart for two, three, four years perhaps, to the heart of Africa! Letters take eight weeks to reach Fort Lamy, so five months to ask a question and get an answer! Fears torment me—the risks of travel, the living conditions, the climate, with so few medical resources." After the cruel final days of December, he showed his anger: "Christiane hands her future to a man who can give her in return only a charged and troubled past. I am too old for illusions. I wanted her to have a marriage, a family." His despair: "Coppet has carried off my daughter in the flower of her youth and taken her away to the center of Africa. I am shattered by it." And his resentment: admitting in his journal, "Whenever I am tempted to worry about Christiane, I recall that she is with Coppet and that she is his responsibility now."[22]

The stress affected Roger's health. Returned to Le Tertre, he caught a cold that became pulmonary congestion and almost pneumonia. Even more serious, he developed phlebitis and a blood clot in the left leg. His physician confined him to bed from mid-March until the end of April, with the warning that if dislodged, the clot could cause a heart attack, a stroke, or a pulmonary embolism. The danger was acute, "Since the war, this is the first time I have passed so close to death." Hélène and *Les Thibault* were much on his mind, Hélène because she nursed him tirelessly and in great fear for him, *Les Thibault* because he had, he believed, so much more to write about his characters.

But of God and of Christiane: "*Not once* did I think of God, of the soul, of life after death," and "I considered how her marriage has 'cut the cords' between us." Soon after he was recovered, he wrote Christiane: "The daughter I had, the friend I had, are no more. Now, I have another daughter, another friend, for whom my feelings are different and with whom my relationship is different, my correspondence is different. Other forms of affection, other forms of confidence."[23]

While Roger lay abed anxious and upset, he conceived the idea for a novella, which he wrote during May and June. In *Jean Barois* and *Les Thibault*, instincts venal or carnal could breech the decorum of bourgeois morality only exceptionally and always at the cost of grief. But outside that ordered existence, which was his own, Roger believed the rules were different—if rules even existed at all. His 1913 *Le Testament du Père Leleu* had celebrated shrewd duplicity. Now in *Confidence africaine* (African Secret), he treated a confession of long-ago sibling incest among North African colonists as neither lurid nor prurient but merely the memory of one more passion gone stale. During the following two years, he would write a play and another novella that implicitly took the measure of amoral behavior, together contrasting the inhibitions he imposed on the characters of his novels to the absence of restraints beyond their bounds.[24]

By midsummer 1930, though his health was improved and the novella sent to Gallimard, Roger had new trouble: increasing financial woes. Part of the Martin du Gard inheritance was a furnished mansion on the Rue Ampère, in the seventeenth arrondissement of Paris near the ritzy Place Péreire, a few steps from the mayor's office where Christiane and Marcel had married, a few more steps to the Champs-Elysées. During the 1920s, the family had consistently rented it to wealthy Americans, who could afford to pay a rent of 90,000 francs a year ($66,218 in 2015). Once the Great Depression took hold in the United States, such wealthy Americans disappeared from Paris. The Rue Ampère mansion had remained without tenants for six months, and no one showed any interest at all in leasing it. Empty, it produced no income for Roger and his brother to divide equally, and even in 1929, Roger had taken a larger share as a loan. And empty, it remained subject to taxation. Now, they made the decision to remove the furnishings and try renting out various sections of the mansion as apartments. From these leases, they could expect only 40,000 francs ($29,430 in 2015), less than half of their original amount but better far than nothing. Roger commiserated with one friend, Emile Mayer, who had retired from the army at the rank of lieutenant colonel and who was finding how little his pension covered: "All around me I see the same gnawing cares, the same financial straits, more or less acknowledged." He was especially anxious about finding 30,000 francs ($22,073 in 2015) to pay the annuity he had rashly promised Christiane as a dowry.[25]

Removing the furnishings from the Rue Ampère offered Roger another telling reprimand. He and his brother planned to sell them, but Hélène asked for the best pieces. Her confessor, the Abbé Sudour, had just been made parish priest for the church of Saint Etienne du Mont, near the Panthéon in the fifth arrondissement, home to the reliquary of Saint Geneviève, patron saint of Paris. Because the presbytery around the corner on the Rue Descartes was stark and barren, she proposed to furnish it for him and supervised the installation herself. For Roger, "The immense satisfaction she found, this revival, this rejuvenation that she showed, made me understand better how painfully she lives constrained in my shadow. She was not born to marry a man with a strong personality, with imperious tastes. She would have been infinitely happier with a good man who was a lawyer or an industrialist, who, with admiration, would have left her to reign supreme over household, family and friends, numerous children, servants. . . . I see clearly that Hélène will never be happy beside me. . . . I do not bring peace to those who live with me."[26]

Roger had not the slightest control over the fate of his investments, over the dividends of stocks, the interest of bonds, the income of rental properties, all of them in decline since the fall of 1929. He hoped that they would recover, but they would, instead, fall much further. The only control he had over his income was through the sale of his writing, and for that, he had to write—more. Yet the many afflictions he had faced had prevented him from doing more than barely begin the next section of *Les Thibault*. He planned to call it *L'Appareillage* (The Setting Off) and to explore at length the worlds of Antoine and Jacques Thibault—now that their father was dead—during the year or so before the war in 1914. He knew this period well, having lived through it and having used its revival of nationalism and religion as the springboard for Jean Barois's return to his discarded wife and Catholic faith. In May, barely out of bed from his bout with phlebitis, he wondered "whether I will have to leave *Les Thibault* unfinished. That would be a fine collapse, a failed life." But by September, he was making rapid progress—"Finally!"— and by December, warned that he was writing so much that *L'Appareillage* would require two volumes.[27]

Then, on New Year's Day 1931, Roger and Hélène drove to La Louvilière, near Le Mans, for a holiday luncheon at the home of Manon, her sister. They brought with them Colette, the daughter of the longtime groundskeeper, Baptiste, because she was a close friend of Manon's maid. On their return that evening, with the sun already down, they reached the point where the road inclined at the entrance to Le Tertre. Hélène was driving and accelerated slightly. As one wheel slipped on black ice, the car veered to the right. Roger reached toward Hélène as she tried to regain control, and she overcorrected, the car falling into a shallow ravine on the left side of the road, crashing into a tree and turning on its side. Riding in the backseat, Colette was able to push open a door and escape to call for help. Her father came running, and they were able to extract Hélène, who was bleeding badly and could barely breathe because of injuries to her neck and chest. Roger was trapped on the side of the car now against the ground and could not move. He lay helpless in the wreckage for three hours until they gathered enough rescuers to pry him loose. A local physician administered first aid, made them as comfortable as possible at Le Tertre, telephoned Roger's brother and Hélène's sister, and arranged for them to be taken the following morning to the Delagenière Clinic in Le Mans. Hélène had pitched forward onto the steering wheel, crushing her sternum, breaking her left collarbone, and cracking six ribs. Glass from the broken windshield and tree branches that passed through it lashed her face, tearing away completely the skin beneath her left eye. An especially large branch punctured her left breast and arm. Roger's left leg had slammed into the dashboard, fracturing his tibia and dislocating his patella. More branches severely lacerated his right hand, left deep contusions on his face, and broke a tooth. Besides their wounds, they were fortunate not to have died from shock. If the accident had not occurred literally at the gate to Le Tertre or if they had not taken Colette, they might not have been found for many hours.[28]

At the clinic, the physicians were able to save Hélène's eye and despite the painful injuries to her chest, had her out of bed and walking by the end of January. The cast on Roger's leg caused a recurrence of his phlebitis, but this time without a blood clot. They both healed slowly and could not return to Le Tertre until March 14, seventy-two days after the accident. While at the clinic, they celebrated their twenty-fifth wedding anniversary on February 19, and then back home, Roger's fiftieth birthday on March 23. Downcast, he noted: "The same age as my father at the time of our marriage. He's been dead seven years now. At fifty, he had less than twenty years more to live." They could not bear the frigid temperature of Normandy as semi-invalids, and in early April they sought somewhere warmer to recuperate, choosing Sauveterre, in southeast France a little inland from the Mediterranean Sea. Roger joked, "We're idiots to settle in the cold fog of the north when such pleasure comes from living in perpetual sunshine. Marseille should be the capital of France." But they had not left bad news behind. His friend Ferdinand Verdier died suddenly of meningitis; without a new installment, sales of *Les Thibault* sagged badly; and new bills arrived with each mail delivery. To Félix Sartiaux, the classicist, with the perspective of Greek and Roman decline, Roger predicted, "a future filled with catastrophic events. Our fifties will no doubt permit us to witness the commencement of vast social upheaval." To Berthe Lemarié at Editions Gallimard, which had cut back his monthly check, he confessed, "The horizon is black; funds are scarce." Worst of all, the injury to Hélène's left breast festered and raised fears of a tumor. They returned to Le Tertre in mid-July, and a week later in Paris, she had an operation under local anesthesia to remove what proved to be a benign adenoma. Roger's relief—"I was terribly afraid"—gave proof of how the torments of the last year had made them so dependent on each other.[29]

While at Sauveterre, Roger had not felt ready, not felt strong enough, to pick up *L'Appareillage* and *Les Thibault* again. But acutely aware of needing a new source of income, he began writing a play, the psychological drama of a brother and sister, middle-aged and respectable, who share a close—almost too close—bond and who each discover a homosexual attraction to another. Because they are unwilling to acknowledge these interior passions, because they withdraw into themselves, Roger titled his play *Un taciturne* (The Reticent One). Once again, he was testing the power of instinct against accepted constraints. To his great pleasure, Hélène guided some of his thinking about this problem, and he dedicated the play to her. The Comédie de Champs-Elysées theatre agreed to stage *Un taciturne*, and it opened to a successful run on October 29. The reviews were mixed: what some viewed as sophistication, others, especially the Action Française, Roger's old enemy from the time of *Jean Barois*, deplored as relativism.[30]

In his own life, Roger was hardly a relativist—and not a homosexual, taciturn or not. Indeed, two years earlier when defending their decision to marry, both Christiane and Marcel accused him of being "conventional." Considering this charge, Roger admitted that he "undoubtedly retained strongly a certain bourgeois atavism: the liking for comfort, remembrances of family, even the paunchy physical aspect of the Louis-Philippe period, a fear of risk and of the unexpected, a preference for the sedentary life. The distinctive characteristic of my bearing for the last thirty years has been, rightly, to reconcile what is solid and respectable in the bourgeois heritage with intellectual and moral emancipation." Returning to Le Tertre after the recuperation at Sauveterre, he declared, "I have been immediately recaptured by this incomparable place, the symbol of my work and success. However heavy the load of debt on my shoulders, the solution surely must never be to renounce Le Tertre but instead to make enough money to have an easy life there. ... Perhaps this *instinct for property* is the strongest, the most central, of my instincts." But having written hardly more than a few pages for *L'Appareillage* in 1931 and with his investments yielding less than ever, how was he to get the money to lighten the load?[31]

In the best tradition of his bourgeois heritage, Roger began the new year in 1932 with a complete review of his finances. He was blunt: "Our situation … is more difficult each year and now has reached the point of catastrophe." They had lived well, during the last half decade spending approximately 200,000 francs a year ($155,224 in 2015). He hoped to reduce this amount to 185,000 francs ($142,657 in 2015) for 1932. He broke down this total into four oddly defined categories. The basic costs for Le Tertre required 75,000 francs ($57,834 in 2015): taxes, insurance, heating, upkeep of the house and grounds, gasoline and servicing for the automobile, and wages for the groundskeeper, Baptiste, and the cook, Mathilde. Another 50,000 francs ($38,556 in 2015) covered Hélène's personal expenses, food, lighting, laundry, housekeeping, and maids, as well as the rent, taxes, and insurance on the apartment in Paris on the Rue du Cherche-Midi. A further 30,000 francs ($23,133 in 2015) went toward Roger's personal expenses, physicians, and a reserve for the unanticipated. And a final 30,000 francs ($23,133 in 2015) were for Christiane's annuity. For revenue, he anticipated 60,000 francs ($46,267), the same as in 1931, from two properties he had inherited jointly with his brother, a garage on the Rue Ampère and an apartment nearby on the Avenue de Villiers. A third and fourth, the mansion on the Rue Ampère, and an apartment on the Rue du Dragon in the sixth arrondissement at Saint-Germain des Prés, remained empty and without prospects. Roger's royalties had been ranging from 80,000 to 100,000 francs ($61,289 to $77,112 in 2015), with 40,000 francs ($30,844 in 2015) of the amount in 1931 from *Un taciturne*. He might expect a similar windfall from *Un taciturne* in 1932, but the total for the year would almost certainly be less because of reduced sales from *Les Thibault* and would remain so until he completed more volumes. They were short, therefore, at least 25,000 to perhaps 100,000 francs ($19,278 to $77,112).[32]

Accustomed to living well, Roger and Hélène had few ideas about how to economize. They were willing to make minor savings in the garden and to give up receiving any friends—to which Roger exclaimed in horror, "A life of reclusion!" Le Tertre contained some minor treasures, but could they consider selling paintings and furnishings that had belonged to their families for generations or books from Roger's extensive library? And what of Le Tertre itself, in which Roger had invested some two million francs ($1,552,240 in 2015) when the purchase price and the renovations were combined? "To sell this family property under the nose of my father-in-law to whom I promised a vacation retreat for the rest of his life? To consummate, in the eyes of everyone, the failure of all that I wanted, of all that I have done with such certainty and sense of permanence? But anyway, doing so would be impossible. Everyone says that for now and for many years, there will be no buyers. No one buys anything, no one risks anything."[33]

"Such certainty and sense of permanence"—Roger wrote these words as if he might never experience their quality again. The test of character is adversity. His past was what he believed he had: fortune, income, Christiane, Marcel. His present was their tarnish. His future was whether he could remake his life with what he had left, Hélène and *Les Thibault*. Had the Furies finished with him?

~

Chapter 5

VINDICATION

ON THE EVENING OF December 1, 1931, Roger summed up his situation: "imbalance, instability, imminent collapse." In all his account books—personal relationships, writing, budget—debits overwhelmed credits. Throughout his life, adversity had always spurred him to attainment. He failed at the Sorbonne, but he excelled at the Ecole des Chartes. His *Devenir!* attracted little notice, but his *Jean Barois* was a best seller. The Great War took almost all his comrades, but he survived with the Croix de Guerre. His father called his literary ambitions foolish, but *Les Thibault* elevated him to the heights of France's literary world. Like his creations, the Thibault brothers Antoine and Jacques, he demanded that fate bend to his terms.[1]

Roger understood that any future security was bound to his relationship with Hélène. Soon after New Year's, he invited her spiritual advisor, the Abbé Maurice-Antoine Sudour, for a week-long visit to Le Tertre. For Hélène, the "sympathy, interest, and attention" Roger offered was "as if the breath of God had passed through the house and purified the atmosphere." Roger himself was surprised at how easily he and Sudour talked away the evenings on all manner of topics. "He told me that he could not believe in hell, that for him, 'hell is unthinkable.' Sudour added that he never worried about eternal salvation because he believed that for almost everyone salvation was assured." To Hélène's delight, Roger even imagined inviting Sudour to his death bed. He did not tell her that he would do so only out of friendship, not for a Barois-type conversion: "no accepting the absurd consolation of religion and so abjure a life lived in total unbelief, *without an hour of worry or doubt*."[2]

Even as Roger played the grand seigneur at Le Tertre for Sudour, he was planning a strategic abandonment of his grand country house, his "Thibauderie." To make economies, he would close up Le Tertre during the winter months, dismiss all the staff but the groundskeeper and cook, and reduce drastically the heating costs. Based on their experience the preceding year in Sauveterre, he and Hélène could live simply in small hotels or in small furnished houses, taking on a local housekeeper for cooking and cleaning. To save money in Paris, they would give up the apartment on the Rue du Cherche-Midi, which they had rented for a decade and a half, and move into the Martin du Gard property on the Rue du Dragon, which was still empty. Le Tertre would remain their home, but only for the summer and the warmer months of spring and fall. They would make the best of their bad times, but as Roger complained to Jean Schlumberger: "My material existence, which over fifty years I took for granted, has been abruptly compromised. ... Properties not rented and impossible to sell, stocks and bonds whose revenues have fallen by two thirds. Even my royalties reduced. And each month, I must find some 10,000 francs [$8,412 in 2015] to pay for servants, taxes, insurance, and the like."[3]

In the south of France, at Sauveterre and then Cassis-sur-Mer (in Provence), Roger made a radical change in his plans for *Les Thibault*. During his long recuperation the previous year, he had read over the pages of *L'Appareillage*. He was engaging his characters in many capacities and exploring in depth aspects of the society around them. And if he continued to do so, *Les Thibault* would require another fifteen volumes. Could he hold his readers for so long? Did he have so long himself? At the beginning of February 1932, Roger made his decision and embraced it triumphantly: "I have found, suddenly, the means to finish my *Thibault* in two volumes [in the end, he would need four volumes], not just in an honorable manner, which would already represent a triumph, but to finish them *masterfully*, giving the work a sense that completes it, amplifies it, endows it with an unforeseen significance. ... The Thibaults die in the war, and it is a whole society, a whole bourgeois way of life that the war annihilates with them. My work will acquire a profound significance, the painting of a world in decadence and the end of this world in bloody catastrophe." As soon as he had the plot in his mind, he reassured Gaston Gallimard about his plans and progress. And he could not resist writing Marcel—perhaps out of long friendship but surely as proof that he carried on. Of course, the carrying on had to be sustained, as Roger admitted to himself: "To finish *Les Thibault* will take me two full years of work, not less."[4]

But Roger could not yet begin the carrying on. As he confessed to his journal in late April 1932, "I am obsessed with the thought that *I must write something from which I can profit this very year.* He decided upon another novella, with the characters rural peasant villagers who almost without exception he made rapacious, cowardly, lecherous, and corrupt. The worst was the mailman, symbol of the government's best intentions, who steams open letters to learn secrets he can exploit. The best were the priest, who has merely lost his faith in God, and two schoolteachers, who have merely lost their faith in learning. Roger wrote this scathing portrait of rural life in three months. He gave it the title *Vieille France* (Old France), and when he read through the page proof in November, added—with elegant spite—a dedication to Christiane and Marcel.[5]

The Coppets had news of their own. For the first time since the end of 1929, Marcel and Christiane would be returning to France for home leave and would arrive in Marseille at the end of May. Roger had long since determined his allegiance: "I recognize that Coppet's death would not lead to my reconciliation with Christiane. But Christiane's death might reconcile me with Coppet." And, "If there is conflict, I know that *I will not hesitate* to side with Hélène." They met at Avignon, and as Roger and Hélène approached the hotel where Marcel and Christiane awaited them, they felt "weak in the knees." Outwardly, everyone was cheerful and happy, but that night, Hélène cried herself to sleep, and Roger wrote in pique, "Marriage has not diminished their difference in age. To the contrary, because Coppet has lost his hair, and his face is harder." A return by all four to Le Tertre in midsummer went well, but in early fall, Christiane announced that she was pregnant. Hélène threw herself onto a bed crying out, "this, it's beyond my enduring!" but later made Roger swear that he would never reveal her reaction to Christiane. Roger's brother and his much younger wife, Marie-Louise, were also expecting their first child: "these two aging husbands, greying and tender." Hélène was, Roger did admit, "in a bad state" and, only half in jest, suggested that the remedy would be "killing four or five people, beginning with every member of Coppet's family."[6]

During the winter, with Le Tertre closed up, Marcel and Christiane stayed in Paris while Roger and Hélène secured new lodging at Cassis-sur-Mer. Roger wrote to his cousin, Maurice Martin du Gard, of "the sun, the blue sky, and the odor of mimosa." As Christiane's pregnancy approached its term, Hélène went to her daughter's side, but Marcel had to call Roger in Cassis on March 20, 1933, to tell him, "*Daniel* is born." Only then did Roger take the train to Paris, where he discovered that all was not well. Christiane was having difficulty nursing and feared for the baby's safety when she returned with Marcel to Africa. He had a new appointment, this time to governor of Dahomey (today Bénin), one of the eight regions composing French West Africa (Afrique occidentale française). They would live in its administrative capital, Dakar, where the climate was significantly milder than at Fort Lamy, and the distance so much less to France that Roger referred to it ingenuously as "a sort of Parisian suburb." Marcel would depart almost immediately, with Christiane joining him in early summer. She proposed that Hélène take care of Daniel, and provide him with a wet nurse from June until sometime late in the fall when he would be slightly older, slightly stronger, and better able to survive in Dakar with a wet nurse there. Christiane would make a special trip alone to pick him up. Hélène accepted with good grace in Christiane's presence, but Roger recognized that she was profoundly shocked: "Hélène continues to regard this marriage as a curse!"[7]

Marcel and Christiane quickly lived down to her opinion of them. They arranged for their infant son to be baptized as a Roman Catholic and then were unhappy that Hélène did not show what they considered proper "appreciation" for this "sacrifice." From Dakar, Marcel railed at Hélène's "hardness of heart and maternal hatred" and revealed that "it was not Christiane but I who had the 'touching thought' of baptizing Daniel. Christiane has always greatly regretted having agreed to this baptism which, far more than to me, was profoundly displeasing to her." Marcel then claimed to have acted in the interest of improving the relationship between Christiane and Hélène because doing so would please Roger. "I have done a great deal for you and Hélène in the past, when it cost me nothing or almost nothing. I have done still more for you and for her since my marriage, when it costs me a great deal and when Hélène constantly treats me in a manner that I do not deserve and that I try to forget. I make Christiane happy, and I have given her a son. What more do you ask of me? Other children, perhaps? Yes, if Christiane wants them. And also a material situation that will suffice for her later on when you and I are both gone and she will have no one to count on but herself and her children."[8]

Alerted by Marcel, Christiane could not contain herself. She wrote her father: "That Marcel was insulted at the moment of our marriage can, perhaps, be excused, but today, no excuses are possible. The way mama treated Marcel during this memorable month of April is perfectly intolerable. . . . That Daniel has been baptized is thanks to Marcel. I would never have consented to it by myself. That we have proposed for mama to take Daniel this summer is out of regard for her, and Marcel had the idea." Seeking a way out of this impasse and knowing that Christiane liked Marie-Louise, Roger wrote his brother, hoping that he would have his wife intercede. His language was unusually blunt: "I have received from Coppet two unqualifiable letters filled with hateful accusations against Hélène, monuments to arrogance and injustice, to which I have had to respond setting matters straight. And Christiane has immediately caught fire, like a lioness in fury, and has showered me with insults and threats of definitive rupture between us for defending her mother against her husband." The imposition of a temporary truce had less to do with cooling tempers than the necessity to care for Daniel. At the beginning of June, Christiane handed her ten-week-old infant to Hélène at Le Tertre and then took the train to Marseille and a ship to Dakar.[9]

What made this episode all the more despicable was that Roger, unknown to either Christiane or Marcel, had stolen more than four months from his writing of *Les Thibault* to prepare a screenplay of Emile Zola's *La Bête humaine* because it would pay him 30,000 francs ($26,260 in 2015), Christiane's annuity for 1933. Afterward, he was "not proud of myself! Four months, almost five months *lost*. Worse still, lost to a task of which I am ashamed." But Christiane got her money, then near the end of November, picked up her child and took the first ship back to Dakar. The experience of caring for Daniel, first at Le Tertre and then at Cassis, was hard on Hélène, Roger fearful that "she is not valiant," that "each year her strength declines to a perceptible degree." And Roger was not impressed by his grandson: "I look at this child. He is not handsome. He has *no freshness*. He looks like a little old man. Some features too prominent: an almost Jewish nose, an ungrateful expression on his face. But he seems intelligent, or so Hélène would persuade me." Nor was he impressed by his daughter, who was both nervous and imperious: her character "aggravated by colonial life, by the importance given to her in the official world."[10]

Worries about money gnawed on Roger. At the end of February 1934, he learned from Editions Gallimard that sales of *Les Thibault* had declined to the point that it could no longer issue him monthly royalty checks. So that Roger would not interrupt his writing, Hélène took the train, on a third-class ticket, to Paris and pled their case. Her revelations stupefied Gallimard, who instantly reinstated the monthly stipend—because, as he said, he wanted to see *Les Thibault* completed. On her return, they cut expenses further, moving from their modest hotel in Cassis to a furnished apartment in the Cimiez district of Nice. They would be on the sixth floor with a sunny view in a building with the impressive name "Grand Palais" but would be paying only 1,000 francs a month ($910 in 2015). With its kitchen, they could save further, as Hélène, "the chatelaine of Le Tertre" did not disdain to cook for them. Even so, they were in straitened circumstances: the check from Gallimard each month was for 5,000 francs ($4,555 in 2015), with just less than half going to pay the cost of Le Tertre, leaving them about 2,700 francs ($2,460) for all their expenses in Nice. When they had paid the rent and for food, they had barely 500 francs ($455 in 2015) for everything else, "personal expenses, clothing, pocket money, books, newspapers, the dentist, café-crèmes." Once in early 1935, Roger had to ask his brother for an advance of 300 francs ($298 in 2015) until the royalty check arrived. A year and a half earlier, he briefly considered taking out a mortgage against Le Tertre despite the attendant shame that such an infringement of bourgeois ideals would heap upon his head. He admitted to Schlumberger, whose friendship he valued all the more since Marcel's betrayal, that he simply could not expect his brother to make further sacrifices by giving him a greater share of their income from joint investments. Schlumberger then offered a loan of his own, to which Roger replied, with embarrassment, "No, reassure yourself, things go badly, but not to that point."[11]

Roger was whistling past the graveyard of his budget. By the summer of 1935, he was in desperate need of 15,000 francs ($14,930 in 2015), to pay the taxes on Le Tertre. In June, he asked Berthe Lemarié, Gallimard's chief assistant, whether she knew of anyone who might purchase a painting by Johan Barthold Jongkind (1819–1891) which had been a possession of the Martin du Gard family for more than half a century. Jongkind was a Dutch artist who had made his career in France, taught Claude Monet, and been well regarded by Edgar Degas. Roger thought it worth at least 15,000 francs but was willing to accept 7,500 francs ($7,465 in 2015). In the end, he got slightly less, 7,250 francs ($7,215 in 2015) and was glad to have it. For finding a buyer, he offered Lemarié a commission, which she flatly refused, haunted by his confession of sleepless nights because "I don't have a penny!" At the end of September, he sought her help again in selling another painting, this one by Giuseppe Palizzi (1812–1888), a member of the Barbizon School, vainly hoping that the buyer of the Jongkind would be interested.[12]

In early 1934, as Roger spent his days writing and his nights worrying, Marcel became governor of French Somaliland (Côte française des Somalis) because the Ministry of Colonies needed a senior administrator to confront the possibility of an Italian invasion in neighboring Ethiopia. Djibouti, its capital, was fiercely hot year-round, but ships made the passage from Marseille through the Suez Canal in only eight days. The task required of Marcel, to deter Italian dictator Benito Mussolini's ambitions and thereby enhance France's position in the Horn of Africa, was, as he quickly divined, hopeless. In letters to Roger, Christiane wrote of Marcel's increasing disenchantment with the colonial service to which he had devoted more than three decades of his life. When Roger commented cruelly that "conjugal happiness seemed to have sapped, little by little, the solid basis of his existence," Marcel sent an angry reply. In May 1935, with worrisome signs in the region increasing, he sent Christiane and Daniel to France, where she announced to her parents that she was expecting a second child in November.[13]

Christiane had no way of knowing how precariously balanced the lives of Roger and Hélène had become despite the obvious need they had for one another. Immersed in his troubles and his manuscript, Roger had "no one I prefer to my solitude. I sometimes regret being with Hélène. I almost always regret seeing Christiane, Gide, Schlumberger—everyone." Yet he called Schlumberger "now my *only* friend. . . . I had Coppet, but not any longer." He tortured himself through a fixation on death: "I remember the agony of my mother, or I imagine Hélène's death from stroke, accident, or cancer, but most often I am the one who dies. . . . I imagine my suicide." Hélène thought herself even more isolated. She was inconsolable over the death of her long-time friend, Mme Dalstein, who had shared her devotion to Abbé Marchand and Abbé Sudour, who indeed had held Abbé Marchand in her arms as he died. Early in 1935, Mme Dalstein discovered she had advanced cancer. She refused all treatment and told not a single one of her friends, for fear of being a burden. Hélène had known nothing of this martyrdom. In profound grief, she cried to Roger, "What I did for our two mothers, *no one* would do for me. *I have no one who has the same thoughts, the same beliefs as me, who can grant me a little of the warmth that I need.* Mme Dalstein was the only one left. Although she was older than me, I always thought that her devotion would enfold me at the moment of my death." Yet she did have another friend, the equally devout Marie Bénilan, and in April 1934, during Easter Week, the two of them traveled to Corsica with Abbé Sudour. While she was gone, Roger asked Gide and Maria van Rysselberghe to visit him briefly in Nice. Was he catering to Hélène's dislike of Gide by timing this invitation for her absence or engaging in equivalent retaliation?[14]

At first, Christiane's visit went well, with Hélène relaxed and in good spirits. But after two weeks or so, Roger learned that she was talking to Daniel of "little Jesus," despite knowing well that Christiane and Marcel wanted not a word about religion whispered in his ear. Torn between her sense of spiritual responsibility and the problem of maintaining peaceful relations, she was now in tears each evening, her face puffy but set. Marcel arrived in June, his presence no longer required in Djibouti because Mussolini seemed determined to launch his invasion and nothing could be done but await results. He anticipated reassignment and likely a demotion for his failure to prevent what could not have been prevented. In the meantime, he was full of opinions, which Christiane shared fully. "They say such stupid things," Roger complained, "and express themselves in such a *peremptory* manner. Everything would go better if we contented ourselves with laughing and taking walks, but they want to discuss! . . . Coppet is intelligent, but as a remarkable colonial governor. His professional capacities are not a basis for his judgment on people, books, and ideas. . . . Christiane's self-assuredness is a thousand times more shocking because so much more unjustified. She has complete faith in her husband, and when she utters a judgment that is hers because he had it first, she believes it to be absolutely and incontestably true."[15]

In August, Christiane and Marcel moved to Paris, where she would spend the last months of her pregnancy, and he would make his case at the Ministry of Colonies. Hélène went with them but would stay alone at the Rue du Dragon apartment. Roger remained in Nice to write. From Christiane by letter he learned that she and Marcel intended to baptize their second child as a Protestant. Hélène could not but regard the decision as a direct attack on her. Roger called attention to the utter lack of religious faith among all the Coppet family, but knowing his argument would be useless, simply told Christiane, "refusing to baptize Daniel would have made everything easier for you." Shortly afterward, he received a letter from Marcel admitting, for the first time, "I did something truly daring in marrying Christiane." Then, on November 9, Christiane gave birth to a daughter, which she and Marcel named Anne-Véronique. During the next four days, Hélène, Christiane, and Marcel all sent letters to Roger, who did not leave Nice to see his new granddaughter. Hélène described Anne as "fine and dear, absolutely the portrait of her mother." In Christiane's telling, Hélène was full of affection until the delivery, when she changed abruptly, saying "I am so disappointed. She looks just like her mother." Marcel recounted that to pray for the newborn child, Hélène visited her sister, Suzon, at the Catholic Hospital of Perpetual Care in Levallois. She took Daniel with her, and in the chapel, told him stories about "little Jesus." He added that he had learned his new post, back to Dakar, but this time as merely lieutenant governor of Mauritania, one of the lesser territories of French West Africa, a "disgrace." In reply to Marcel, Roger played up the material advantages, the mild climate, the greater safety, and the proximity of West Africa—compared to a more important but also more dangerous assignment. About Hélène and her "unauthorized" religious instruction, he urged caution. She was, he feared, spoiling for a fight, and such a fight would certainly be "envenomed." Christiane and Marcel should "wait until you are back in Africa" because Daniel would then be far from Hélène's influence. They should write Hélène "a measured letter . . . entreating her to refrain from interfering with their parental responsibilities." Roger then warned that if relations came to a rupture, "My duty is absolute. As long as Hélène is alive, I will not hesitate to choose between her and Christiane: I owe everything to Hélène."[16]

The Martin du Gard-Coppet drama had as its backdrop the increasing sense of anxiety—even fear—in France. During 1932, Roger made two brief trips to Berlin. On the first, he had the impression of "a people returned to paganism (and a little obsessed with sex)" and thought the only followers of Adolf Hitler were "imbeciles." On the second, he attended a Nazi rally and was appalled by "stupidity on the faces." Not half a year later, referring to Josef Stalin, Mussolini, and Hitler, he wondered, "Are we seeing a reaction against the principles of 1789 [Liberty, Equality, Fraternity]? Already in Russia, Italy, and Germany they are abandoned and ridiculed. And it seems to me remarkable that even in the democratic nations, the majority of young people, whether consciously or not, have turned against 'liberal' ideas." He read Hitler's *Mein Kampf* and had new respect for the dire analyses offered at least every week by Wladimir d'Ormesson, foreign policy analyst for the influential Paris newspaper *Le Temps*. D'Ormesson was a former diplomat who had warned of Nazi ambitions as early as 1928 in a book then widely discounted, *La Confiance dans l'Allemagne?* (Confidence in Germany?). By May 1935, Roger wrote facetiously that if Hitler waited to start a new war until the following spring, he would have time to finish the new volumes of *Les Thibault*. Of course, Mussolini was not waiting, at least in Ethiopia. Roger described *Il Duce* as "one of the baleful monsters Hell periodically vomits forth to the misery of mankind." Because the League of Nations, because the leaders of the democratic countries, France and Great Britain especially, were unwilling to act forcefully against Mussolini, "Law and Civilization have been shown up as shameful impostors. . . . Let us find a deserted island and establish a splendid little colony."[17]

Establish a colony because France itself was threatening to blow apart: in January 1934, sensational revelations about the Stavisky Affair brought the accusation that high government officials had engaged in financial corruption to an unprecedented degree. Massive and bloody demonstrations on February 6 by the political right, and on February 9 by the political left, made clear a new taste for violence in a profoundly divided France. To his brother, Roger warned that "the riots would have *incalculable* consequences." He imagined "a new French Revolution . . . hours of violence in a long rising turmoil"; "we must accept a yaw into disorder and nothingness before reaching the period of reconstruction"; "we enter the domain of civil war"; "the fourth French revolution has begun." And because so, as he wrote to Christiane, "under the pretext of order and authority, a clamor arises for discipline and obedience . . . the regime of the barracks." To Marcel, he added, "You should congratulate yourself on being far from the home country at this moment, whatever may be the difficulties of your proconsulate."[18]

In May 1935, Roger wished for one more year to finish his writing before a new war. Ten months later in March 1936, war threatened, when Hitler remilitarized the Rhineland and eliminated the buffer zone between Germany and France established by the Versailles Treaty. For a week until France and Great Britain made clear that they would not contest this provocative violation, Roger and Hélène "hung on the radio." In July 1936, civil war began in Spain between the Nationalists, supported by Hitler and Mussolini, and the Republicans, supported by Stalin. Roger saw them as "two dictatorships doing battle. . . . Both terribly and *equally* fearsome for humanity." Within France, the

Popular Front, a coalition of political parties from the center-left, the left, and the far left, the Radicals, the Socialists, and the Communists, respectively, won the May 1936 elections. Demanding the spoils of victory, industrial workers initiated massive strikes that won them previously unimaginable concessions: the forty-hour workweek, two-week paid vacations, and substantial wage increases. Earlier, considering himself as much a victim of the Great Depression as anyone else, Roger had not scrupled to contend, "I believe that capitalism is the cause of the troubles from which we suffer and that we cannot be saved from them by the delegates of capitalism." Now with the delegates of capitalism defeated, he worried about a dictatorship of the proletariat à la française: "The day when the Communist Party finally reveals its *real* program, and substitutes it for the watered-down version it brandished for the elections, France will see *widespread panic* and then a rush to the center-right parties, which in the name of Order and Liberty will strangle us in a French fascism well camouflaged as liberalism." Roger believed that the Spanish civil war was the precursor to a future general war in Europe between communist and fascist nations. And before that possibility, recalling the horrors he had lived through and the friends he had lost between 1914 and 1918, he took a stand: "*Anything rather than war!* Even fascism in Spain! ... Even fascism in France! ... Nothing, *no hardship, no servitude,* can be compared to war, to all that war can engender. ... *Anything*; Hitler, rather than war! And besides, war would straight away become civil war, with the triumph perhaps of communism after years of blood, of destruction, of sorrows without name."[19]

How Roger completed three new volumes of *Les Thibault*, collectively titled *L'Eté 1914* (*Summer 1914*), in the midst of such tribulation in his life as a man, a novelist, and a citizen testifies to an extraordinary perseverance. *L'Eté 1914* was more than 300,000 words long, the typescript manuscript more than a thousand pages. Roger began planning it in the spring of 1932 and thought then that he would need at least two years. Instead, he needed three and a half. The many personal crises and financial reverses, the writing of *Vieille France* and the Zola screenplay, delayed his preliminary work until the beginning of November 1934, but then he wrote in a frenzy until he declared himself finished at the end of December 1935, only fourteen months later. He worked every day, never less than "six or seven hours." In the evening, he read his pages aloud to Hélène, "Her judgment aids me greatly in maintaining a *lifelike* quality to the work, avoiding any literary tirades." His "return to the past" inured him to the "great lies and deceptions found today from one end of the political spectrum to the other." To his impatient publisher, Gallimard, he responded: "I work. I do absolutely nothing else. I read almost nothing. I see no one. I am terribly impatient to finish, and I assure you, *I am doing everything I can!*" And then he was finished, turning the manuscript over to Schlumberger, his editor. The pages are filled with magnificent and stirring drama. The characters are, as he intended, "leaves blown about in the tempest of war." Equally important, they are, especially brothers Antoine and Jacques, endowed with the flaws that Roger had discovered in himself, his wife, his daughter, and his best friend.[20]

Jacques Thibault has returned to Switzerland following his father's death. He has refused his share of the estate and lives humbly in Geneva, renting a single room on the income from writing occasional articles for obscure newspapers and magazines. His milieu is the collection of socialists and anarchists who congregate at a cheap hotel. He sees them as two types, either "Apostles," "generous-minded mystics" hoping for a new internationalism of peace and freedom, or "Experts," professional revolutionaries ready to use violence. Their acknowledged leader is Meynestrel, called "The Pilot," an Expert who preaches insurrection because reformers underestimate the resistance of the bourgeoisie, capitalism, and the nation-state. Beside Meynestrel, beside most of them, Jacques is a moderate, replying, "I'm positive that no true progress can be achieved by sordid methods. It's sheer nonsense glorifying violence and hatred as means to bring about the triumph of justice and fraternity." Because Jacques cannot escape his heritage as bourgeois and French, another Expert retorts, "A dilettante, that's what you are!" The date is June 28, 1914, but none of them have yet heard news of the assassination in Sarajevo.

Three weeks later in mid-July, Jacques recognizes the threat of war and has volunteered for the effort to encourage a general strike of the European working class to prevent it. When he arrives in Paris, he seeks out his brother, Antoine, who has spent the last months taking full advantage of a substantial inheritance. Now, he calls himself "Antoine Oscar-Thibault," wears only the finest clothes, has lavished money remodeling his father's house, and has converted one floor into a modern laboratory. His father's investments were gilt-edged equities and bonds that generated modest but stable returns. Having spent so much and requiring a greater income to support his new pretensions, Antoine has shifted to Russian state obligations that pay higher interest but at greater risk. He has taken on an additional risk, an affair with a married woman, Anne de Battaincourt, older and of dubious reputation, whose daughter was once his patient. Frustrated at finding Paris oblivious to any danger of war, Jacques turns on Antoine: "How at home he seems in all this luxury! . . . He has Father's vanity, the aristocratic vanity of the bourgeois." "What made me a revolutionary," he exclaims, "is having been born here, in this house, the son of a bourgeois father. It's having had to witness as a child, day after day, all the injustice which keeps our privileged class on top." Antoine replies with condescension, "Every social system's doomed to reproduce the failings, the incurable defects of human nature. So what's the use of running the risks of a general upheaval?"

The next scene is the only one in the more than 700,000 words of *Les Thibault* that seems contrived. Martin du Gard has to bring the Fontanin family into *L'Eté 1914* and does so by having Jenny burst into Antoine's house begging his care of her father, Jérôme, who has shot himself in a nearby hotel. Four years earlier, Jenny and Jacques were profoundly, and innocently, in love, but Jacques disappeared after his father vehemently rejected any relationship between his son and a Protestant. He has not seen or contacted her since, and she believes that he has utterly rejected her. Neither finds a word for the other, and Jacques vows a quick return to Geneva. Antoine displays his professional calm and competence, telephoning for a surgeon to meet him at the hotel. A telegram goes out to Daniel de Fontanin, Jenny's brother and Jacques's childhood friend, who is completing his required military training—extended an additional twelve months by the three-year service law of 1913—as a sergeant at Lunéville, near the border with Germany. At the hotel, Antoine and his associate immediately recognize that Jérôme is without hope. Estranged from his wife, Thérèse, he has recently arrived from Vienna, where he left behind a young mistress and accusations of fraudulent financial dealing. As he put the gun to his temple, he must have thought no escape remained. The papers, bills, and letters he leaves behind are painful for Thérèse to examine.

Jacques's return to Geneva is brief because he is unique among the Apostles and Experts in having access to a fortune, the inheritance he refused, which Antoine has honorably kept safe awaiting his possible change of mind. When he reveals his willingness to turn the money over to the "International Socialist Committee" for use in an antiwar campaign, he becomes, dilettante or not, Meynestrel's most valuable asset. Back in Paris on July 23, to retrieve the funds, he learns that Jérôme has died, that Thérèse will go to Vienna to clear her husband's name, that Daniel will sell his new paintings to pay his father's debts, and that Jenny—well, "How was she to quell that insensate yearning to be happy that her meeting with Jacques had revived?" Jacques tells her, "when once there has been between two people what there has been between you and me, when they've been drawn to each other as we were drawn, glimpsed such boundless hopes, such visions of the future, what difference can the lapse of four years, ten years make?" He also discovers a Paris now suddenly and intensely concentrated on the threat of war. After Jérôme's funeral on July 25, Daniel waits for the train to take him back to Lunéville, aware that the first battles of a war will engulf him. Antoine recalls that he is to report to a military medical unit at Compiègne on first day of mobilization. On July 26, his mentor, Dr. Philip, who is old enough to remember the Franco-Prussian War of 1870, warns against hoping for the best, "at my age it's hard to count on reason vanquishing stupidity." Rumelles, a high official at the Quai d'Orsay (the Ministry of Foreign Affairs) and long Antoine's friend and patient, acknowledges that war is likely, "What would you have us do? . . . Let Russia down and stand entirely alone?"

While awaiting the settlement date on the sale of the securities constituting his inheritance, Jacques anxiously haunts left-wing gatherings. To Jenny, who tags along dreamily, he explains his choice, "I realized that it was absurd to fancy justice would triumph easily or quickly, . . . my instinct of revolt . . . joined forces with other rebellious spirits like mine for the betterment of mankind." When he finds most French labor leaders succumbing to nationalist propaganda, he is bitterly disappointed and eventually demands to speak. "My friends, you ask, 'What is our duty?' Well, it's simple, and it's clear. We must have one aim only: peace. We must drop party differences and unite. Unite in saying 'No!' and fighting against war." His words thrill Jenny, but the workers walk out. Later, an old-time syndicalist printer sums up: "Nine out of ten of our famous revolutionary leaders—shall I tell you what I really think about them? They'll never be able to bring themselves to adopt 'unconstitutional' methods. That being so, well, the conclusion's inescapable."

Antoine as well is suffering the collapse of the ideals in which he has believed. On July 30, Russia ordered general mobilization, and on July 31, Germany announced "a state of threatening danger of war," refused to guarantee Belgian neutrality, and sent an insolent ultimatum demanding French intentions. Antoine's "morale, till now intact, was badly shaken. . . . . . He was suddenly discovering the impotence of intellect; and . . . the futility of the virtues which had been the mainstay of his industrious career: common sense, moderation, wisdom and experience, the cult of justice." Even so, he still had a moral order to defend when Jacques—representing Martin du Gard's position—cries out: "Anything rather than the madness, the horrors of a war! . . . I won't take part in any war, whether they label it 'just' or 'unjust,' whatever its origins and motives." Antoine upbraids him, "the man who joins his regiment when he is called up for service is obeying the collective will of the nation— whatever his personal views may be." The Thibault brothers stand on opposite sides of the social contract. Jacques insists, "I deny that the state is justified in forcing a man, for any reason whatsoever, to go against his conscience." Antoine replies, "To refuse to do one's duty at such a moment is to sacrifice the public's interest to one's own."

That night, a nationalist fanatic shoots dead Jean Jaurès, leader of the Socialist party and the most eloquent spokesman for preventing conflict between nations through a general strike of their workers. Confronted the following day by the German declaration of war against Russia, Jaurès's lieutenants quickly promise support for whatever decisions French leaders take—meaning the order for mobilization that goes out a few hours later with the injunction, "We rely on the loyalty of every Frenchman, knowing full well not one of us will fail the call of duty." Had he survived his wounds, Jaurès almost certainly would have done the same. Reading the posters declaring that August 2, was Day 1 of Mobilization, Jacques feels "a cold, disdainful rage. . . . For weeks he had lived in a fool's paradise, fondly trusting that justice, truth, and man's fraternity would triumph in the nick of time." He knows he must leave France quickly to avoid being arrested as a pacifist, a dissident, or even a traitor. He asks Jenny to flee with him, to make a life together in Geneva.

On August 2, just before the border closes, Jacques does take the train to Geneva. He has the money from his inheritance but not Jenny. With both of them overwrought from the announcement of mobilization and thinking her mother still in Vienna, Jenny has Jacques sleep beside her—both fully clothed—at the Fontanin apartment. Thérèse arrives unexpectedly and is mortified by her daughter's conduct. The following morning, Jenny cringes as her mother says, "You've been led astray by an infatuation I'd never dreamed possible. . . . You should be ashamed of yourself!" Later at the train station, she tells Jacques that she cannot go with him, that she cannot abandon her mother with Daniel on the front line and Jérôme in his grave only a week. Maybe she will join him soon. Jacques has been planning, in that quaint nineteenth-century expression, "to make her his own" after they reach Switzerland. Now, they have only a couple of hours before the train leaves: "She dared not refuse him this last joy. Her cheeks crimson, she looked away with a wan little smile."

Jacques is free from every emotional commitment, free—in the existential sense—to pursue a defining act which, though likely futile, is magnificent in conception. Using a portion of his inheritance, he will print up many thousands of leaflets denouncing the war, load them into a small plane, and release them to the wind as he flies over the French and German lines in nearby Alsace. He thinks, "How it would grip the imagination of the world at large! 'The Peace Plane!' 'A message from the air!'" When brought to account, he will proclaim, "There is a higher law than yours, the law of conscience." But on August 10, when the preparations are complete and he is waiting for the plane to take off, he recognizes bitterly, "I'm acting as I'm doing only out of despair. To escape from myself. I shan't stop the war. I shan't save anyone—except myself." Over the battlefield, both sides open fire on the unmarked plane, which crashes to the ground before he can toss out a single leaflet. Jacques is badly injured. French troops reach him first and assume he is a spy. He is being carried to the rear on a stretcher when a German attack makes him an unnecessary liability. A soldier shoots him dead, muttering, "Scum!"[21]

L'Eté 1914 was a literary vindication for Roger. Eventually, its publication would be a financial vindication as well, but not immediately. Evoking the threat of war, the loss of innocence, the collapse of values, the narrative and the characters resonated strongly in a France that was facing so much of the same. After publication in November 1936, it was an immediate best seller, but before Editions Gallimard paid him from new royalties, it would deduct the advances it had made him since early 1934. As a result, "*I am a prisoner of Nice for another year*, because I do not know any other place in the world where I can lead a normal and agreeable existence at so little expense." But what was wrong with a minor celebration, meaning an invitation for Gide and Maria van Rysselberghe to visit them. The answer was Hélène's strong aversion. Roger went ahead anyway, believing that he had sacrificed this friendship sufficiently during his long bout of writing. He had attended the Pontigny retreat only twice since the fateful one in 1929 with Christiane and Marcel, once in 1930, for a discussion of abnormal psychology, and again in 1934, for a depressing account of intolerance in totalitarian states. Gide had been Roger's guest at Nice that same year, in April 1934, but Hélène had been away on a religious pilgrimage to Corsica with Abbé Sudour. Now, two years later, Gide and Maria arrived at the beginning of May, bringing with them Catherine, her only grandchild and secretly his daughter.[22]

The presence of Catherine conjured an emotional fury within Hélène. The girl, now just twelve, tutoyered Roger and called him "uncle." Hélène imagined that Roger hoped to adopt Catherine, because Gide was sixty-seven and not well, as a substitute for Christiane. To her horror, Hélène had learned the truth of Catherine's parentage and blamed Roger for lying about it. Confronting him, she demanded to know what "ascendancy these people have over you that they make you perjure yourself? *You swore on the head of your daughter and on the head of your mother that Gide was not the father of Elisabeth's child!*" For Hélène, further proof of the influence this infernal couple had on Roger came when the three of them discussed pages of *L'Eté 1914* while relegating her to domestic duties. Through the closed door, they could hear her crying out, "You are all louts! You trample on everything I hold dear! You hold me apart from everything!" Gide sought to apologize, but she refused to see him and replied with "a flurry of invective and insults." Roger sent his guests away and confessed: "I am broken. I fall from on high. For the last three years, I have lived with Hélène in perfect intimacy and good camaraderie, which seemed to me solid and accepted. . . . I believed that our love had entered a phase of definitive calm, but I was wrong."[23]

In the early summer, Hélène went north to Le Tertre, while Roger remained in Nice. He waited until late August and then wrote asking that she decide her future relationship to Gide and Maria van Rysselberghe: "In the first solution, you will never see them again, and you will never hear me speak their names. They would be a compartment in my life from which you would be excluded. In the second, I would ask them to act as if nothing had happened, and you would continue to meet them with at least a modicum of cordiality. If you prefer a third solution, breaking with Gide but maintaining relations with Mme van R., that is also possible." Hélène replied bitterly, "Why should I make a decision about a situation *you* have created? . . . You are the one who has excluded me completely from a chapter in your life that you believe so important that you have sacrificed our happiness to it. You are free to continue or not distancing me from this 'compartment in your life.' The pain I experience will have no influence on you because it will be discreet." In the same spirit, Roger answered, "Replying to your letter, a monument to thoughtlessness and arrogance about which, to maintain peace between us, I shall not comment, I think it preferable that we pick up relations where they were rather than have a definitive break." Hélène insisted on poisoned last words: "You accuse me of arrogance because I have agreed to see your friends, as you prefer? So of what would you have accused me if I had refused? But no matter—I accept it freely if, in accusing me, you lighten your own conscience. . . . I accept it with a smile, for our mutual peace."[24]

Such were the joys of the Martin du Gard marriage. Yet the year had left two surprises that can be entered on the credit side—the vindication side—of Roger's ledger. The first was a chance to reconcile with his daughter and former best friend through celebration over Marcel's utterly unexpected and dramatic elevation. The victory of the Popular Front made one of his political allies, Marius Moutet, minister of the colonies, and at the beginning of August, Moutet made Marcel governor-general of French West Africa. Roger addressed his congratulations to Christiane as "Madame Governor-General." Marcel now had "the position that he hardly dreamed of but to which he has aspired for the last thirty years! The most important position in the most important colony, the colony he cherishes above all." He acknowledged his reservations only to his old friend, Lt. Colonel Mayer: Was Christiane, still only twenty-nine years old and mother of two small children, prepared to play the social and political role her husband's exalted post required of her?[25]

The second surprise came from the ever-resourceful Schlumberger, friend as well as editor. At the beginning of December, he sent Roger "one of those complicated and discreet letters for which he has the secret" containing a check for a thousand francs ($1,387 in 2015). He claimed to have sold his heavily annotated copy of *Jean Barois* to a specialty bookstore for fifteen hundred francs ($2,080 in 2015) and that the check he enclosed was "naturally" Roger's portion. Of course, Roger knew that these thousand francs were a gift: "I played along with his delicious subterfuge shamelessly because I knew with what heart he offered me this money and because I had as much pleasure in accepting as Jean had in giving." He invited Hélène to go with him to Rome. She accepted, and their complicated life together continued.[26]

Chapter 6

~

TRIUMPH

ROGER WAS BENDING FATE to his terms, but for how long could he keep fate bent? And what had the bending cost him? Still in Rome at the beginning of 1937, he walked to the end of a jetty and considered how appropriate the place was for suicide. Briefly, he touched the revolver he sometimes carried in his coat pocket. When he returned to Nice, he analyzed his feelings: "I am not tired of life but of *my* life. . . . I am tired of my wife, of my work, of my friends; I am tired of the places where my life plays out; I am tired of the anxieties that my life has caused me."[1]

Yes, the publication of *L'Eté 1914* stemmed the financial rout, but only a recovery in the value of his properties and his investment portfolio could restore the sense of ease he once took for granted. As he confessed to Christiane, "Below a certain level of affluence, the sense of liberty no longer exists: preoccupation with expense bridles all fantasy, the atmosphere is left heavy, and life is made ponderous." He had never accommodated himself to being "an impoverished bourgeois," and he idled by imagining "a packet of checks and money in my account. I would begin by paying the five thousand francs [\$4,624 in 2015] of taxes I owe, next buy myself some underwear, a pair of shoes, two suits, and an overcoat, and then spend two months in Italy or Morocco." By contrast, Hélène "had truly accepted poverty," "cutting the hours of the maid, spending only fifteen francs [\$16.20 in 2015] for gas and six francs [\$6.50 in 2015] for electricity each month, living for eight days on chicken porridge or a beef tongue." Once, he had thought her "fragile"; now, he thought her "a rock." Jean Schlumberger's surprise gift made the Christmas trip to Rome possible, but Hélène returned to Nice after only ten days so that Roger could have a longer stay.[2]

Although Roger valued such solitude, friendships had always been vital to him, and he felt increasingly alone. The betrayal he continued to associate with Marcel's marriage to Christiane deprived him of both as confidants. He had hoped to see Christiane develop "a feminine intelligence formed through culture and human experience," but she had become "a mother hen, ridiculously proud of having made two beautiful children, living only for them and for the man who gave them to her." She had also become arrogant, the result, Roger believed, of being "not only queen of her household but queen of the colony." And Marcel: having achieved the summit of his ambitions as governor-general in French West Africa, he found the toils of maintaining imperial glory increasingly discouraging. In one letter, he declared that his sole interest had become his wife and children. The company of André Gide and Maria van Rysselberghe was delightful to Roger, but he always regretted entrusting Gide with confidences, and he could not imagine doing so with Maria. Only Schlumberger was left: true, kind, generous, but bizarrely ascetic, living in a single hotel room, taking all his meals alone there, preoccupying himself with problems of hygiene, and going to bed early each night. He was born six years after Roger, but "he is much, much older than me. His horizon is so much narrower than mine. He lives in the past, with all that he acquired long ago."[3]

Most of all, life with Hélène was an eternal recurrence. In March 1937, Maria arrived in Nice to spend two weeks away from the northern cold, her first trip south since the previous May and Hélène's indecorous rejection. This time, she stayed in a hotel, never ventured near the Cimiez apartment, and saw Roger for only an hour or two in the late afternoons. But her mere presence in Nice was sufficient to unbalance Hélène, who once again exclaimed bitterly that Roger had "stolen her daughter" and that under the influence of Gide and Maria, "lies took firm hold in our house." As before, her special grievance was Roger's having concealed that Maria's granddaughter was Gide's daughter, and she claimed to have learned this secret from Marcel. "*We no longer love each other*," she lashed out at Roger. "Our life together makes no sense. We have nothing in common but our worries about money, our poverty, our obligations. Everything else is dead. I no longer have any confidence in you. *I no longer believe anything you tell me*. Doubt eats away at me. . . . *We have to separate*. Because we have nothing in common, let us live our own lives without causing each other suffering. . . . I do not know where to go or what to do, I just know that this life is intolerable and that I must, must finish with it!" After spending two days in bed, she got up to tell Roger—almost bragging—that she was leaving for Paris to stay at the Rue du Dragon where she "would be without heat, without anyone to care for me, without anyone to pay me attention because all my friends will be away for Easter, but at least I will be away from here!"[4]

Schlumberger suggested that Hélène was demanding Roger choose: either her or his friends. In exasperation, Roger replied, "When I look back on my life, friendship has enriched me, conjugal love has brought me my only sufferings; the joys I owe to conjugal love are drawn from the moments when conjugal love became conjugal *friendship*. To sacrifice friendship to love would be the essence of ingratitude." Writing his brother, whose marriage to a much younger woman had brought him great happiness, Roger admitted, "I am going through a rotten period in my life. Since December, I have done nothing and am able to do nothing. . . . The secret to my troubles is the sadness of our daily life because things go badly between Hélène and me. . . . She has said, 'We no longer love each other. Let us separate.' Yet, a separation is difficult to imagine, for Hélène is absolutely alone in the world. She has neither family nor friends. If she left me, she would quickly die in arid solitude. She has no one else, and she has made immense sacrifices for me. I am her only reason for living. Pathetically, this exclusive love that ought to make us happy instead turns against us and poisons our lives. I would not wish my worst enemy to be loved like that!"[5]

Then, near the end of March, only days after Hélène threatened a retreat to Paris, they found the means to reconcile yet again. Maria's departure removed a principal irritant between them. Hélène's exhaustion after two weeks of turmoil left her amenable. Roger's loneliness made him fear losing her all the more. They took the train back to Rome, leaving in "good spirits." *L'Eté 1914* was selling spectacularly well, earning Roger one hundred fifty thousand francs ($104,040 in 2015) in royalties since its publication four months earlier, but Editions Gallimard had not increased his monthly check because it had advanced him so much during the previous three years. From Rome, Roger wrote asking for a small sum to cover this new trip and was annoyed because the reply took two weeks. When she had Roger all to herself, when she did not have to compete with Christiane or Marcel or Gide or Maria, Hélène brightened, calmed her nerves, and regained her strength. As before, she left ahead of him, as much to display her self-sacrifice as to grant him a few extra days. Roger had hoped for this return to their regular existence, but he had no illusions: "I need a friend, and Hélène is the opposite of a friend. She is the lover who can never be satisfied, who demands exclusivity, who is hypersensitive, who is endlessly inflamed. Unfortunately, I know well." When Roger despaired of his marriage, he sometimes imagined that Hélène would have been better off as the wife of some prosaic specimen from the French upper bourgeoisie, sometimes as the chaste companion of either Abbé Marchand or Abbé Sudour. Now, alone in Rome, he thought that life had cheated Hélène, was "monstrous," in having denied her "sensual experience" other than with him. Still, he added in his journal, "I do not mean that if Hélène had deceived me I would not have suffered from it."[6]

In the first days of June, Roger and Hélène went north to Le Tertre, which they would open fully for the first time in three years as a symbol of having prevailed against misfortune. Christiane, Daniel, and Annique, as they were calling her, arrived soon after, all three "beautiful, happy, brimming with health." Outwardly, Roger was exultant. "The old place has unshuttered its windows and shaken its dust," he wrote Schlumberger. "I feel ten years younger," he wrote to Marcel, "I am supremely happy." Yet he was not. All the crises, the anxieties, the travails, and the torments he had endured welled up in him and left him in a state of "an indescribable *anguish*, which comes without warning during the day or at night when I am sleeping or in the morning when I wake, a sudden *terror* without reason, the sense of an imminent and frightful catastrophe, a *panic*, which makes me unable to breathe, soaks me in sweat, and leaves me trembling."[7]

Throughout the rest of the summer and early fall, Roger put on a brave face—aided by the lack of any serious upsets. With her usual "inflexibility of the rule," Hélène ran Le Tertre like "a sort of convent, where nothing is left to fantasy." Unusually, Christiane had the sense and the tact to say nothing, and neither did Roger, except in his journal. At the end of July, Christiane and her children left to visit Marcel's mother in Quiberville before returning to Dakar. Roger and Hélène were once again alone and "Le Tertre the domain of the old, the prey of shadows from the past, the museum of family memories and customs." In the middle of September, they spent four days of "perfect harmony and amusing companionship" in Paris touring the Universal Exposition of Art and Technology. Roger dissipated these good feelings by immediately leaving—and leaving behind Hélène, as always—for the retreat at Pontigny, which dealt with the "social vocation of art in questions of mental disease and despair." On his return, he was, as always, surprised at her dissatisfaction. Then, on October 16, the Paris municipal council awarded its annual literary prize of twenty-five thousand francs ($18,360 in 2015) to Editions Gallimard for *L'Eté 1914*. Gaston Gallimard was so delighted that he ordered the entire sum handed over to Roger instead of retaining it against his debt. Roger used five thousand francs ($3,670) to pay some taxes due at the end of the year, donated a second five thousand to various philanthropic endeavors, pledged a third five thousand to Hélène for a cruise, and banked the final ten thousand ($7,340 in 2015) against future needs.[8]

This windfall and this validation came as Roger was literally closing Le Tertre for the winter and figuratively closing years that had severely tested his resolve. The splendid seventeenth-century country palace endured. The brilliant narrative of *Les Thibault* endured. If Roger could not yet claim a triumph, no one could contest that he was ascendant. With his characteristic introspection, he took this moment to reflect on the only relationship in his life that had survived with him through this time of tempest and storm: "How do I resolve these two contradictory truths: that it is marvelous to be loved and that Hélène's love has been the source of sufferings without solution for her and for me? In her love she has found only the bitter joys of a perpetual sacrifice, . . . Instead of being for her a source of strength, stability, and joy, this love appears to her, I am almost certain, as an infernal bewitchment, a kind of curse. And for me, I am compelled to recognize that this love, from which I have egotistically *profited*, has been responsible for all the discord, all the sorrow of our existence together. . . . I have given Hélène all the love I am capable of giving. I need her. I need her tenderness, to the point that I am literally unable to live with her when this tenderness is shadowed by daily clouds, to the point that I prefer to be alone rather than to live beside her when she suffers from loving me. But my love has never had the impassioned, unhealthy, overly sensitive character that renders hers so heavy to bear for both of us."[9]

On October 24, Roger wrote Gallimard that he was heading soon to Nice, where he would begin the composition of one final volume for *Les Thibault*, an *Epilogue* that would tie up the lives of the remaining principal characters. He had hardly been at the Cimiez apartment a week when he received a telephone call in the midafternoon on November 11, from his sister-in-law, Marie-Louise. She told him that Swiss journalists, unable to find Roger's telephone number in Nice, had been calling their house for the last hour with the news that he was the 1937 Nobel laureate for literature. In addition to the supreme honor for his work, he would receive a monetary prize of one million one hundred thousand francs ($807,850 in 2015). Roger was not just possessive of his privacy: he had an "obsessive passion for living hidden . . . a horror of being recognized, of being called 'Monsieur Martin' by tradesmen and shopkeepers, of being photographed." Realizing that French journalists were certain to be hunting him, he took the first train to Cannes and anonymity in a hotel. When he returned to Nice the following day, the concierge told him that journalists had indeed besieged the building the previous evening but were now gone. What did await him were nearly a hundred telegrams and letters. He wrote Hélène with generous praise for her comments on his pages: "This work that we have done together, every evening at your bedside, day after day, that the world hails today as if it is something truly important. Mama would have been so happy." His letter crossed with one from her at the Rue du Dragon: "I have so many telegrams announcing your glory, and the telephone will not stop ringing. . . . [Georges] Duhamel came by to say that *your* coronation is that of *France*, rendering homage to French literature, and that you have an official role to play in accepting this prize at such a troubled time. . . . I am so sorry to be far from you. Love to my glorious husband." A few days later, she added, "For me, your coronation will always be a natural outcome, exactly right, almost expected! But the happiness of this confirmation is not lessened in the least." From Dakar, Christiane exclaimed, "Would that I could kiss you, I am so happy, so proud of you. I have always been proud of you, but today all the more so because you have just won the greatest literary prize in the world. Dakar is in a commotion, the bookstores selling out of *Les Thibault*, the libraries overwhelmed." She could not help adding, "Everyone is astonished that the father of Madame de Coppet is such a great man." Coppet did better: "You cannot know how pleased I am that not only your work but your noble moral attitude throughout your long literary career have been so highly rewarded by this Nobel Prize which your true friends have for long known you deserved."[10] Note how international renown and renewed fortune had an immediately beneficial impact on these relationships.

Roger now had to contend with many details. Having expected to take up his abstemious life in Nice, he had almost no funds readily to hand. After spending ninety-six francs ($73.50 in 2015) replying by telegram to the Swedish Academy with his acceptance of the Nobel Prize and then approximately the same for his flight to Cannes, he had less than fifty francs ($38.25) left in his wallet. He had to call Gallimard requesting that he send some money immediately. In a letter following, he promised that nothing would change between them, "I have no intention of being either demanding or presumptuous." But after considering the expenses he would incur just accepting the Nobel, he asked Schlumberger for an advance of fifteen thousand francs ($8,100 in 2015) to cover the cost of the formal dress required for the ceremonies and travel from Paris to Stockholm. Schlumberger was already writing him with suggestions for how to handle himself. The French press, he reported, was celebrating, an exception made for some of the right-wing newspapers that had been campaigning for the well-known Catholic novelist François Mauriac. Roger should, therefore, be accommodating about allowing photographs, especially because tradition decreed that he present a formal autographed photograph portrait to the Swedish sovereign. At Stockholm, he would have to deliver a speech accepting the Nobel Prize and another, in an academic setting, discussing either his own work or the current state of French literature. If the latter, Schlumberger urged praising contemporaries such as Gide, Duhamel, Paul Valéry, and Paul Claudel—he did not include Mauriac.[11]

Schlumberger ended with a note about Hélène. Roger had sent Gide a letter proposing that he and Maria van Rysselberghe take advantage of this moment to seek an accord with her, in the hope that she might "*leap* to restore amicable relations." They did so, proposing a celebratory luncheon for November 16, with Schlumberger as the fourth at table. Hélène wrote Roger to say that she had accepted and to wonder at the "unexpected effects" of his award, at how much was "unforeseeable and contradictory." Afterward, Gide sent a brief note, "Well, everything went marvelously, and our little luncheon was charming."[12] Whether or not Hélène merely pretended her good gratitude, here was another example of the Nobel influence.

For another ten days, until November 25, Roger hid away in Nice to prepare what he would say in Stockholm, to consider the changes this new distinction would bring to his life, and to deal in some haphazard manner with all of the congratulatory messages. He had an exact count of the telegrams, 286, but not of the letters, which exceeded a thousand. The Popular Front cabinet, still in power but only barely, wanted to elevate his rank within the Legion of Honor from "Knight" (*Chevalier*) to "Officer" (*Officier*). As he wrote Hélène, who had opposed his accepting the initial appointment in 1926, "I declined, of course. I was courteous, but I expect my refusal will be taken badly." Hélène was radiant and had, at least, made an effort with Gide and Maria as she enjoyed the first celebrity of her life: the best Paris fashion houses vying for the right to design her prize ceremony gown. Roger's prestige as Nobel laureate would lead to translation of *Jean Barois* and especially *Les Thibault* into many languages and important new sales. The check from the Nobel Foundation would remake his fortune. No more debt to Editions Gallimard. No more asking his brother for an uneven share of the income from their jointly owned properties. "I can buy la Fouquerie's property [bordering on Le Tertre] and get a dog—two long-held dreams." Most of all, he assigned a meaning to his new honor, writing to Per Hallström, permanent secretary of the Swedish Royal Academy, "I am convinced that the Swedish Academy chose the date of November 11, anniversary of the Armistice, to attract attention to the author of *L'Eté 1914* because my books of anguish, where I have tried to resurrect the anxious turmoil of the weeks preceding the mobilization, might, in their manner, serve the cause of peace in recalling to all the tragic lesson of the past."[13]

As soon as Roger arrived in Paris, he found himself absorbed by formalities. He and Hélène took a suite at the Lutetia, perhaps the grandest hotel on Paris's Left Bank, because the apartment nearby on the Rue du Dragon was cramped, and because he was, he had finally realized, a "millionaire." No longer worried about how to pay for his clothes, his trip, or anything else, he could indulge in grand gestures, as in promising to pay the travel expenses to Stockholm for his brother, Marcel, his publisher, Gallimard, and their wives—they had, after all, been extraordinarily generous to him during the preceding years. He had a briefing at the Ministry of Foreign Affairs, where Jean Marx, director of cultural relations, solemnly enjoined him to be "amiable with everyone," and another at the Ministry of Education, where the minister himself, Jean Zay, pressed him, unsuccessfully, to accept the new rank in the Legion of Honor. He committed to memory the long list of appearances he was to make in Stockholm and reluctantly posed for an album of photographs required by the Nobel Foundation. On December 2, the Swedish legation in Paris held a grand dinner presided over by Prince Bertil, a grandson of Swedish King Gustaf V. Four days later on December 6, they boarded a train to Hamburg and the following evening a ferry that landed at Malmö early the next morning. The passage across the Baltic Sea had been uncomfortable, and Roger was in a bad mood. When the many journalists and photographers waiting at the dock called out his name and questions in French, he replied, "Non capisco. Italiano"—"I don't understand. I'm an Italian." This shabby ruse did not confuse them for long, and the press turned vehemently against him. Appalled, Roger Maugras, head of the French legation in Sweden, quickly intervened and the next afternoon organized an informal meeting between his rude charge and about forty journalists. By then, Roger realized how badly he had blundered and was open and agreeable, answering every question, whether silly—"Are you a Communist?"—or personal—"Did your child make her First Communion?" They left satisfied: "their daggers in their pockets and smiles on their faces, writing that I was a Frenchman full of cordiality and humor, not at all an unpleasant stuffed shirt."[14]

The presentation ceremony took place in late afternoon on December 10, at Stockholm's magnificent Concert Hall. Amid pomp, splendor, music, and tributes, the Nobel Foundation formally announced its 1937 laureates for Physics, Chemistry, Medicine, and Literature. In turn, each laureate heard his work summarized and praised and then received a diploma and medallion from King Gustaf. For Roger, the encomium came from Per Hallström, who insisted that Roger's selection was based on the totality of *Les Thibault* and not because his *L'Eté 1914* resonated so strongly in a Europe once again threatened with war. Indeed, the Swedish Academy had almost chosen him in 1936, before *L'Eté 1914* had even appeared. He praised especially Roger's ability to define his characters through their habits, thoughts, and actions, and concluded that through "his pointed and skeptical analysis of the human soul, which almost consumes its object with its often extreme exactness in detail, through the most minute realism possible, Martin du Gard finally pays homage to the idealism of the human spirit." As always, the laureates offered their acceptance speeches a few hours later following a grand banquet at the Stockholm City Hall. Often, these remarks lasted less than five minutes, but Roger spoke for almost a quarter hour. His voice strong with conviction, he emphasized how he had led the characters of *Les Thibault* into the Great War and how much in the present "the noise of arms does not let our minds rest." He bore down especially on his last phrases, "an atmosphere polluted by misery and fanaticism ... this exceptionally grave moment through which humanity is passing," beseeching that his books might "remind all—the old who have forgotten as well as the young who either do not know or do not care—of the sad lessons of the past." After Roger finished, Crown Prince Gustaf Adolf took him aside to praise these sentiments, called them his own, and then declared to all that he "wished every newspaper in Sweden would publish them in their entirety." Maugras, the ranking French official in Sweden, had asked for a copy of Roger's remarks ahead of time and had fretted at their tone, but now he positively beamed.[15]

A giddy round of festivities began the next day, December 11, with a gala luncheon for Roger, Hélène, their guests, Marcel, Marie-Louise, and the Gallimards, and some thirty more at the French legation. A dinner sponsored by the king at the royal palace followed that evening. The turn of Sweden's most distinguished and powerful publisher, Albert Bonnier, came the next day, with a party at his estate outside Stockholm. On December 13, Roger delivered a lecture before the Swedish Academy, shrewdly choosing the analysis of his own *Jean Barois*, to guarantee its exposure and possible sales. That evening brought a spectacular moment with the celebration of St. Lucia's Day, which combined commemoration of a young martyr, whose story was told by the monks who brought Christianity to Sweden, with the pagan ceremony of the Winter Solstice—the date taken from the old "Julian calendar." On the stage of a large music hall, a dozen girls stood in a semicircle, each dressed in a long white gown with a red sash, her head of thick blond hair surmounted by a crown of candles. As the large orchestra behind them began playing *La Marseillaise*, the several hundred guests clapped, cheered, and stood on their seats seeking a glimpse of the Nobel laureate. One of the young women was then designated "Lucia" for 1937, and she went immediately to Roger demanding a kiss. Afterward, he was besieged for autographs and later believed he had signed five hundred.[16]

The only false step came on December 16, when at the urging of Jean Nogué, head of the French Institute in Sweden, and even more so Hélène, Roger agreed to visit the Ecole française (French School) for girls established by a Catholic nun, Mademoiselle Roullier. At his arrival, the more than one hundred fifty students, who were arrayed on a grand staircase decorated with flowers and French tricolor flags, sang *La Marseillaise*, after which one of the older girls approached him to recite passages from his work and to express the hope that he would one day follow the edifying example of his own creation Jean Barois in returning to the eternal truth of faith. Profoundly offended,

Roger nevertheless maintained his composure sufficiently to thank the students, teachers, and Roullier for their welcome, but he could not resist adding that he brought them greetings from a "secular" France. Some months later, he learned that not only Maugras at the legation but Marx from the ministry in Paris had sternly rebuked Roullier for this performance.[17]

Otherwise, as he wrote Christiane, the visit to Stockholm was "two weeks that surpassed imagination. . . . I became something of a star—impossible to walk along the street, to enter a café or a store, without being hailed, asked for autographs, stopped by women and children, flowers sent anonymously to the hotel, people spontaneously singing *La Marseillaise* on seeing me. . . . But I hope *it's finished*—forever!" To Lt. Colonel Mayer, he called these days "a fairy story. Incredible. But I am not made to play the star, and I sense myself emptied of all instinct for sociability."[18]

Wealthy again, Roger and Hélène decided to take the long way home. They left Stockholm on Christmas Day, crossed by ferry to Copenhagen, and then spent the next month visiting Berlin, Dresden, Prague, and Vienna before returning to Paris at the beginning of February 1938. They might better have saved their money, because what they saw raised their gravest fears: "Germany is led by a handful of all-powerful *madmen*, truly dangerous madmen because they have no opposition"; "From Germany, we bring back the most sinister, the most appalling impression." Prague impressed Roger as "a disappointment . . . something unkempt and upstart," but Vienna enchanted: "the charm of an old civilization, cheerful and sophisticated." Six weeks after their return, Adolf Hitler, Germany's madman in chief, annexed Austria, with France and Great Britain merely protesting, and that not loudly. Roger feared a new war, this one, as he described it to Marcel, would have Germany, Italy, and Japan mounting a vast attack against the Soviet Union, Great Britain remaining neutral, and France surviving as a small power if it observed neutrality, or becoming reduced to the status of a Portugal or Holland if it sided with the Soviet Union.[19]

While awaiting this disaster, Roger took refuge at Le Tertre: "The world is insane, all is absurd. . . . Here is calm and overwhelming silence." And there, he counted his money. Of the one million one hundred thousand franc Nobel Prize ($807,850 in 2015), he had now roughly 600,000 francs left ($440,650 in 2015) after paying off his debt to Editions Gallimard and the cost of travel to Stockholm and then home through central Europe. He set aside 150,000 francs ($110,150 in 2015) as an endowment to Hélène, to replace in small measure her marriage dowry that they had "nibbled away" between 1906 and 1914. With the remainder, about 450,000 francs ($330,500 in 2015), he bought conservative Swedish securities that would yield fifteen thousand francs ($11,000 in 2015) annually, a return of 3.33 percent. As soon as possible, he intended to address the issue of the properties he had inherited jointly with his brother, who had always been extraordinarily accommodating: "Between Marcel and me, *there has never been the shadow of a shadow of difficulty.*" Because his brother had been far more prudent in his spending, and because he now had a young wife and two children—and because the properties were currently generating less income than anticipated—Roger wanted to give him far more than an even division of the assets. He knew that doing so would antagonize Christiane, who was already anticipating what she might inherit herself, and who had an ugly "*taste for accusation.*" As a complication, the two Marcels had never liked each other, and Christiane's Marcel would surely encourage her.[20]

Otherwise, Roger's retreat to Le Tertre, with Hélène going to Nice and leaving him alone, was to begin the final volume of *Les Thibault*, an epilogue based on the journal of Antoine Thibault, who is "gassed late in the war, knows that he has no chance for recovery, and records his thoughts in a tête-à-tête with death." For company, he kept a promise made to himself after learning of the Nobel Prize and bought a little black French bulldog, which he named "Guadeloupe" and spoiled: "She sleeps on my bed, never leaves me day or night, and we make a good couple. She has only a single fault, snoring like a cracked bellows." "I lead her around to 'go pipi,' and that forces me to get out a little." As Roger began writing, he got word that Gide's wife, Madeleine, had died. From Nice, Hélène urged Roger to invite Gide to Le Tertre "for a time of rest," implying that her absence would make doing so easier—perhaps the celebration luncheon in November had softened her heart. Gide came, spent eight days, and offered this explanation for his unconsummated marriage: "I was thus; she was thus; the result was great suffering for us both." Hélène returned from Nice soon after Gide left, and two weeks later in early June, Christiane and her children arrived from Dakar by airplane, Marcel to follow in mid-July.[21]

By then, any hope of retreat was gone. The play of Daniel and Annique made work impossible for Roger, and he longed to gather up his papers and flee. Perhaps unnerved by so many people, Guadeloupe began spending more time outside and was run over by a passing car, dying in Roger's arms as Hélène sobbed beside him. When Roger gently asked about her grief, she answered that this dear little dog had shown her love, "*and it was so good for me to find a bit of tenderness.*" At the end of July, saying nothing to Hélène, Roger joined Schlumberger at the mayor's office in the seventh arrondissement of Paris to serve as witnesses when Gide formally petitioned to adopt Catherine van Rysselberghe, who was, of course, secretly his daughter. Whether cynically or not, both Roger and Schlumberger signed a declaration attesting to Gide's good morals and to their belief that he met all the requirements necessary to be an adoptive father. Finally, the crisis over Hitler's demand that Czechoslovakia cede the Sudetenland region to Germany raised the first serious fear of war in Europe since 1918. For Roger, "I am on the eve of completing my *Thibault*, and something tells me that I must hasten, that unforeseen evils menace us and, if these ordeals befall us, the suffering for me would be increased by my not having finished my work when I could have done so with greater application." But could he work with so many distractions? By the end of August, he wrote this note to himself: "The political horizon is black. . . . I do not believe there will be a war, but I have no good reasons for thinking so." At the beginning of September, the Ministry of Colonies ordered Marcel to cut short his home leave and return by the first plane to Dakar, with Christiane and their children to follow if war broke out. Roger imagined himself "reading the newspapers of July 1914" and thinking, "nothing has changed, and no one has learned anything in these twenty-four years. I should write a 'Summer 1938.'"[22]

The announcement on September 28, that Hitler's ally Mussolini had proposed that Germany, Italy, Great Britain, and France resolve the crisis through a conference to begin the following day at Munich drew from Roger this acidulous response, "We have reached such a point that the intervention of the other gangster, the Italian, is considered salvation." Yet salvation of any sort was not to be disdained: "I believe the immediate danger is now averted." As it was, for at Munich, France and Great Britain avoided war by agreeing to Germany's seizure of the Sudetenland, despite France's having a mutual defense pact with Czechoslovakia. To himself, Roger admitted, "Czechoslovakia is dismembered and pays for our peace. . . . We are ashamed of such a solution, and this shame prevents our rejoicing." But the accusation that the Munich Agreement was a "humiliation" infuriated him: "We had to choose either a negotiated *capitulation* or *general war*! A war that would have cost forty million lives, ruined a civilization, and which would have begun with the massacre and devastation of these Czech 'friends,' in whose name, for the sake of 'honor,' we 'should have' unleashed the conflict! . . . Nothing is worse than war. It is not inevitable, no matter what anyone says."[23]

Spared war, Roger contended instead during the next months with death, implacable and close. The painter Maurice Ray, a friend of Roger's parents and then a friend to him, died in late November. Utterly gaunt, he whispered to Roger, "I don't have much longer. It's hard. I have loved life. I thank you, infinitely, infinitely, you and Hélène." The same week, a heart attack took Emile Mayer, the stoical and withdrawn former army officer whom Roger called "my dear colonel" and trusted almost as a confidant. Far, far worse was the almost simultaneous news that Hélène's sister Suzon was failing rapidly from tuberculosis she contracted through the nursing responsibilities she gladly assumed as a Dominican sister. Hélène was holding her as she died three weeks later on December 21, her last words, repeated several times, "I no longer understand anything. I no longer understand." After hearing the news of Suzon's death, their father suffered a cerebral hemorrhage and died two days later. Hélène was distraught, inconsolable, and quickly spiraled into a dangerous state, heart palpitations combined with aching pain in her left arm. Roger worried even more about her spirit: "Her resilience is broken. Her grief is like a poison."[24]

More and more, Roger and Hélène thought of fleeing everything. The telephone still rang many times each day with congratulations or requests. Mail arrived from around the world, and one week, Roger counted stamping sixty letters in reply. They worried at the attacks against Marcel by the right-wing press, beginning in *L'Action française* and then picked up by *Candide*, *Gringoire*, and *Je suis partout*. Their real targets were Georges Mandel, minister of the colonies in the cabinet Edouard Daladier formed on April 8, 1938, and Léon Geismar, the colonial official Marcel had chosen as his chief assistant—because they were Jews. But with Marcel the link between them and himself a Freemason—Freemasonry a longtime bogeyman of the political right—he was fair game. Marcel believed that his own political friends could protect him, but as Daladier leaned away from the Popular Front after Munich, he became expendable. In April 1939, Mandel would move him to Madagascar. He retained the title governor-general, and Christiane would "reign over the Malagasy," but the change was an obvious and public demotion. As Roger and Hélène cast about for a means of flight, a financial windfall made almost anything possible. The Viking Press in the United States had commissioned a two-volume English edition of *Les Thibault* by the gifted translator Stuart Gilbert, and after the announcement of the Nobel Prize, the Literary Guild decided to adopt both as "Books of the Month," the first in 1940, the second in 1941. They had considered the idea of going to the French Antilles and now impulsively embraced it.[25]

On March 3, 1939, Roger and Hélène boarded the French ship *Barfleur* at Marseille bound for Basse-Terre, Guadeloupe, arriving thirteen days later. From the outset, they realized that they had made a serious mistake. Conditions on Guadeloupe were primitive compared to what they were accustomed in France: "The lack of comforts is unbelievable . . . the filth, the negligence are beyond description." Within two weeks, they took a night ferry to the neighboring island of Martinique, where in Fort-de-France they were at last able to find "a good colonial hotel." But when they looked for a villa to rent, the disappointments multiplied because the only ones they found acceptable were unfurnished. Eventually, they took the least undesirable, a villa at La Redoute, and purchased the necessary beds, tables, and chairs. They might have escaped France, but they could not escape the news from France. On March 15, Hitler violated the Munich Agreement by seizing the remainder of Czechoslovakia. Ten days later, he demanded the Polish Corridor, which granted Poland access to the sea through German territory, and the port of Danzig, which the Paris Peace Conference in 1919 had made an international city. On March 31, in reaction, Daladier and Neville Chamberlain, the prime ministers of France and Great Britain, declared that their nations would aid Poland in the event of German aggression. On April 6, they expanded this guarantee into a mutual defense pact. On April 7, Mussolini invaded Albania. The "anguish of Europe" pursued them. The unpleasant conditions and anxiety over the threat of war aggravated Hélène's condition. Roger located a Paris-trained physician in Fort-de-France, who measured her blood pressure as 157/142, far worse than her last reading at Nice, 137/97, and truly dangerous, predictive of heart attack or stroke. What had they done, coming to this barbarous land? Would they ever find their way home? And what changes would await them?[26]

For the Guadeloupeans and Martiniquais, people of African or mixed-race descent, Roger had an immediate disgust. He displayed typical European colonial racism, but his bitter disappointment with this escape to the Antilles sharpened his scorn. "They are essentially natural, and by that I mean animal. From the age of thirteen or fourteen, the girls and boys couple. . . . They bathe and perform their needs with almost no shame. The women are 'easy,' in the sense that they give themselves generously to men of color, but they are less 'easy' for Europeans, by whom they are intimidated." "The savagery of the past is not far gone. . . . They are very close to being animals." "Beneath the apparent gentleness and kindness among people of color, I discover their fundamental hatred of white people. . . . They are ignorant of *effort*, incapable of energy, of perseverance. They prefer that things go badly rather than take the slightest pains. No increase in wages will make them decide to work harder." "If I write a book about Martinique, I will not give it the title *Madinina*, 'Island of Flowers' in Carib, but instead *Merdinina*, 'Island of Shit.'"[27]

When Roger boarded ship with Hélène in March 1939, he brought with him a draft of his *Epilogue* for *Les Thibault*. In case of disaster, he left behind two copies, one with Schlumberger in Paris, another in his study at Le Tertre. He planned to make some small revisions and to run through the pages one last time while away. And in spite of the disagreeable conditions, in spite of Hélène's health, in spite of—or perhaps because of—the frightful portents from Europe, he proclaimed himself finished on May 26. Over the last years he had proved beyond question that he could write, and write brilliantly, under pressure. With confidence that in retrospect appears foolhardy, he entrusted the manuscript to international mail on June 5, and enclosed a letter for Schlumberger, "This enterprise, during nineteen years the framework of my life, has reached its conclusion, the Thibaults exist, independent of me, whole and complete." For himself, he wrote, "I have a phobia of the unfinished. How many times I sweated with fear that events in my private life, events in the world, or my health would cut short my undertaking and prevent me from pushing it through to its end! So today, I can say, *What I began, I finished.*" Then he added, "I think of Hélène with gratitude. I am alone in knowing the part she has taken in the work of this venture. Without her, I would never have been able to carry on so well this work—leaving aside her unfailing counsel, the revisions and corrections we make together, her sure sense of life and its beings."[28]

Whether or not Hélène deserved the credit, never in all his writing did Roger display a surer sense of life and its beings, a more profound appreciation of tragedy and loss. For the Thibaults are finished indeed: The *Epilogue* opens in May 1918, with Antoine recuperating at a hospital near the Mediterranean, in Le Mousquier, after exposure to mustard gas six months earlier. Persuaded by his physicians that he will eventually regain his health, he is keeping a detailed record of his symptoms and treatment for future publication. He has avoided Paris entirely since his mobilization nearly four years earlier in August 1914. Through Rumelles, his contact at the Quai d'Orsay, he learned of Jacques's death in Alsace. From letters, he discovered that Jenny became pregnant from her single tryst with Jacques and gave birth to a son, Paul. Now, he has news that his father's longtime housekeeper has died and decides the funeral is reason enough to go home. The trip by train is exhausting and reminds him of how weak he remains. At the Thibault house, which has been closed and empty since his departure, he has an overwhelming sense of loss: "He saw the past now bathed in roseate light, the glamor of youth and health. Ah, what would he not have given to retrieve the atmosphere of that bygone family life, that lost serenity!" An accumulation of mail awaits him, and he picks out a package, postmarked March 1915 from the General Hospital, Konakri, French Guiana. Within, he finds a necklace of honey-golden amber set with tiny rings of ambergris between the beads, the necklace that Rachel Goepfert always wore—"And suddenly the past had risen before his eyes, vivid as reality." That night, he dreams of his father. Is he recalling a world long gone, or does a conscience uneasy at his departure from his father's values assail his sleep?

Thérèse de Fontanin and Jenny have converted the old Thibault country retreat northwest of Paris at Maisons-Laffite into a hospital for soldiers recovering from their wounds. Daniel is there with a prosthetic leg. Antoine is not surprised to find Thérèse superbly capable of running things because she managed to fend for herself and her family with a husband like Jérôme. Jenny as well knows how to get things done and has charge of the laundry. She is defiantly defensive of Jacques's memory and entirely indulgent of her son. Antoine notices that while "maternity and its obligations had filled out her hips and bosom, thickened the lower portion of her neck, . . . the expression of her eyes . . . still had that far-away look—of loneliness, serene courage, and melancholy." Other than play with Paul, Daniel does almost nothing, and his sister says harshly that he "has never had any sense of his duties to society." She does not know that the shell fragment that tore off Daniel's leg also left him emasculated. The burden of nostalgia weighs heavily on Antoine as he remembers when "all of them were young, rejoicing in their youth and prospects for the future, without an inkling of what lay ahead—the cataclysm the statesmen of Europe were preparing for them behind the scenes."

The following day, he goes to the office of his longtime mentor, Dr. Philip. They agree about the war and its impact, Philip saying, "Who knows if, in the years to come, historians won't write us down as a generation of fools and simpletons who gulled themselves with wishful thinking, with illusions about man and his capacity for civilization?" He examines Antoine, listening carefully to his lungs and heart, and try as he may, he cannot prevent himself from revealing the result. "Philip's look, his whole expression, seemed to be saying: 'Your case is hopeless—and there is no escape.'" For the first time, Antoine admits to himself, "Way down deep I too knew it: I knew there was no hope." And so Antoine returns to Le Mousquier prepared to die, but true to his organized nature, he first has preparations to make. In a series of letters to Jenny, he discloses his condition and declares his intention to make Paul his sole heir. Ever bourgeois, he suggests that Jenny marry him to give Paul legitimacy, but she adamantly rejects the idea as a betrayal of Jacques. After writing to Guiana, he receives a note explaining that Rachel was brought to the hospital suffering from yellow fever. Before dying a few days later, she entrusted her nurse with the necklace and Antoine's address in Paris. Because no one claimed the body, she was buried in a pauper's grave. She left behind a black French bulldog called "Hirsch."

Antoine now knows all he can ever hope to know about his life and its meaning. He begins a diary that he hopes Paul will find and read some day. Memories of his father haunt him. "He was a difficult man to love. I judged him with much harshness and, I suspect, did him less than justice. . . . His defects set everyone against him and his very real virtues won him no liking. . . . I believe he was aware of this and that the knowledge of his isolation made him suffer terribly." He questions his father's wish for his sons to adopt the name "Oscar-Thibault": "There was much more to it than the proprietary instinct.... It was something finer—a craving to leave some trace behind him, not to be utterly blotted out by death." Memories of his only true love haunt him even more. "Thought of Rachel. In these sultry nights the perfume of the necklace is overpowering. She, too, had a stupid end, in a hospital bed. Alone. But one's always alone, dying.... The associations of this necklace may concern a paltry love affair, but, when all is said and done, that paltry love affair was about the best thing in my paltry life."

As Antoine approaches his end, he casts aside his remaining baggage. On July 8, 1918, he records, "Thirty-seven today. My last birthday." He warns Paul, "Impossible to rid one's mind wholly of the futile desire to find a 'meaning' in life. Even I, reviewing my career, often catch myself wondering: What was the point of it? It had no 'point.' None whatsoever.... And nothing matters— except perhaps, to get through this short lease of life with the minimum of suffering." When the chaplain asks to hear his confession, he thinks, "Could bring myself to do it if I thought it would give anyone pleasure. But nobody that I can see would be the happier if I pretended to die a Christian death." He lives to see the Armistice, but a week later he is in great pain and fears he may slip into a coma. He wants to die on his own terms and has prepared a lethal dose of morphine: "High time—or my strength may fail. All's ready; I need only steel my will, reach for the syringe. Struggled all night. High time. Monday, November 18, 1918. 37 years, four months, 9 days. Simpler than one thinks. Goodbye, Paul."[29]

During the months of June and July, Hélène's health slowly improved, her heart palpitations all but gone, her blood pressure lower, and her red blood cell count higher. To celebrate, she and Roger embarked on a three-week cruise around the Caribbean, with stops at Barbados, Trinidad, Colombia, and Panama. They left aboard the French ship *Flandre* on August 9, and had a perfectly delightful trip until August 22, as they were steaming back to Martinique from Panama. The ship's captain announced to the passengers that because the threat of war in Europe subjected the *Flandre* to immediate requisition as a troop carrier, he could not guarantee their return to Fort-de-France. Roger refused to worry, convinced that war would be averted at the last moment just as in the previous year. He was wrong, of course, but they were able to regain La Redoute on August 27, before he had the proof of his fatuity, which came on September 1, with the radio broadcast announcing that Hitler had invaded Poland.[30]

The following day from Tananarive (now Antananarivo), Marcel sent Roger a letter by the last scheduled airmail flight: henceforth, mail service between Martinique and Madagascar would require at least two and a half months by sea. At this moment of high emotion, he was no longer the libertine who had seduced Christiane—all that was nearly ten years of marriage and two children ago. Instead, he wrote: "We are saying farewell to our youth, my dear, old, faithful friend, farewell to the grand hopes of that youth, to the liberty, to the art, to all that made life worth living. I sense myself profoundly lost. Something within me is dead."[31] More than any apology for the past, this poignant, even intimate, message made amends.

Fulfilling their pledge to Poland, France and Great Britain responded to Hitler's attack with a declaration of war on September 3. At La Redoute, the great question for Roger and Hélène was whether to remain in Martinique or go back to France. Hélène imagined Le Tertre pillaged and ruined, perhaps overrun by refugees or seized for some military purpose. She was "inconsolable at being so far away" and insisted that they take passage on the first ship available. Roger replied that "thousands, millions of people in Europe would like to be where we are" and warned that in France they would risk "a life of daily anguish and material privation." Still, emotion trumped reason when Hélène's anxieties brought on a new crisis of hypertension and "a nervous state approaching breakdown." By the end of September, Roger reluctantly agreed that they should return as soon as possible.[32]

But what of the dangers and the difficulties? The Atlantic Ocean lay between them and France, with German submarines lurking in the sea lanes. Initially, they counted on taking the French ship *Bretagne*, which operated between the Antilles and France, but in mid-October, two weeks before their voyage, it was torpedoed and sank. This news heightened Roger's anxieties, and he wrote to Schlumberger with "testamentary" instructions: "If some mishap should befall us before we can return to Europe, try to get my *Epilogue* into print, and then issue a complete edition of *Les Thibault* in two or three volumes. At Le Tertre, I have left a journal written during the 14–18 war. I ask that Christiane deposit it with the Bibliothèque nationale and that it *remain under seal until her death.*" Then, over the next three weeks, Roger learned that they simply could not any longer reach France directly from Martinique or from anywhere else in the Caribbean and that they would have to leave from New York. But reaching the United States required an expensive and roundabout procedure. On November 11, they flew in a small airplane from Martinique to the Dominican Republic, where both the French and American consulates proved eager to help a Nobel laureate obtain the necessary visas. Three days later on November 14, they boarded the American ship *Borinquen*, which headed north at full steam and reached New York in less than a week on November 20. As they passed Cape Hatteras, Roger wrote to his brother that the cost, while enormous, would have been greater still if a Dominican Republic official had not accepted an autograph in return for waiving their exit tax of fifteen hundred francs ($900 in 2015). Once in New York, they learned that for fear of submarines, no American ships were sailing the Atlantic route, but that they could have a cabin on the *Conte di Savoia*, the largest and most luxurious of the Italian passenger liners, which was departing in five days for Genoa and Naples. Italy and France were not at war, and because Mussolini was Hitler's ally, German submarines would not target an Italian ship. The tickets were, consequently, a fortune.[33]

In early December, Roger could write to Christiane that he and Hélène had finally reached their Cimiez apartment after landing in Genoa and taking the train to Nice. Hélène would remain there to rest, while he headed north the following week to look after Le Tertre. Despite the wartime censorship prohibiting publication of weather data, he heard that winter in northern France had turned fearsomely cold, perhaps the coldest in a century, with low temperatures close to zero degrees Fahrenheit, and the daily average well below freezing. Roger went first to Paris, where Noël Margaritis, Pierre's widow, presented him with a two-month-old boxer puppy to take the place of Guadeloupe. He wrote Hélène, "Brace yourself, we have a new dog!" At Le Tertre, the heating system had been inadequate to prevent the water pipes from freezing, and when Roger brought in a portable stove to raise the temperature, the pipes burst and sprayed until he shut the main valve. Despite damage elsewhere in the house, his study was dry, though cluttered with his nine pieces of baggage and the seventeen trunks he had sent up from Nice before leaving for the Antilles. If regular shipping could be restored, he expected seven more eventually from Martinique. On Christmas Day, with no running water and only limited heat, Roger and the puppy sat at his desk shivering.[34] Exactly two years earlier, he had left Stockholm as the reigning Nobel laureate, the pinnacle of any literary career—an extraordinary triumph. Did he recall from his classical studies at the Ecole Fénelon that when the Roman Empire celebrated a victorious general with a "Triumph," custom required a companion to remind him frequently how he was but mortal: memento mori?

Chapter 7

~

DISPLACED

AFTER GERMANY INVADED POLAND on September 1, 1939, France supported its ally by undertaking a tentative advance into the Saar Valley on September 7, halted it five days later, and on September 21, decided that Poland was lost and that France's military interests were best served by withdrawing to its Maginot Line fortifications and forcing the Germans to mount any attack. Great Britain supported Poland by doing nothing and by encouraging the French to do no more. Perhaps Germany would content itself with command of Eastern Europe, or better still, turn on the Soviet Union, despite the non-aggression pact the two nations had signed at the end of August. Perhaps with Poland destroyed, the declaration of war by France and Great Britain could be forgotten in a bloodier version of Munich. Such thinking defined what the French would call *la drôle de guerre*, the "peculiar war," or, as the British preferred, "the phony war": out of sight and out of mind.

Stuck at Le Tertre, Roger was not worrying about the war. He was braving the burst pipes and the cold, with nighttime temperatures still near zero Fahrenheit throughout January. He envied Hélène's relatively "tropical" climate in Nice. He busied himself with emptying the trunks, glad to find "nothing ruined, nothing eaten by moths." He upbraided Christiane for a letter of "diatribes against colonial life and the duties and drudgery" inspired by her unhappiness at the demotion to Madagascar: "Compare your situation with Marcel and the semi-royalty you enjoy to the comparatively mediocre existence of your friends in France." He contemplated a new project, one he first imagined while on the way home from the French Antilles, about "growing old, discouragement, and bitter wisdom." Most of all, he contended with the problem of his *Epilogue* for *Les Thibault*. Editions Gallimard, and Schlumberger especially, worried that its account of the Great War's horrors might attract official censorship, which could mean seizure of the entire print run, some ten to fifteen thousand copies, at the cost of perhaps eighty thousand francs ($41,130 in 2015).[1]

Ultimately, Gaston Gallimard made the shrewd judgment that the government would not censor the culmination of a book crowned with the Nobel Prize, and *Epilogue* appeared at the end of January 1940. The reaction in the press was negative but not strident, taking the general tone that its publication was "singularly inopportune," sometimes adding the accusation that it was "a defeatist book." Roger protested that he was relating the meditation of a man dying in 1918 and had written *Epilogue* in 1938 and 1939 before France entered this new war. He was glad to cite letters to him from readers, many of them men who had served at the front during the Great War, who praised his having captured the mood that continued to haunt them. But was doing so, reviving these sacrifices, wise in the spring of 1940? Perhaps Schlumberger had a point. When Roger came to Paris in February, he found the city "truly sinister, empty, cold, grey, and infinitely dismal." In Normandy, he had noticed with anxiety that "the vitality seems to lessen week by week, the shops closed or empty" and that "the countryside around me is dead, the stores hardly bothering to restock their shelves." Roger sensed a spirit of resignation, but to what?[2]

Then with a vengeance, the war ceased to be phony. On April 9, 1940, Germany launched an assault on Denmark and Norway. To Hélène, who was preparing to join him at Le Tertre now that the pipes had been repaired, Roger was confident: "the Allies will respond energetically." Within a week, an Anglo-French expeditionary force did land in southern Norway, but it was decisively driven out by May 3. Exactly a week later on May 10, Germany began a broad invasion of Western Europe, attacking Belgium, the Netherlands, and Luxembourg. Within two days, their troops crossed the Meuse River at Sedan into France. By May 20, they had pushed back the French and British lines to reach Arras, Abbeville, and Amiens near the English Channel. On that same day, Hélène, at Tertre since the beginning of May, slipped on the stair landing and broke her right arm close to the juncture with the shoulder. Roger took her to the Delagenière Clinic at nearby Le Mans where they had recovered in 1931. After three days of treatment, she left practically encased in a cast that extended down to her thigh, making it difficult for her to sit or lie down. By now, with the Germans less than two hundred miles away, Roger was seeing caravans of civilian refugees in bullet-ridden automobiles along the roads. For the first time, he called the news "truly terrifying."[3]

Roger had not heard the worst: In the last week of May, the Germans trapped the British Expeditionary Force and the French First Army in a pocket around Dunkirk. Although nearly 340,000 of them were rescued by sea, about 50,000 others were taken prisoner, and all of the heavy weaponry was lost. The fighting had become a rout. The Germans now held almost as much territory as they had during the Great War, and had seized it in only three weeks. Paris was their objective now, and in taking its environs, they would certainly envelop Le Tertre. Roger was right to be fearful: the Nazis had burned his books in Berlin. On June 7, he wrote his brother, "I remain firmly persuaded of final victory by the Allies, but perhaps only after unforeseeable tribulations, terrible and long. Anything is possible, even the forty years in captivity of the Hebrew people." Roger would not wait to see what his reception might be, but the preparations he made for flight were insufficient. A week later, on June 14, the day the Germans entered Paris, he and Hélène left Le Tertre at dawn, taking with them in their automobile only a few suitcases of clothing and some of his papers. They stopped first in Le Mans, where they convinced the physicians at the clinic to remove Hélène's original cast and replace it with one much smaller. In a letter that evening he wrote: "We have fled Le Tertre, leaving behind everything. Profound distress." The following day, they headed south and west, toward the coast on the Bay of Biscay. The distance was just over two hundred miles, but the going was slow because of all the other refugees on the roads. After two days, they reached Vaux on June 17, where they took shelter with one of Roger's correspondents, the classicist Félix Sartiaux. That evening, they learned from an official French government radio broadcast that Marshal Philippe Pétain, a hero of the Great War, had become prime minister and had asked the Germans for an armistice.[4]

On June 23, from a second broadcast, Roger learned "the appalling conditions of the capitulation." By its terms signed the day before, Germany annexed portions of northern and eastern France, notably Alsace and Lorraine, and occupied three-fifths of the country, everything north of the Loire River and the entire Atlantic coast. Italy, which had declared war only when France was clearly beaten, received a small occupation zone in the extreme southeast, from the border about five miles to the town of Menton. The French army was demobilized except for a force of 100,000 to maintain order, the navy disarmed and interned at its home ports, the one and a half million prisoners of war to remain in German hands until a final peace, and the French people to bear the cost of occupation, at four hundred million francs a day ($205,000,000 in 2015). The remainder of France, the south and the Mediterranean coast, would remain under the control of the French government as the "Free Zone," but from the outset its dependence on the goodwill of Germany was obvious to all. For Roger, "It is the abyss, the depths of despair."[5]

Convinced that his liberty and perhaps his life were at stake, Roger decided that he and Hélène should seek visas and permission to leave for the United

States. Doing so meant approaching the Pétain government, which had charge of the Free Zone and eventually established its capital in the spa town of Vichy, where the many hotel rooms could be easily converted into offices. Roger arrived in Vichy on July 11, the day after the senators and deputies of the Third Republic voted its abolition and entrusted Pétain with the power to promulgate the constitution for a new regime. Left unsaid was the presumption of seeking a favored position in a German-dominated Europe. Roger quickly discovered that "all who could help me are in disgrace." As he wrote bravely to Maria van Rysselberghe, "New York having been refused me, I shall rally to Nice." But to Schlumberger he confessed, "These upheavals are the overturning of everything, and for those of our age, the end of all we held dear. The future is *terrifying*, and few dare to recognize it."[6]

Evidence of the future to come caught up with Roger and Hélène when they got to Nice at the beginning of August. From Madagascar was Marcel's telegram with the news that he had been dismissed as governor-general because he had refused to accept the authority of the Pétain government and had instead proposed handing over the colony to Great Britain. He would be returning to France with Christiane and the children, but exactly how was unclear. And from Le Tertre was a letter reporting that a German unit arrived on June 18, and "searched through everything, not an armoire, not a compartment in my desk, not a drawer, not a cupboard that was not opened, emptied, and scattered.... I would a hundred times more have preferred that an incendiary bomb had set fire to Le Tertre and that nothing remained!" No matter what, Roger and Hélène were not returning to the German Occupied Zone: "I believe in neither their guarantees nor their promises. It would be foolhardy to place ourselves within reach of their paws." They found their Cimiez apartment undisturbed, and there they huddled as best they could, cut off at least temporarily from Roger's sources of money and with only the clothes they packed hurriedly before fleeing Le Tertre.[7]

National disaster elicited varying responses from Roger's literary acquaintances. Finding himself in Nice, the aristocratic novelist Henry de Montherlant, an anti-Semite and misogynist, invited Roger to dine with him. They had never met despite admiring each other's work. Afterward, Roger commented on Montherlant's hauteur: "The important thing is not that France escapes its servitude and its people their hunger but that he maintain his health, eat his fill, have sufficient money to live as he pleases, and pursue in complete independence his work and his pleasure." André Gide was equally solipsistic: his principal anxiety that Catherine van Rysselberghe, his unacknowledged but adoptive daughter, now seventeen years old, was playing coy with one of her professors—"It's disgusting," he had exclaimed. But Roger, in the most severe commentary he would ever write about their ambiguous friendship, recalled that "Gide has passed his entire life committing far graver abuses of confidence! How many times has he cultivated a family for the sole purpose of approaching the young son of the house, sometimes a schoolboy of thirteen, to awaken in him sexual curiosities, to teach him certain pleasures! More cunning than Catherine's professor, more diabolical in his temptations." A few months later, Catherine would tell Roger that she had always hated Gide, and hated him all the more now that she knew he was her father. Finally, there was the mystical Catholic poet Paul Claudel, another anti-Semite and misogynist, whom Roger had known since the 1920s. Claudel was now a favorite of the new Vichy government and threatened to resign from its radio broadcasts of literary works if they ever featured anything "by a certain Nobel Prize winner whose anti-French opinions are known and whose last book is a crime against the nation."[8]

In counterpoint to these monsters of egotism, Roger could place Hélène. By November, her arm had healed, and she volunteered every day at the local center for demobilized soldiers. With her compulsion for service fulfilled, she was "cheerful, open, kind, indulgent, spirited, and full of life." And he could place Marcel, who had sacrificed his career to oppose a government compliant with the Germans. On Christmas Day, he, Christiane, Daniel, and Annique finally reached Marseille after an uncomfortable forty-five days aboard a freighter that had already made stops at Cape Town, Dakar, Casablanca, and Oran. Roger and Hélène awaited them on the dock in the midst of an unaccustomed snow storm and then took them, "worn out and freezing," back to Nice, where they moved into a neighboring apartment. Christiane seemed especially glad to see them, and despite having been so recently a reigning queen of the colonial service, she was soon getting up before dawn to stand in the ration line for vegetables. Hélène had begun helping the families of men who were prisoners of war, and while she was away, Christiane and Roger cautiously patched their relationship through idle chatter. Daniel, now seven and a half years old, had become "serious, attentive, thoughtful, curious about everything," but also "capricious and demanding." Annique, just five, was quieter, even docile, "exquisite, tender, engaging." Marcel was unbowed, "talking, perhaps too loudly, of 'duty' and 'honor.'" Marcel's "bitterness," Roger agreed, "is more than legitimate. But beneath an outward stoicism combined with haughty scorn, he conceals a rage that eats away at him and renders him capable of any excess: a violent and cruel appetite for reprisals, leading him to express the hope of 'gunning down' adversaries once his 'side' regains power."[9]

How were the tortured questions to be answered? To deny them was to be Montherlant or Gide. To exploit them as a bludgeon was to be Claudel. To cry vengeance was to be Marcel. Roger recalled how until Munich he had insisted, "Anything rather than war!" but afterward he revised his opinion: "prudence, conciliation, but no new capitulation." By August 1939, he had decided, "*this time*, this war is 'just.'" Now, he added, "I was mistaken." But besides his idealism, he had nothing to oppose the German aggression with all its cruelty and terrors. He acknowledged the belief among many, certainly by Marcel, in "the final victory of England and America." But such a victory, Roger believed, would inevitably lead to an England dependent on America and a France dependent on England. He worried that any outcome would mean a world in which the "individual will be more and more muzzled, eroded, subjugated to the community, and proud of having been sacrificed." He tried to imagine how the last of his characters from *Les Thibault*, Paul, born in 1915 from the union of the Thibault and Fontanin families and therefore twenty-five in 1940, would have chosen to act: "Would he be a soldier? A deserter? A prisoner of war? A pilot for the Free French of General Charles de Gaulle? A journalist in Lyon, slipping propaganda under closed doors? A Communist in a concentration camp? A partisan of the Vichy government determined to remake France?" The confusion he attributed to Paul was simply the confusion he felt himself. The solution was both easy and impossible: "If I were younger and alone, I would go live in America."[10]

No, Roger was not younger, and he had the symptoms of age, urinary difficulties as a result of benign prostatic hyperplasia. When he sought treatment in Nice, he was diagnosed with an enlarged but not cancerous prostate gland and told that he should undergo an operation to increase urinary flow. He reacted with dread because he had heard stories of death from acute hemorrhage during such a procedure—especially that of his early mentor, Abbé Marcel Hébert. Both Marcel and Gaston Gallimard strongly advised against it and insisted that he see a specialist at the medical school in Marseille. This second examination blamed his problems on a "localized infection" and rejected any need for surgical intervention. Roger had comforted himself with the thought that "death by hemorrhage is rapid and painless," and even the relief at escaping the scalpel did not cheer him. Less than a month later, he noted his sixtieth birthday by commenting, "This year, I have, clearly, become an old man," and "certain days, I imagine that everything is finished for me."[11]

A large part of his discouragement arose from his inability to make a start on his new writing project, which was itself about the bitter wisdom of age. All he had done so far was work on some background materials, which he had prepared in the hope of having "my subject impose itself upon me." And it did so. On May Day 1941, he went to bed early, suffering from digestive upset and fearing that he might be catching the whooping cough that had kept Daniel and Annique in bed for more than a week. Unable to sleep, "I little by little constructed in my head the entire project of a book, which will be Maumort's journal. . . . It will be a book where everything that preoccupies me will find a place." He imagined his protagonist as a retired colonel in his seventies, composing his memoirs in the wake of the German invasion and thereby commenting on the entire course of his life and the life of all around him. Maumort would resurrect the past and parade it for inspection. The following day as Roger recorded his sleepless night, he was exultant, concluding, "Alleluia!"[12]

Then, the rest of the month passed in a burst of activity. Marcel had made more enemies than friends in Nice through "his political intransigence and his rancorous, partisan attitude." He and Christiane decided to move with the children to Figeac, in the Lot region about 275 miles east but still within the Free Zone. Marcel had family connections there and "would be king in his village"—more like his position in the colonies. Roger's financial situation had improved because the armistice permitted the restoration of rudimentary banking connections between the Occupied and Free Zones. His brother and Schlumberger could now send him money, but those amounts, even if multiplied several times, could not solve the problem of scarcities. Almost everything was in short supply, especially food. Just as in every other urban area of France, rationing in Nice meant that each day was a search for nourishment: Hélène had waited in line more than an hour for a single artichoke. Vegetables were uncommon, meat rare, and the bread adulterated. They had both lost weight, and their clothing hung ever looser around them. Now that he could afford to do so, Roger proposed that they spend the summer in the mountains at Evian, about two hundred miles north on the French side of Lake Geneva. Food was said to be more available in rural areas, and they could buy directly from the local farms. In the brisk air and with large portions at meals, they could regain their strength. And get well: they had to delay heading north for ten days when Roger suffered acute prostatitis from urinary colibacillosis. When they did reach Evian in mid-June, they were delighted. Their villa was spacious and set on a scenic plateau. Food was more available: always vegetables, often fresh meat, and occasionally even butter and cream. After setting out his writing materials and notebooks, Roger declared that he was ready to begin serious work on what he was calling his *Maumort*.[13]

Then came the shocking news that Germany had invaded the Soviet Union on June 22. Roger rightly concluded that this extension of the war would significantly increase the degree of Vichy France's "collaboration" with Germany. The Germans would demand additional support, and Vichy leaders had long made clear that Communists and the Communist homeland were anathema.

About that collaboration Roger was ambivalent. He believed that Pétain was "honorable, energetic, well intentioned" but that the men around him were "the adversaries of Jean Barois and Luce," men who favored an "evolution toward fascism." About Pétain, he was too generous; about his underlings, absolutely correct. In March, the Vichyite weekly *La Gerbe* featured an attack on Roger as one of "the false witnesses of our time," his *Jean Barois* exalting "the new cult of laicism," and his *Les Thibault* "conducting the trial of the bourgeoisie." "We cannot pardon such a shepherd." Roger credited Pétain with having saved France from the kind of German atrocities reported in Poland but did not flinch from calling the result "subjugation." He hoped that Great Britain could hold out long enough for "America to come and play the role of liberator." He also pondered whether France, having surrendered so quickly to Germany, might have become "definitively suspect" in the view of the United States. He asked himself, "Is it wise to renounce battles that are already thought lost? *I believe that there are decisive hours in history when what must be saved cannot be saved unless it is defended at all cost, without reserve, no matter the repugnance of the wise man to take part.* There are hours when neutrality is not only culpable but noxious, even criminal. And we may be at one of those hours."[14]

Roger had already entered the mind of Maumort: "An old colonel, retired, living in the Orne on a property called Le Saillant (which is, of course, Le Tertre), is subjected in June 1940 to invasion and occupation. Before the Germans arrive, he has, through an excess of caution, destroyed the journal he has kept during forty years. Closing himself off in one wing of the country house while the rest of it and his garden are the prey of the occupiers, he begins his journal 'of captivity.' He is inconsolable at having burned the notebooks in which he had consigned, day by day, the episodes of his eventful life. He uses his enforced leisure to repair, to the extent possible, this loss by writing his memoirs at the pleasure of his fantasy and his recollections, that is to say without chronological order." Through Maumort, Roger could comment on everything: "reflections of all sort on topicalities, the meditations on life of a cultivated old man, the portraits of people he has known, the adventures he has had." From the first moment, Roger understood that he and Maumort would overlap but that his protagonist "must exist by himself and be clearly different from me, whether by his military life, his cultural and spiritual upbringing, his aristocratic tendencies." He spent four or five hours each day with his notebooks preparing the background, telling Christiane, "the work brings me great calm." But already he had decided, "This will certainly be my last book. . . . I am in no hurry, I have no desire to see it published, and I embrace completely the idea of it as a posthumous work."[15]

During the summer, Evian exceeded every expectation for Roger and Hélène. The villa was comfortable, the climate brisk, and food plentiful enough that they both regained some of the weight they had lost. Hélène remarked that "her life had not been so easy since the death of our parents, fifteen years ago." Having Roger all to herself without any interlopers, she created around them "a calm atmosphere of love, gentle and placid." They had planned on returning to Nice in September but stayed on because "we want to extend this sojourn where we have found so much peace and have so many material advantages. *I work, and we eat potatoes.*" But when October brought freezing temperatures and snow, they discovered that the villa had no heating apparatus and only a single fireplace, for which they had difficulty obtaining wood. They were soon "bundled up like polar explorers," "*frozen to the marrow,* and literally *paralyzed* by the cold." At the end of October, "the toothpaste tube was frozen, hard and heavy like an ingot of lead." Although desperate to leave, they could not because only three trains a week ran from Evian to Nice, and all of the seats were reserved until early November. They could have bought standing-room tickets, but they were afraid that they could not endure the more than twenty-hour trip, twelve hours of it at night, holding each other up in the corridors. At last, their turn for seats came on November 6—they had been in Evian almost five months—and they "returned from the pole."[16]

The weather was only slightly warmer in Nice, as this winter was vying to equal the last in its cold. Heating fuel was hard to obtain, and Roger sat in his study "dressed like an Eskimo" because the temperature inside the apartment was forty-five degrees Fahrenheit. He apologized for his handwriting: "My fingers so cold that the pen is a bit epileptic." The cold was harder to bear without sufficient food, which had become even more difficult to obtain in Nice than during the previous spring. Roger grew thinner again, much thinner, his weight eventually falling from 200 pounds to slightly less than 170. He was unaccustomed to standing in the ration lines, and Hélène was not there to do it because she was braving the danger of Paris in the Occupied Zone to liquidate her father's estate. He had died fully three years ago, at the end of 1938, but the normal complications and slow pace of legal procedure had pushed the formal disposition into late summer 1939, after which the effects of the war and German Occupation significantly extended the delay. Alone, Roger was despondent, all the summer optimism gone. His urinary problems had improved, but rheumatism in his left leg, the one prone to phlebitis, forced him to use a cane. He thought of his father, who in his sixties had appeared to him "so diminished. Premature old age runs in the family, but why does it have to come on so suddenly and so rapidly?" He worried most that his memory was failing and that its "weakening would leave me helpless" in the face of the work required to complete his book. Yet the year was ending with a sense of hope because the United States had finally entered the war after the Japanese attack at Pearl Harbor. "If all goes well," Roger dared to predict, "1942 will be a year of uncertain combat with Germany ceasing to be everywhere victorious, and 1943 would mark the decisive turning point when the Anglo-Saxon forces will regain the advantage."[17]

Roger sounded so pathetic that Christiane left her family behind to visit him in early January. He found her "resplendent in health, ... robust like a country girl," and was so glad to see her that he easily forgave her adamant opinions. Those French "who thought like her husband," she exclaimed, "were in possession of the truth, while the rest were self-seeking reactionaries, treacherous, stupid, and wicked." She added that this war "confronted good and evil, with Churchill, Roosevelt, and de Gaulle the apostles of good." She had been there a week when Hélène returned on January 15, and despite her mother's appearance of exhaustion, left the next day. Hélène did not revive quickly, and when she had a fever of 102.5°F and swelling on the side of her face, the initial thought was a simple abscess of the parotid gland. Instead, she had the mumps and was in bed for more than a week. She got better—and exchanged the mumps for morosity.[18]

They were a pair, Roger and Hélène, in their Cimiez apartment, each mourning for a world lost. Hélène came back from Paris burdened by great sorrow. Roger assumed, naturally enough, that the trip had stirred memories of losing both her sister Suzon and her father during the same week. Yes, it had, but while in Paris she had also learned that her dear friend Marie Bénilan, who had shared with her such devotion to Abbé Sudour, was to enter a Benedictine convent that summer. However much Roger rejected their profound and mystical Catholicism, he understood that Marie's decision would deprive Hélène of "her last and ultimate source of trust, of spiritual exchange, where she might take shelter." And in his own unhappiness, he imagined that the solution for Hélène was that "I die, and that she, in her turn, enter a religious community where she will finally find her home. Alive, I can do nothing for her. Only through my death can I deliver her." If not exactly death, a sense of decline as its prelude was certainly heavy on his mind: "I have experienced such a crisis of premature aging that I have twice almost taken the train for Lyon to consult with a famous neurologist whom I count among my friends. I have experienced unaccustomed anxiety, absolute incapacity to work, loss of memory and the impossibility of tying two ideas together. My eyesight has diminished. In conversation, I can no longer come up with the right words. I say one thing when I mean another. During these last few weeks, I have truly wondered whether I am a helpless witness to my own decrepitude." Roger was, in fact, neurasthenic, but the tumultuous quality of his dozen years past had indeed combined with the precarious nature of his present to wear down his tenacity, while the uncertainties of his future gave him good reason to fear. As before—as always—the remedy for his discouragement was concentration on a vast writing project. Hélène would, again as always, find a certain solace in being his partner, his sounding board, his confidante, his choice—in spite of all their differences.[19]

Only a single day after complaining about his infirmity, Roger was analyzing his lack of progress on *Maumort* since the fall and realized that he had failed to heed his own warning from the early summer to make clear the distinction between himself and the colonel: "the use of 'I' in this journal has led me to write more and more *in my name*, unconsciously to substitute myself for Maumort." The solution, he recognized, was "to write a complete biography of my good fellow from his birth up to his sixty-second year: purely preparatory work that will take several months but that will finally give me the necessary basis to begin my book." Maumort's actions could then derive from the prior course of his life. Roger added a piquant metaphor to describe the importance of this background before attempting the narrative: "When I am going to make jugged hare, I begin by skinning the hare and cutting it up. Once I have all the pieces of the animal in front of me, I make the sauce." The denser the background material, the more Maumort would ring true. Roger had done the same for *Les Thibault*, and he attributed this passion for accuracy to the training he had received at the Ecole des Chartes: "I acquired a kind of scientific conscience, the taste for truth, an obsession for documentation, and the habit of precision." Soon, he was chasing down details about the school Maumort would have attended, the sense of making progress anew revitalizing him: "In this anguished world, I have found—illusory or not—a reason to live, a goal, a vast project that I would truly like to accomplish before becoming empty and finished." At the beginning of May, Roger and Hélène declared their independence of "this anguished world"—whether illusory or not—by leasing a villa for the summer at Cap d'Antibes, less than twenty miles west along the coast but far more rural. They escaped the drear of Nice and found vegetables and fruit "without lines."[20]

Roger meant to work, and he set about it but from a remarkable perspective. He had already decided that his *Maumort* would include "all that I still wish to say, all that I have in my drawers from unfinished projects, a summing up, the totality of life and experience, the notes accumulated over forty years, the testament of a generation, on the eve of a complete scission between two ages of humanity." Now, he declared, "it is a work that will never be completed, that can expand indefinitely and perfect itself, a work *that will never be finished by me* and that can be interrupted at whatever moment by my death, *without its being an unfinished work*, because Maumort's journal can always be stopped short by his death." Here, then, was Roger's plan: "I will need two or three years to give the work its preliminary form, but afterward, there will only be additions, improvements, which will go on for years, or not, depending on the length of my life."[21]

Throughout May and June, Roger prepared background material. "My characters take shape, autobiographically and psychologically. I build up 'reserves,' from which I will have only to gather passages when the day comes that I compose Maumort's journal. These reserves must be abundant and varied. I have already sorted out the life of Henriette, Maumort's sister." By early July, he was moving "step by step through the early childhood" of Maumort himself. "I want to know *as well as he does himself* all the periods of his life, even the least prominent, the more to be at ease in the center of *his* memoir. . . . At this moment, I am emphasizing sexuality, for the years from ten to eighteen are the 'sexual' age. . . . Right now, I appear to be making it the principal subject, but that is not at all my intention! Everything will take its rightful place in the overall scheme." A month later, he boasted that the thick stack of pages covered with his cramped handwriting had taken Maumort to his eighteenth year: "I have given special care to his childhood, his education, the development of his personality, and especially his sexual awakening. If I were to die tomorrow and if someone poked around in this scribble, they would think that I was writing a study of adolescent sexuality and even that I was obsessed with these questions." To Christiane he wrote, "*No work has ever brought me such joy of creation.* Absolutely none." And to her he even revealed his conception of a book that would never be completed: "I am like an old stone mason who, in his declining years, is put in charge of beginning a cathedral. Surely, I will die leaving behind only one or two roughhewn columns, the beginnings of a keystone, a few meters of balustrade. . . . But I can no longer conceive of any other occupation for my old days, and I am now the slave and prey to my folly."[22]

Hélène spent two weeks in mid-August at Figeac charming her grandchildren. She also managed to remain on friendly terms throughout with both Christiane and Marcel, though doing so required her to inhibit every censorious thought. That exhausting suppression of emotion was, in fact, the cause of her trip: to ensure that she thought as little as possible about how Marie Bénilan was about to begin her novitiate at the Benedictine Abbey of Jouarre outside Paris. Roger considered again how "God will have refused Hélène this last refuge: after having taken from her successively *all* the pious beings to whom she was attached, Abbé Marchand, Suzon, Monsignor Sudour, *all dead, one after the other.*" He feared that she was becoming passive and vacant: "She is more and more indifferent *to everything, me included.*" "The curse is that two beings so profoundly different and irreconcilable have loved each other, faithfully and cruelly their whole lives! ... A love that for me has been unique. ... Her vocation was to be a nun, to become a despotic mother superior like her great aunt, her godmother." He recalled a remark his mother made shortly after their marriage: "'Hélène,' she said smiling, 'does not much like hearing the truth about herself.' I thought then that this disposition arose from Hélène's fear that my mother, by pointing out her little faults, would make me notice them all the more and turn me against her. But thirty-five years of marriage without my ever having heard her confess an error, a mistake, an imperfection, have taught me that this attitude is a kind of fierce pride, which is her principal and central armament."

Without an answer to their perpetual quandary of misunderstanding each other, he wrote in his journal, "Friends tell me sometimes that I am old for my age, that I have abdicated too soon, that I am inward-looking, a recluse. But how could I be otherwise? All my impulses to undertake something new, to organize our life in some other manner, collide with Hélène's passive sadness, Hélène, who waits for her death and who believes, deeply, 'Why bother?'"[23]

Roger and Hélène extended their stay at Cap d'Antibes until mid-November, and by the time they returned to Nice the relatively good times of the summer and fall were about to worsen considerably. A week earlier, on November 8, American and British forces mounted an amphibious invasion of Morocco and Algeria in Operation Torch. Germany reacted by extending its occupation throughout the rest of France, with Italy given a slight expansion westward to include Nice. The Free Zone was no longer "free," and Roger was now subject to the Italian authorities. Christiane sent him a worried letter, but he replied that "the risks are not immediate." More pressing were scarcities: less and less food, no heating supplies whatsoever, and empty shelves in the shops. For more than a month, no matches could be found for sale anywhere in Nice, and when Roger asked about shoes to replace the ones he had worn out, he learned that there were two hundred pairs and nine thousand requests. Hélène's mood turned dark, and she had a recurrence of heart problems, dangerously high blood pressure with the systolic reading reaching 180. She lay in her bed and got up only for meals. Bitterness flooded her: Christiane, she reproached for her adolescence, marriage, and loss of faith; Daniel and Annique, she complained were being reared contrary to her principles; Le Tertre, she described as a hell where she slaved to serve Roger's hateful friends; and Roger himself, she accused of "creating this emptiness around her." She was determined, he believed, to present herself as *the most unhappy of all creatures.*" Still, Roger was familiar with Hélène's recurrent depressive storms. He had thirty-seven years of experience with them and knew how quickly they could flare up or dissipate almost without warning or justification—at least that he could discern. The new component was her heart condition and peril. The fear that he might lose her, lose his only true companion, left his meditations to himself about her a tangled mélange of exasperation and apprehension, hopelessness and desperation.[24]

While tending to Hélène, Roger received "a sort of moral S.O.S." from Christiane: the accounts of fighting in North Africa had impressed upon Marcel his uselessness in Figeac and made him "sad and easily offended." Roger replied that Marcel was "suffering in his solitude, a king in exile dispossessed of his throne," but would recover when given an opportunity to play an active role once again. Christiane rallied at this reassurance but added: "Marcel's solitude makes me suffer terribly, because, despite himself, he catches me up in this solitude, and emptiness surrounds us. Realizing it, I have decided that in a more normal future I shall create around me a life of friends and society. I fear for my older years." Sensing that real trouble loomed, Roger dared entering German-held territory to make a hasty visit to Figeac at the beginning of March. Out of caution, he stayed in a hotel but spent most of every day with Marcel and Christiane. He found much to encourage him. Their house was spacious and comfortable. Food was so abundant that Roger called it "cuisine from before the war." Annique at seven was charming and resourceful. Daniel at ten was sensible and studious. Marcel was even more dogmatic in his moral rigidity about the politics of the war, "as if he had truth in his pocket"—like the Abbé Marchand—but he showed no sign of gloomy irritation. With his usual derogation of religion, Roger imagined that Marcel was returning to Protestant roots and a kind of "Puritanism." Christiane did, however, alarm him: he thought her close to nervous exhaustion. "She is highly emotional and has a morbid imagination. At any moment, tears fall from her eyes. More than ever, she submits to her natural disposition of dissatisfaction with everything, dreaming of what she does not have, and believing that all would be better otherwise and elsewhere." Like Hélène, Christiane had returned to form. Roger could sum up the Figeac drama in a couple of sentences, as if Maumort were recounting it for his journal: "Coppet is a man in his sixties who no longer expects much from his life, even his rancorous ambition visibly attenuated by a certain weariness, a certain desire to give up the fight. Christiane is thirty-five with a great appetite for living and a sense that her colonial life was only a prelude; she is fatefully impatient watching the months pass while her husband ages and her youth flees. . . . Matters can only get worse."[25]

Except that Maumort might not be keeping his journal, for Roger began questioning the very form of his new project. He had, he believed, been seduced by the ease with which he wrote Antoine Thibault's journal for *Epilogue*. But there, he could draw upon Antoine's entire past as it had played out in the previous volumes. If he left the recollections to Maumort, he deprived himself of "*presenting my characters in action.*" The difference would be similar to "reading the script of a movie instead of watching it on the screen." His new plan was to present Maumort's life through a series of short stories or novellas, overlapping and sometimes repeating each other as they came to Maumort's mind. "Each would have its own unity but together they would create the extended work. ... Thus, the autobiography of Maumort would constitute itself gradually *by slices.*" Roger thought that the preparatory work he had already accomplished would fit perfectly into this scheme, becoming in fact the basis of these "slices." The depiction of critical moments was his greatest strength as a writer: their extraordinary realism and profoundly developed characterization. To do so, he relied upon what he called his "interior vision: to imagine the characters, the setting, the décor, the gestures, the dialogue with sufficient *intensity* as if having seen and heard myself." For him, "a scene for a novel is not prepared, not ready, not ripe until it has the *intensity of a recent experience.*" And if so, "*imagination* no longer has much to do, its role is finished, because I work with my *memory*, which brings to my eyes the vision of something as real as if it had truly taken place, and with my *intelligence*, which aids me in ordering the elements, sorting out the details, finding the appropriate structure and the right words."[26]

What was the structure and what were the right words for the relationship between Christiane and Marcel? In mid-August, Christiane left Marcel behind in Figeac while she took Daniel and Annique with her to Paris and then to La Bourboule, in the Auvergnat region of central France. To Marcel, Roger made excuses, "She has reached that terrible age: regret at the passage of youth, disappointment at hopes unfulfilled, and rage at obstacles standing before her." But to Christiane, he was stern: "You are delivering yourself to the demons that you carry within you, an incurable sadness, an incurable impatience, a morbid need for something else, a refusal to accept what is, an impossibility to recognize what is happy, a juvenile quest for some 'bliss' as imaginary and inaccessible as a mirage, always fleeting. *And the consequences are of an extreme gravity.*" Christiane was beyond such warning. She replied that she was returning to Figeac but only briefly and would then take her children back to Paris "to see if life there is possible," because relations between her and Marcel "have become *impossible.*" Marcel was exasperated, convinced that "Christiane seeks out difficulties. She does not want to be helped: she wants to be pitied." In a second letter he confessed, "I cannot do much because my influence is nil or has the opposite effect of what I wish for Christiane. . . . You are the only person in the world to whom she will listen." Apparently, she did so, because after returning to Figeac at the beginning of September, she decided to remain there at least for a while.[27]

Christiane was a problem at a distance, Hélène was a problem at home. Because her physician in Nice warned that she avoid "all physical and psychological fatigue," she accepted an offer to spend four weeks during the summer in the French Alps. The invitation came from their neighbor, Marie Rougier, who was acting as Roger's secretary and whose family had a home in Tines, near Chamonix. Once Hélène arrived in early July and learned that Marie shared some of her Catholic mysticism, they became fast friends. Back to Roger a month later, she claimed to be "resuscitated." "Too much, perhaps," Roger commented. She began attending daily early Mass, and when she learned that he had visited Catherine Gide, who had come to Nice, she "grew swollen with venom." He vented his anger at Hélène's family: "These devout Foucaults seem to bear all the curses of heaven. Hatred is congenital to them. . . . Is their religiosity the proof that they sense the need of a check against their natural iniquity?" After a month, he wrote his brother, "I find in her attitude toward me the same kind of exasperation without cause that the presence of her father caused in her! That promises us a charming winter."[28]

In fact, by late September, Christiane's marriage and Hélène's mood were far overshadowed by the course of the war. The Anglo-American invasion of Sicily provoked the overthrow of Benito Mussolini on July 24, and almost immediately, the Germans began to take control of the Italian occupation zone in France. At the end of August, Marcel urged Roger and Hélène to join him in Figeac: "Think about it!" Roger himself was so worried that the fighting would engulf Nice that he sent a trunk containing his journal and most of his preparatory work for *Maumort* to the apartment on the Rue du Dragon in Paris. By October, the Germans had installed their security apparatus in Nice, with the Gestapo hunting for Jews and partisans of de Gaulle's "Free French." Roger worried that he and Hélène might have to prove that they were "Aryan" and wrote to his brother asking him to search for baptismal and wedding documents. In December, he warned Christiane that the wrong opinion or a single suspect piece of paper could lead to arrest. "The world of tomorrow will be a world of slaves," he predicted, "It will be born in the blood of civil wars and revolutions, in an atmosphere of reprisals and injustices." He feared that the resistance movement in France, the majority of whose participants were Communists, was working not just to handicap the German occupation but to "prepare the revolution, by constituting an army of young fanatics, hardened and accustomed to massacres and ready for anything." He was exhausted and fearful and suffering anew from prostatitis.[29]

With every aspect of Roger's life in turmoil, the progress of his writing had slowed drastically. While Hélène was away during July, he began composition of the episode recounting how the German forces occupied Le Saillant and how, out of respect for Maumort's rank and aristocratic heritage, their commander granted him the use of one wing and its library. He also gathered notes for Maumort's army career after graduation from the military academy at St. Cyr. But for the more than eight months since he had revised the structure of the book, he had nothing else to show. At the end of 1943, his morale reached low ebb: "I have renounced nothing, and I still hope to finish my book, if circumstances and health permit me. But the idea that it may never be completed does not provoke a violent reaction in me, does not make me despair at all."[30]

Chapter 8

~

DISCOMFITED

AFTER THE GERMANS TOOK control in Nice during the fall of 1943, their security apparatus began hunting down the usual targets: Jews, Communists, active members of the Resistance, and prominent opponents of Vichy, beginning with the outspoken. Six months later, by the spring of 1944, they were ready to search out the quieter ones, men and a few women whose names appeared on a black list compiled by French collaborators. In 1941 and 1942, several prominent French literary figures, among them Jean Paulhan, François Mauriac, Paul Valéry, and Georges Duhamel, created the clandestine "National Committee of Writers" (Comité national des écrivains) as an "intellectual resistance." Roger joined near the end of 1942 and would later claim to have played no role other than "to learn afterward what had been done in our name." But he did, in fact, take risks. At the beginning of February 1944, the Gestapo arrested Oscar von Wertheimer, a Hungarian Jewish author of historical novels, who had taken refuge in Nice. Local Resistance leaders hid his wife and daughter but needed money to get them away. Without hesitation, Roger sold the manuscript of his *Confidence africaine* to pay for their escape to a convent near Toulouse. And so he was a target. By the end of April, his friends in the Resistance warned him to leave as soon as possible. Since the beginning of the year Christiane and Marcel had urged him to take refuge in Figeac, and now he agreed.[1]

Roger and Hélène began packing, and remembering how little they had carried away from Le Tertre, decided to take almost everything they had at the Cimiez apartment. The Resistance provided a trusted driver who loaded his truck with almost a ton of their belongings, and they set off on May 12. Three days later after hard going through neglected roads, they arrived in Figeac—actually, about eight miles outside Figeac, at the Château de Roquefort, which Christiane had rented to keep them out of sight. She had expected that it would be in poor condition, but the reality was far worse: a ruin, huge drafty rooms, filthy with years of dust, a haven for rats and spiders, no running water, no gas, no heat, no telephone, no mail, no automobile. Heroic efforts by all rendered it "habitable," but nothing more. In a letter to his sister-in-law, Marie-Louise, Roger called it the "Château of Misery" and compared it to the dilapidated Russian country houses in Nikolai Gogol's *Dead Souls*. He wrote Maria van Rysselberghe that they had "the life of the sixteenth century." Far worse, Christiane had unwittingly placed Roger close to the caves where the local Resistance hid their weapons and took refuge from German patrols.[2]

For the next three months, Roger and Hélène, who were now sixty-three and fifty-seven years old, respectively, and far from good health, did their best to survive in this isolation. Almost pathetically, they tried to get around on bicycles until August 18, when Hélène caught a wheel in stony ground and fell on her right elbow. She made it back to the château before fainting. Roger's only option was hastening to the nearest farmhouse, where he convinced "young Francesca" to ride his bicycle to Figeac and alert Christiane. She in turn called a physician with an automobile who picked up Hélène and brought her to a hospital. Fortunately, Hélène's elbow was merely dislocated, but she had a large hematoma that greatly delayed the healing. They both remained at the hospital for almost a month, and Roger ate lunch with Christiane and Marcel each day. Until then, he had only sketchy news of the Anglo-American invasion of Normandy, but now from Marcel's radio, he heard that Allied forces were advancing across France, that the German army was everywhere in retreat, that Free French forces had liberated Paris, and that General de Gaulle had led a victory march down the Champs-Elysées on August 26: "Days of exaltation and excitement." A couple of weeks later, de Gaulle's provisional government summoned Marcel to Paris, "apparently," in Roger's words, "needing his competences."[3]

Immediately afterward on September 15, Roger and Hélène moved in with Christiane. Hélène was stronger and in less pain, but there could be no question of a return to the dilapidated château. Marcel's departure made this transition easier because he and Christiane were now quarreling about money, the children, his sense of caution, her desire for independence—in essence, disputing the state of their marriage. For the moment, she played the loving daughter, and because Roger wanted to believe that he could recover the Christiane he had lost, he wrote, "She is no longer the stranger that she had become. Life and hardship have matured her." Hélène remained dubious, but they avoided "collisions." Christiane knew that within a few weeks she would be moving to Paris with her son and daughter to join Marcel. There, she would take up anew the contest between them on a field of play given far greater scope. She might well need the support of her parents, and used these days to cajole them. And indeed, almost as soon as Christiane arrived in Paris at the end of October, she and Marcel exchanged ugly words. Christiane quickly sent Roger cries for freedom: "I no longer believe that Marcel loves me," "marriage is a fucked-up institution!" and "happiness is reserved for imbeciles."[4]

But freedom has costs, and to pay them, Christiane mentioned selling some possessions, especially a diamond barrette given her as a child. Roger protested: "We have lived for some years in a poverty beside which your current life is a luxurious existence, but never for a single instance did we succumb to the temptation of selling any jewel or treasure. We refused to do so not only from attachment to memory but to keep them in the family." This admonition, certainly disingenuous in its claim of penury, infuriated Christiane, who let the mask of devotion slip. Her reply was venomous: "At the time of my marriage, you gave me neither dowry nor trousseau, not even a pair of sheets or a soup spoon. That was your right, but I have not brought dishonor to the family, and I have two beautiful, charming children, worthy of their ancestors, so I do not see why I should be disinherited. ... Since you won the Nobel, things have been better, and I have not forgotten your generosity of these last years, but for a woman, nothing is more painful and more difficult to bear than to have no personal fortune and no profession to earn her crust of bread."[5]

Christiane's words provoked Roger's outrage: "You were not married 'without trousseau' because we allotted twenty-five thousand francs [$18,600 in 2015] for it during your engagement, ... but you preferred to buy dresses and riding breeches and I know not what instead of sheets and napkins. ... You were not married 'without dowry,' because we promised you an annuity of thirty thousand francs [$22,330 in 2015] a year, which we paid for the first three years until we fell into penury. ... But during that time, Marcel received the salary of a viceroy, and you led a sumptuous life. ... And since the Nobel, I have constituted a small fortune for you." Roger was so upset that even when promising "we are ready to give you all the money we can," he added sternly, "but regarding the jewels, antique lace, pieces of silver, and fine furniture in the midst of which I have lived since childhood and which remind me of my grandmother and my parents (who had the same reverence for them as I), do not expect that I shall relinquish them to you. No, I do not have confidence in your feelings about them. You do not have respect for these things. As long as I live, I shall try to protect them." A few days later Christiane's groveling reply arrived, but Roger—as if scales had fallen from his eyes—did not answer in acceptance. For fully fifteen years, the relationship between them had foundered on his sense that she had betrayed him—betrayed his love, his trust, his dreams for her—in marrying Marcel. And every time he came close to absolving her, because she surpassed his expectations as a wife and mother, she acted in some fashion that he defined as a new treachery.[6]

With Hélène, Roger's bonds were so much stronger, but for the tormented relations they had as husband and wife, no sudden clarity of vision could offer resolution. Their joint epiphany was their essential antimony: a consuming love mated to a despairing antagonism. No sudden apprehension was left to them. The previous March, Hélène had reminded Roger of their first meeting, thirty-nine years before, when they could hardly imagine where destiny might lead them. She was certain now that they would never separate and implored him to find with her a way to "support one another in our respective failings while never forgetting our compensating virtues. . . . Let us not lose courage at this risky turning in our lives together." Roger thanked her for "this sad wisdom" and pledged that "to seal this pact, I embrace you with all the love of which I am capable, and of which you will have been, throughout my whole life, the *sole* beneficiary."[7]

Yet in July, Hélène revived her diatribe: "I am the most miserable of creatures. You stole my daughter and destroyed her faith through your attitudes, your books, and Pontigny! If she made this marriage, it's your fault, yes, your fault, because you made her the way she was. . . . You wrecked my life, my life that should have been happy! You deprived me of a family. You made my daughter a stranger, an atheist! I would have preferred never to have had a child than to have had a child with a man like you! I want only one thing, to disappear." An hour later, she took Roger's arm, crying: "Tolerate me, my darling. Take me as I am. I ask only a little understanding, some tenderness. Put up with me!" A month later, Hélène slipped a note under Roger's door, "one of those messages that I never see without breaking into a cold sweat." She accused him of poisoning her life, saying that she was "*without descendants,* because 'Christiane is not of my blood, to your great satisfaction.'" Perhaps the hard trials at the Château de Roquefort were to blame. By September, with the fighting in France almost over, Roger imagined finding a refuge where he could "forsake the provisional and settle *definitively,* assemble my papers from their various shelters, and finally, in the midst of my books, consecrate the end of my life to work!" The reverie collided with reality: "This frantic hope comes up against difficulties of all order, not the least of which is finding with Hélène an acceptable *modus vivendi* where our tastes, our needs, so different and contradictory, may be reconciled without too great a sacrifice on either of our parts."[8]

Nice was hardly the end of the provisional, but Nice had to be the first stop for Roger and Hélène if only to return all their belonging to the Cimiez apartment. Getting back was harder than leaving because in a liberated France everyone had some place to go and needed a truck. They had to wait until the end of December and harsh winter weather: snow and a temperature of fourteen degrees Fahrenheit as they left. Their arrival in Nice on New Year's Day 1945 was "a return to civilized life. Figeac has left us only a memory of hardships and grime, of mortal cold and discomfort, a little French province in all its unwelcoming bitterness and its inalterable routine, beneath a low sky, walled in by its cloudy horizons." The long delay in Figeac had made Roger ungrateful. In October he had written, with greater truth, that "while all the other regions of France were devastated, pillaged, and ravaged by fighting, we had extraordinary good fortune. We left Nice at the right time, to avoid the arrests, the bombs, and the famine."[9]

Once settled back into the Cimiez apartment, Roger experienced a sense of exhaustion. The thought of restoring Le Tertre—the clerk-of-court at Bellême, the nearest town, estimated the damage at 280,000 francs ($67,175 in 2015), a figure Roger thought far too low—left him overwhelmed: "I am without courage before such a daunting task, even if I had the funds." He rejected outright entreaties to play a role in postwar France, even membership in the Académie française: "*I do not want anything. . . . I want to isolate myself all the more.*" He tried to end the possibility of election even if nominated by writing to Schlumberger that "the Académie *dishonored* itself *by its silence* during the Occupation," and he rejected out of hand Duhamel's insistence that he accept election "to *serve* French letters." Roger was, in fact, ill-suited for this time of settling scores: "I do not have the disposition to dispense justice." He applauded the sentence of life imprisonment for Charles Maurras, leader of the Action Française whose anti-Semitism and integral nationalism were the basis for some of the Vichy government's worst policies, but he grieved over the suicide of Pierre Drieu La Rochelle, the novelist who embraced the Nazi regime and would almost certainly have been condemned to execution for "collusion with the enemy."[10]

Roger was not clear in his own mind about the Vichy regime. He could not forgive its willingness to hand over Jews and refugees to Nazi torture and death: "Indelible shame for France! . . . For that, the Pétain government will be forever condemned before history." And he recognized the stupidities of Vichy's everyday repression: in reply to his submission of a comment to *Le Figaro littéraire* about the suicide of anti-Nazi Stefan Zweig and his wife in Brazil, the editor replied, "*It is forbidden to say that Zweig is dead, forbidden to say that he lived, and forbidden, of course, to make the slightest reference to his work.*" But like many in France, Roger credited Pétain's armistice and Vichy's collaboration with preventing the kind of atrocities in France that the Germans carried out in Eastern Europe. He also believed that by refusing to fight on from North Africa, Pétain saved the French Empire. Playing history in the subjunctive: if, to force a French surrender, Hitler had invaded Algeria and Morocco in 1940, he would have turned the Mediterranean Sea into a Nazi lake, with incalculable consequences for the outcome of the war. His invasion of Russia might have turned out differently with the oil resources of the Middle East at his disposal.[11]

Because de Gaulle and not Pétain was on the winning side of the war, Pétain had to answer for his conduct, and from late July until mid-August, he stood trial on the double charge of plotting against the security of the state and intelligence with the enemy. Schlumberger covered it for *Le Figaro*, and when Roger and Hélène came up to survey Le Tertre's the damage, he got Roger a seat at one of the sessions. "An unforgettable day," Roger called it, and described Pétain as having the "courteous detachment of a man *who is already no longer of this world*, whose soul is elsewhere, who is not truly there, who is prepared for any contingencies but is passionate about nothing, a man for whom the affairs of men no longer hold any interest." Roger considered that trying Pétain for defeatism and concluding the armistice—the meaning of the formal charges—was absurd, for history alone would be the judge of such matters. The court might call its proceedings justice, but Roger denounced them as "a settling of scores." His most revealing comment was that "all the sense of nobility is on the side of the accused." The cries for Pétain's death, the vindictiveness of the grinning victors, he found appalling, vulgar, the very definition of "canaille." They represented the end of a certain kind of life and civilization, which he had foreseen and feared: "I have a taste for order, equilibrium, and security. I have a need for justice and peace. … I am, without doubt, only a filthy bourgeois? But the bourgeoisie of the nineteenth and twentieth centuries … will perish as we watch for the same reasons, the same causes, that led to the end of the ancien régime's nobility, lack of will combined with arrogance."[12]

For Roger, staving off such a world might be possible at Le Tertre. Despite his fears, his country house masterpiece did not lie in ruin. The damage to the structure itself, the exterior walls and roof, the water pipes, the electrical system, was not extensive and could be repaired without difficulty or even major expense. The interior was worse off, a true mare's nest. Almost every piece of furniture showed some injury—a missing leg, deep scratches, broken marble tops, the seats slashed or staved. The curtains were ripped or pulled down altogether. The rugs were scarred from rough-soled boots. Every cabinet, every drawer, every file had been rifled. Yet, hardly anything had been taken, not even the silverware and the antique lace. The contents of the cabinets, drawers, and files were piled, sometimes carefully, in corners and could be retrieved. Roger's library, his retreat where he wrote, was almost untouched, most of the books still in their places on the shelves, and the ones that had been removed were waiting to be found all over the house or sometimes in the garden. Before leaving in June 1940, he had buried some of his most important papers, correspondence, and documents in iron trunks. The Germans had not found them, and though a little water had seeped in and caused mildew, he believed that most could be salvaged. Almost immediately, Roger felt himself "recaptured, reconquered, repossessed by my universe, created to my measure, adapted to my most indelible particularities."[13]

Throughout the summer and fall, Roger and Hélène set to work restoring, aided by the longtime groundskeeper Baptiste, who had kept what watch he could on Le Tertre during the war and who now recruited all his local friends to help. The progress went faster than Roger and Hélène ever believed possible, and for this moment they created between themselves "a *perfect understanding*. Reciprocal concessions, accorded without effort, easy relations, no quarrels." Roger even imagined "that we will have gentle years to live here together." After so many abrupt changes in Hélène's affections, he was hoping for the best. Did he realize that this enormous effort of reconstruction exactly corresponded to Hélène's compulsion for sacrifice and service? She returned to Nice in November and left him to reclassify his papers and documents. There, without a daunting task and without a Roger who needed her, she summoned her recriminations and wrote him yet another letter filled with her usual bitter griefs. After beginning an anodyne reply, he surrendered to frustration, writing that he almost destroyed her letter so that she might not find it after his death and be overwhelmed by her own injustice. And despite his aversion to winter, he also decided to stay on longer at Le Tertre or the Rue du Dragon apartment rather than join Hélène in Nice.[14]

Roger was hoping to take up again his work on *Maumort*, but on his own terms. When writing in January 1945 to Gallimard, who would be the publisher of any manuscript he completed, he declared his ambition to consecrate the years he had left "to getting under way this last work that I have been preparing for three years and that demands to be born." Then, he added, "More than ever, I have the desire to write but less than ever the desire to publish. ... Truly, I am writing only for myself. I have no presumption of offering something new. I seek only to put in this last work the experience of a life. I know my limits. I am conscious that time has passed me by." By now, he had a refrain: the author forgotten, the book posthumous or perhaps unfinished. The previous summer, he had written Maria van Rysselberghe, "My project is insanely vast." That winter, he insisted to Duhamel, "I simply wish to finish my life as I have lived it, not as a misanthrope ... but as an individualist resistant to cooperation and obstinately independent," and to Pierre Marois, "My only aspiration is finding some peace and dedicating myself entirely to the work that I am preparing, a work that will, without doubt, be posthumous." He was making some progress, in the weeks before he and Hélène went up to Le Tertre, writing an extended scene, "La Baignade" (The Swim), a pivotal moment in the life of Xavier de Balcourt, Maumort's tutor. Roger thought it some of his best writing, "so much detail, so minutely precise that no one would believe it entirely fictitious." Yet because this brilliant fragment connected only tangentially to Maumort, he wondered why he wrote it even as he answered his own question: "I enjoyed myself enormously." On his own terms indeed.[15]

Yet these terms were slipping from Roger's control. In February and March after returning to Nice, he wrote more about the tutor Balcourt but not about Maumort himself because he had, once again, come to question the basic structure of the book as a whole. Originally, he meant to begin the narrative in 1940 and to describe the course of the war and occupation as Maumort reconstituted his memoirs. Now, he believed that a single character's view could never compete with the enormous volume of information that had become available: "Pending the passage of years, everything that can be said has been said." His solution was to advance the beginning of the book to 1945, with the material about the war and occupation merely additional elements in Maumort's recollections. But doing so meant "a complete revision of my story. I have prepared the elements of his life so minutely that this change upsets everything and requires a readjustment to all the elements of the book. I have to modify my entire chronology, delaying by four years Maumort's birth [from 1866 to 1870] with repercussions for every aspect of his biography." Roger would have to discard much of his work from the last six years, however intermittent. The very thought of beginning anew sapped his desire to proceed, and after the early spring, he set the *Maumort* project aside for the rest of the year. This capitulation, with the restoration of Le Tertre unfinished and many of his files still in disarray, provoked anew in him "a perceptible physical and intellectual *aging*."[16]

Roger's profound fatigue in body and mind had other causes as well, the usual ones. When he got to Nice in mid-February, he found Hélène in bed with a low-grade fever and symptoms of influenza. She had sometimes before relished a solitary existence, but more than three months alone this time had left her in low spirits. Roger's presence encouraged her to greater activity and lifted her mood. Even so, her weakness gave proof of the toll exacted by heart and circulation problems. When she seemed better by late April, he went north to Paris and prepared the Rue du Dragon apartment for her arrival several weeks later in mid-May. They moved to Le Tertre in July and stayed there until December, overseeing further renovations that came close, after eighteen months of work, to restoring its magnificence. During these months, Roger endured increasing pain in his legs. Inflammation of his right heel was only a nuisance, but swelling from edema and grievous pain in his left leg was serious. He limped badly and could not walk more than fifty yards without resting. His cardiologist attributed the condition to residual damage from the phlebitis episodes of 1930 and 1931, which had collapsed some of the interior circulation in his left leg: "thus, varicose veins, swelling, puffing-up, cramps, and distress." The only treatment was rest with the leg elevated. In December, he added pulmonary congestion to his list of ills, though for it, sulfonamides were a rapid cure. As the year ended, Roger and Hélène took the express train to Nice. They limped up the steps to their passenger compartment holding each other for support, a middle-aged couple with chronic disease, unrecognizable as the toast of Stockholm nine years earlier. They were "fleeing the cold, the overcast sky, the mist, the perpetual half-night of northern winter. At Nice, we will revive"—he hoped.[17]

Another cause of Roger's exhaustion—and about this one he could do little but watch—was the disintegration of the Coppet marriage. Both Christiane and Marcel appealed to him as an ally, and each insisted that the events of the war were the precipitating cause. Marcel claimed that when the Vichy government revoked him as governor-general of Madagascar, he wanted to offer his services to the British in their nearest colony: "My place was in London. Christiane's pusillanimity was the reason I remained at her side." Christiane claimed that Marcel "had not done his duty. He tried several times to join up with the Free French but always hoped that he would not succeed. . . . He fell forever from the pedestal where I had placed him." They quarreled repeatedly at Figeac, and by the fall of 1943, Christiane thought of creating a new life for herself and her children in Paris. The arrival of Roger and Hélène in the late spring and summer of 1944 restored a surface calm, but once the provisional government restored Marcel to the Ministry of Colonies that September, with Christiane, Daniel, and Annique joining him in the capital at the end of the year, their incompatibility became obvious. Christiane wanted to live a life that was "lively, dazzling, and luxurious." Marcel wanted to live a life that was "cloistered, solitary, and familial." She accused him of stifling her independence. He accused her of neglecting their children.[18]

After Marcel had served in various posts for almost a year and a half, his moment came at the end of December 1945. Marius Moutet, his ally, was once again minister of the colonies and appointed him first his chief of staff and then in March 1946 high commissioner of the Republic—a new title for a new time but the equivalent of governor-general—in Madagascar: "the revenge for all his reverses ... the crowning of his career." With this new power and position, Marcel was determined to assert his authority over Christiane and demanded that she and the children accompany him on his return in triumph to Madagascar, seven years after the Vichy government had, ignominiously, sent all four of them back to France aboard a slow freighter. When she adamantly refused, Marcel departed in May 1946 with Daniel, leaving Christiane and Annique in Paris. He also spoke openly of his plan to divorce Christiane and to do so under the harshest possible conditions, demanding retention of his house in Quiberville and apartment in Paris, which were his before the marriage, and custody of both children, with Christiane deprived of all maternal rights "as if she were a woman of loose morals [*une gougandine*]."[19]

Christiane expected that Roger would support her. When he did not, replying that she should indeed have gone with Marcel to Madagascar, she was beside herself with rage and wrote coldly, "Your last letter could have been signed 'Oscar Thibault!'" But his warning that in a divorce proceeding the civil court was likely to favor Marcel and that the best she might hope for was retaining custody of Annique made her fear about the future. By the fall, she talked of finding a means to reconcile with Marcel when he returned to France. Reading their correspondence to him, Roger rejected such hopes: "After what they have said and written, I believe any patching up will be difficult because they have completely lost respect for each other. Christiane speaks of her husband with hateful scorn: he is *false*, hypocritical, vain, and tyrannical. Coppet says that Christiane is a poor fool who believes herself 'intellectual,' is without character, without dignity, and, as he told me, 'from now on *unworthy of rearing his children.*'" "I can do nothing," Roger concluded, "I try to be fair, but the truth is *they both exasperate me.*"[20]

In Madagascar, Marcel faced a revolt against French rule that began shortly after he arrived. As it spread throughout the colony, he sent Daniel home in late spring 1947. The Ministry of Colonies recalled him at the beginning of 1948 because the French government gave up on any negotiated solution and turned over responsibility for suppressing the uprising entirely to the military. This time, Marcel received a reward for attempting the impossible. In February 1948, Moutet appointed him chairman of the board of directors for the Bank of West Africa (Banque d'Afrique-occidentale), essentially a permanent sinecure with a high salary. Throughout, he and Christiane made a show of reconciliation—from caution for how the civil court might rule on a divorce, custody, and financial arrangements. Roger learned the reality from Daniel, now fourteen years old, who spent the five days of vacation for Pentecost with him at the end of May 1947: "He talks about his parent's household with measure and perspicacity, and without hope. His mother irritates him, and he considers her failings especially odd and blameworthy. But he recognizes perfectly her merits, and in the marital dispute, he places much of the blame on his father. He knows him well and admires his character but not without seeing that this character is irreconcilable, 'Papa forgives, but he does not forget.' He does not believe that his father and mother will ever find any means of conciliation, and he speaks of that failure as a kind of fatal destiny."[21]

Roger himself was less restrained, especially about Christiane. To him, her pleas for regaining their "closeness of before" were utterly insincere, "as if this closeness had not ceased because of her absurd marriage! ... Of all the people to whom I am tied, she is the one with whom I would most obstinately refuse to live." He feared her manipulation, her meddling, her desire "to supplant her mother beside me. This need for domination irritates everyone around her and is a principal cause of her conflict with Coppet and Daniel. She would be most proud of exercising it over me, and doing so in the view of others." During the summer of 1947 when Roger and Hélène were entertaining Daniel and Annique at Le Tertre for a month, Christiane came herself for two days. That time in her presence was sufficient for Roger to write in his journal, "I suffer thinking what I have just written: Christiane is more and more the kind of person whom I would not want to have as a friend for anything in the world." The following day he added a cryptic note. "With Christiane, you have the sense of being with someone whose intelligence does not quite make contact with reality, whose spirit and reason function on a different plane, obeying a different logic, with someone who would affirm, with supreme good faith and inflexible assurance: two and two make four, thus four and four make *nine*."[22]

Clearly, the return to the sunshine in Nice was not enough to brighten his mood. On this year's birthday, he exclaimed, "*Sixty-six years*! An old man. The end approaches. How good it would be to know that I will die in my sleep without anguish." Once the idea was in his head, he could not shake it: "I think often of my death, and this idea, though it always distresses me profoundly, never provokes within me any regret at being a complete nonbeliever." He wondered what funeral arrangements Hélène would make for him if he died first, but "if I survive her, I shall request a civil service and cremation." He imagined an indulgent priest at his deathbed arguing that he has, through certain passages in *Jean Barois* and *Les Thibault*, revealed a religious inspiration: "'When you think of your failings in life, do they not awaken in your conscience a sense of contrition?' To Roger's reply, 'Of course,' he continues, 'My friend, I ask you nothing more. You believe in God, and you repent of your sins. *Absolvo te*. You may die in peace!' I protest in advance, and may my protest be heard, in the name of truth." This frame of mind could hardly energize him to make progress on a book, especially with its protagonist a septuagenarian preoccupied with the memories of his past and acutely aware of how little time he has left to live.[23]

And so Roger did not make much progress. In his journal, he was blunt: revising the chronology of the book was "a thankless task, hard to get started" and complained of all the trouble getting "the genealogy of my colonel straight, but I have to situate my character's ancestors in his century." This preparatory work, which he was having to repeat because of changing Maumort's birth date, he compared to creating a framework of hexagonal wax cells, the comb that beekeepers place in their hives and into which the bees deposit their honey. Likewise, he would place his "honey," the story, "all that was living, personal, moving, and new," the best of his work for the last six years, the "tasty goblets," into his "comb," the framework of his preparatory work. Just as the honey transformed the comb into a "honey cake," his vignettes representing Maumort's memoirs would transform the preparatory work into a rich and complicated novel. But did Roger really believe so? "When friends ask where I am in my novel, I often reply that it is moving ahead but that I hardly 'believe' in what I am doing. I mean that while I am in the midst of this preparatory work, I have the tedious sensation of composing pages that do not matter, which are without real value. I also mean something more profound, that I am not certain about the quality of the honey itself. I fear that when I finish, when I deposit my honey, the cake will not be any good." Then he confessed his true discouragement: "I hardly 'believe' in what I am doing because I doubt that I will add a single nuance to the solar spectrum, and to work with 'faith' requires the illusion of 'revealing' something." He was increasingly convinced that whatever readers his book might have would find only minor interest in Maumort's comments about the war and occupation— because he himself had less and less interest in the details of those terrible years. He had to concentrate on Maumort's life beforehand, to demonstrate "how deeply rooted he was in the world overturned by the war." He had to make his book a testimony to what was lost, but in doing so he was diverging even further from his original conception.[24]

By turning Maumort's eyes to the past, Roger was consciously rejecting— for himself—the literary fashion of the day, "committed literature" (*littérature engagée*). He had high praise for the work of the "committed" writers: of Albert Camus's *L'Etranger* (*The Stranger*) and *Le Mythe de Sisyphe* (*The Myth of Sisyphus*) in 1942, and *La Peste* (*The Plague*) in 1947, and of Jean-Paul Sartre's *L'Age de raison* (*The Age of Reason*) and *Le Sursis* (*The Reprieve*) in 1945, both of them Gallimard authors and Camus a good friend. He was also close to André Malraux, whose prewar novels were a precursor to committed literature, his *La Condition humaine* (*Man's Fate*) almost its definition. But Roger recognized that to them, he was an anachronism, that his *Maumort* risked being "regarded as old-fashioned, a fossil" and that "my book will be rowing against the current." Even so, he rejected committed literature because he saw its danger: "They are all *partisans* with a philosophic and political view of the world that they hope will triumph. The goal of their campaign is to force writers who have remained independent to declare themselves, to make their opinions *public*, a question of seeing clearly on the field of battle to come who are the allies and who are the adversaries."[25]

Roger knew himself: in the June 10, *Le Figaro*, François Mauriac, a superb novelist, a devout Catholic, and a hero of the literary resistance, railed against the death sentence imposed on Jean Benoist-Méchin, a right-wing politician and writer, for his collaboration with the Germans during the war. Certainly, Benoist-Méchin deserved conviction, but his crimes had been less than many who had escaped with a lighter penalty. Mauriac questioned the "terrible spirit of revenge" led by the Communist Party, which for its prominence in the Resistance had an important place in French government since the liberation. He asked why men of decency like Gide and Martin du Gard had failed to protest, why "the best appear resigned to this supreme decadence, a country without justice." Roger responded the following day with a letter that appeared in *Le Figaro* on June 12, seconding Mauriac and deploring a France torn by "fanaticism, where there are only 'partisans.' What good is it to preach clemency, or simply justice, in this jungle?" To Mauriac himself, Roger wrote praising "your role as Public Conscience" but insisted, "to each his measure, to each his possibilities and limits." He explained by referring to the Dreyfus Affair: "I wrote *Jean Barois*, as you recall, and not without vigor, but I would never have written 'J'accuse.' My sphere of expression does not extend past the book."[26]

Early December 1947 began with the Communist Party provoking something close to a general strike in what may have been an effort to overthrow the often inept Fourth Republic. Lasting more than a week during bitter cold weather in Paris, the strikes meant no trains, no natural gas, no garbage collection, frequently no electricity, and sometimes no water. Roger and Hélène were at the Rue du Dragon apartment holding useless train tickets for Nice. Inside, the temperature was forty-one degrees Fahrenheit; outside, an embankment of stinking refuse lined each side of the street. Christiane called every morning with some new complaint about her husband, her children, or her friends. Whether from the conditions or from the stress, Hélène suffered a sharp increase in her blood pressure and had to remain in bed—where at least she was warmer. They were finally able to leave on December 19, and reach Nice the following day. Hélène did not rebound this time as she had often done in the past. Her elevated blood pressure persisted, with chronic kidney disease a complicating element. More and more, she was an invalid.[27]

Was a sense that time was running out the motive for inclining their lives toward each other? During the late spring and summer at Le Tertre, Roger willingly agreed to long visits from Jesuit Father Auguste Valensin, Hélène's new spiritual advisor, and from Marie Rougier, now her best friend. Doing so cost him nothing because he found them both congenial. What did cost was denying Le Tertre to Gide, who in 1947 had joined Roger as Nobel laureate for literature, and to Maria van Rysselberghe: Hélène had finally won. Alone with his journal, Roger could lament that his friends were old, seventy-nine and eighty-two years, respectively, that "they are going to die, and I will be inconsolable at not having long visits in the country with them, those hours of irreplaceable closeness." Hélène made concessions of her own, and Roger supposed that "she has memorized her long list." Whatever else might have been on it, at the top was the vow not to repeat her diatribe against Roger for destroying her life and stealing her daughter, and right below it was calming her compulsion to impose order. Perhaps for Hélène, sickness had left her recriminations a burden she could no longer bear. Perhaps for Roger, the debts he owed Hélène had come due. Perhaps for both of them, their anguished love, alternately attracting and repelling, demanded a final truce.[28]

Regarding Gide: During the occupation, Roger saw him only once, for dinner in Nice on New Year's Eve 1941. Immediately after, Gide took refuge in Tunis and once Paris was liberated, returned directly to his apartment on the Rue Vaneau, in the Latin Quarter. When Roger came up to Paris from Nice in the summer of 1945 to begin repairs on Le Tertre, the Belgian novelist Georges Simenon invited them both to dine with him on July 24, at the Claridge Hotel. Roger had never met Simenon but had heard that he made "millions" through his dozens of crime thrillers published in cheap editions and translated into many languages. With fascination, he heard Simenon describe finding inspiration each morning through vigorous sex with either his wife or his chambermaid and then rapidly completing a new chapter before noon. Afterward in private, Gide, who seemed "restless and preoccupied but not unwell," entrusted Roger with two confidences as if he feared dying suddenly. The first was a dossier of letters from Paul Claudel and Francis Jammes, both important and profoundly Catholic poets, calling on Gide "to repent from his vices or at least not to avow them publicly." The second was a sealed envelope: "'It is my testament,'" Gide told him, "'You will be among the first to be notified when I die. You will open it, and you will do what is necessary.'" His outward appearance aside, Gide sensed that he was ill, and three years later in June 1948, Roger described him as "thin, with bad color, his skin a deathly pale because of a weak heart." Since the dinner with Simenon, their only contact had been through a few letters, with Roger insisting that his progress on *Maumort* was far from what he wanted. He was now visiting Gide at the Rue Vaneau apartment—in Hélène's calculus of concession, for Roger to meet him in Paris was not openly objectionable. Gide described himself as "'no longer good for anything'" but listened with keen interest as Roger read aloud from a chapter about Maumort's childhood. Until that moment, contrary to his previous habit of sharing pages with Hélène, he had shown "nothing to anyone" from his manuscript. Gide praised what he heard unreservedly, saying that he preferred these fragments to everything else that Roger had ever written.[29]

With such an endorsement, Roger gained new enthusiasm, boasting in September that he had been working all summer for "seven or eight hours a day without stopping." He was writing more about Balcourt, who had arrived at Le Saillant as the tutor for Maumort and his cousin Guy Chambost-Lévadé and had introduced them to a premature sexuality. If Roger were writing Maumort's memoirs from beginning to end, composing these chapters first was not unusual. But earlier, he had declared that Maumort would recall his past in a disordered fashion, and if so, did Roger write about Balcourt because he was thinking of Gide? Certainly, he was aware of possible interpretations: "If I were to die without having treated other episodes of my book, I would no doubt be accused of having ended my life in the midst of sexual obsessions!" This burst of energy did not mean that he was changing his mind about the fate of his grand scheme. "I sense myself truly devoid of all ambition. I have completely lost my taste for 'getting ahead in the world.' I experience incomparable relief in writing a 'posthumous' book, no need to explain myself, to justify my judgments, to be accountable." So of course, he took an interest in *Citadelle*, the last essays of the philosopher-aviator Antoine de Saint-Exupéry, "left in unfinished form, a commendable and noble book," because Saint X, as his ardent readers called him, was shot down over the Mediterranean on July 31, 1944, flying for the Free French. And of course, a spiteful observer could conclude of Roger that he was "finished."[30]

That spiteful observer was Christiane. Marcel's appointment to the Bank of West Africa, the kind of reward to politically connected officials referred to as "working in bedroom slippers" (*pantouflage*), complicated disentangling their outwardly reconciled household. Christiane feared that divorce could cost her custody of Daniel and deny her any right to Marcel's property, while Marcel feared that divorce could cost him custody of Annique and require him to make a substantial financial settlement in Christiane's favor from his new wealth. Living in Marcel's apartment but hardly speaking, they waited, and as Roger characterized them, "Coppet hopes that Christiane will do something

stupid, such as engaging in an affair, and thereby provide him with a spectacular and decisive fault. Christiane hopes that her old husband will die." In his
journal, Roger denounced his daughter as "*mediocre*, violent, arrogant, brutal,
and lacking all *rectitude*." In premonition, he wrote, "She has made a complete
mess of her life, and, out of genuine fear, I am trying to avoid her making a
mess of mine in the years I have left to live."[31]

Yet Christiane was Roger's daughter, and just as her failures of "rectitude"
profoundly offended his essential bourgeois nature, that same essential bourgeois nature valiantly defended her public good name. In November 1948,
without warning, Marcel declared that he would no longer accept any invitation that included his wife or be seen with her. Roger sent a stiff letter laying
bare Marcel's despicable motive: "I shall not hide from you how personally
disagreeable to me has been confronting the grave, perhaps irreparable, prejudice you have caused Christiane's reputation.... You have led all who know
you to say, 'If M. de Coppet inflicts this public insult on his wife, then Mme
de Coppet must surely have engaged in shameful and manifestly scandalous
behavior!' You are aware that I have never blindly defended Christiane, but
on this occasion, I find that you have been cruelly unjust toward her." When
Marcel simply ignored this intervention, Christiane argued that to preserve
her dignity, she had to establish a residence of her own. Indeed, Marcel's das-
tardly behavior united Roger and Hélène behind her. They rented Christiane
an apartment on the Rue Villaret-de-Joyeuse, cramped but chic, in the seventeenth arrondissement two blocks from the Arc de Triomphe. They also
opened a small line of credit in her behalf. To pay for this defense of their
daughter's honor, Hélène sold the silver serving pieces they had received as
wedding gifts forty-two years ago. Four years earlier, Roger had sworn that he
would never sell family treasures, but what good were they if not to defend the
family? As a provision for the future, they also agreed that Christiane could
use the larger Rue du Dragon apartment when necessary—the ambiguity giving Roger pause.[32]

Christiane's response to their loyalty and generosity was to prove Roger's
doubts about her "rectitude." She explained her relationship with Marcel to
her sister-in-law, Yvonne de Coppet, as if it were the new fashion: "In the eyes
of the world, we are two people who live separately but rear their children in
common. That makes matters clear, neat, and exact." She immediately had
new calling cards engraved with the name "Madame Christiane Martin du
Gard," as if to spite Marcel. She boasted gaily to Roger, "Here I am with two
names, one legal, for identity papers, business, and passport, the other social!
The concierge at Joyeuse and the concierge at Dragon say that they can take
mail for me under both names, and that permits me choice and diversity!"

For New Year's Day, she sent her cards out to everyone she knew or hoped to know. In exasperation, Roger wrote his brother, "Christiane, who has never before said 'Happy New Year' to anyone has now inundated France and beyond with her calling card filled with best wishes so that everyone will know that she has taken back her name. . . . I have truly no argument to defend this childishness, but I have not even told Christiane what I think because doing so would accomplish nothing."[33]

Roger was now like Hélène—"Why bother?" Neither Christiane nor Marcel cared what he said, nor did he have anything left to say to them. Hélène was an invalid, her life with him a congeries of love and regret that they would never resolve. He was writing *Maumort* for himself alone, "the interior monologue, supreme resource of the old." He had survived a second war and restored Le Tertre but to what end? His answer was simple: "I am waiting for death. The worst of it is the uncertainty, not of the date, but of the path I must follow to reach the inevitable, through what bodily suffering, what moral anguish must I pass before ceasing to exist."[34]

Chapter 9

~

BEREFT

ROGER MADE ONLY A single entry in his journal for January 1949: "No desire for publication. More than that, repugnance mixed with dread. Cowardice? Perhaps. But by pursuing my work in silence and isolation, I satisfy two vices of my nature, *the need for tranquility*, a horror of everything that disrupts me, and *the taste for secrecy*, a penchant strong and even morbid." Seeking both, he embraced his approaching mortality and his present marital conciliation. When composing *Les Thibault*, he had always shown Hélène his drafts and asked her opinion. Now, he revived this old habit for his pages about an aging soldier rejecting the future for the past. Together, Roger and Hélène slipped into a peace that was a presentiment of the graveyard—but peace, nonetheless, and for the two of them.[1]

Then, Gide arrived at the end of April. In Roger's terms, this coming was a "disruption"; in Hélène's terms, this coming was the penetration of evil. For Roger, he was welcome; for Hélène, he was anathema. Gide was now seventy-nine and seriously unwell, with kidney and liver failure added to his heart disease. He had come south, like Roger and Hélène themselves, to escape the cold of Paris. Would Roger risk the quiet calm he had established with Hélène for his often ambiguous friendship with Gide? Certainly he did so: though he did not impose Gide on Hélène, kept the visits brief, and multiplied his attentions to her in compensation. Would Hélène risk the quiet calm to complain? Certainly she did so: because while she regarded Gide's apartment in Paris as his territory, she regarded Nice as hers. She did not revive her usual diatribe, but by mid-June she did succumb to "a state of unbelievable nervous agitation." Even when Gide moved inland to Saint-Paul-de-Vence, "the Devil was only forty miles away," and if Roger displayed the slightest moment of distraction—forgetting to write a letter or to take his keys when he went out—she exclaimed, "Of course, you think only about Gide!" "It would be comic," he wrote, "if it were not monstrous and even infernal."[2]

A resolution of sorts was easily available. Hélène did not enjoy the hot summers of the Riviera and would go up to Le Tertre, where Baptiste and Mathilde would look after her. Roger would remain in Nice and live abstemiously—he was worried about paying his taxes. Immediately afterward, every trace of antagonism between them disappeared. Hélène had left the Devil behind, and Roger could visit Gide without censure. They exchanged letters about their helplessness before the "ancient drama" of Christiane and her marriage, with Hélène suggesting the need for psychoanalytic treatment. And in letter reaffirming their love and devotion despite all—"the embers that glow beneath a thick layer of cinders"—she pledged her hope for "a certain gentleness between two old companions that we are in the last years that remain before one of us leaves the other forever." She was even glad to read his accounts of meeting with Gide because these conversations appeared to advance Roger's work on *Maumort*, work that he was now sharing with her.[3]

Indeed, in mid-July when Gide recovered from an especially serious hepatic crisis at the Hôtel de la Colombe in Saint-Paul-de-Vence, Roger took a nearby room and sat with him for four days. As he had the previous June in Paris, Roger read aloud to Gide from the material he was composing for Maumort's memoirs, but this time at much greater length, for some twelve hours. And once again, Gide declared "his approval without reservation of both the plot and the structure." A month later, with Gide improved and taking the sun at Juan-les-Pins, a few miles down the beach from Nice, Roger returned to seek advice: should he include material about the war and reconstruction in *Maumort* or should he renounce the initial plan and write instead a book entirely of memoirs? He had been in a quandary about this issue for more than three years and because he could not resolve it, had left the opening chapters unfinished and turned to Maumort's reminiscences, especially of his youth. After Gide encouraged him to trust in his original vision, Roger sensed a revival of ambition for the first time in many months. A few days later he recounted this new determination to Hélène: "I am attacking the first part. It will be hard to pull off, but I now believe that I know how to make it work. I have been suffering from having to drag it behind me rough and incomplete, and it will be a great relief to establish solidly the departure point of the work, to have written, before going on to anything else, a version of the beginning that is essentially definitive. And if I were to die, the unfinished work would no longer be just a series of isolated 'pieces' but an actual book, of which the first two or three parts would be in place. I think that doing so will bring me the enormous relief of having cleared the disorder, and I will continue with the satisfaction of having the beginning behind me and at a high standard."[4]

Roger worked six or seven hours a day for six or seven weeks—how many times had he had just such a stimulating interval since conceiving *Maumort*?—until Hélène returned from Le Tertre. Her appearance was unchanged: she looked older than her sixty-one years, she moved slowly and sometimes unsteadily, and her fragility was too apparent after more than a decade of complications from heart disease. Still, before she left in July, her physician had found nothing alarming about her blood pressure or electrocardiogram. On November 16, a month after her return, she experienced sudden pain from angina, and a new examination revealed some deterioration from the results four months earlier. She rested for ten days and then went to early Mass on November 27. When she came home, she told Roger, "See, I am completely all right. I've had enough of being sick. This week, I'm going to begin living like a normal person again." The following day, she was happily expecting a visit in the late afternoon from Suzanne Parent, a childhood friend who was passing through Nice. To avoid interfering, Roger left the apartment just as Parent arrived about 5 p.m. A little later, Hélène was describing the flight from Le Tertre in June 1940 when she felt a new attack of angina. She insisted that if she lay down the pain would pass, but in fact she was suffering a massive acute myocardial infarction. Not knowing where Roger might be, Parent alerted the building's concierge. The concierge telephoned a physician and Marie Rougier, Hélène's closest friend. Rougier then tried to reach Father Valensin at the Jesuit residence, and when she could not, left him a message and called the local parish office seeking a priest.[5]

Just as Roger entered the Cimiez building lobby shortly before 7:30 p.m., the priest who had been sent approached him asking if he knew the apartment of "Monsieur Martin du Gard." Roger smiled and introduced himself before realizing what the request might mean. In dread, they rode the elevator to his floor and found Rougier standing in the doorway. Roger cried out, "Hélène? What? Tell me!" Rougier murmured, "It's over." Inside, the physician, the concierge, and Parent were clustered around the bed where Hélène now lay dead. The priest knelt beside her and began to recite prayers. Overcome with emotion, Roger could hardly stand. The physician embraced him, insisted that no medical intervention could have saved her, and assured him that she had lost consciousness quickly and had not suffered. A few moments later, Father Valensin arrived to console as he could. That night Roger began the preparations. Hélène had always made clear that she wanted a Low Mass for her funeral and the presence of as few mourners as possible. She had also agreed with Roger that they should be buried together and that this tomb should be wherever the first died, whether Nice or Le Tertre. Roger asked his brother and Christiane to stand beside him, and they came immediately. He asked no one else, not Marcel, Daniel, or Annique, not Marie-Louise and her children, not Manon, Hélène's remaining sister. After the simple service early on the morning of November 30, Roger had Hélène's casket placed in a temporary chamber at the little Cimiez cemetery near their apartment. He permitted only Father Valensin and Marie Rougier to accompany him. Three weeks later on Christmas Eve when the permanent tomb was ready, Roger asked them to be present again as he moved Hélène to her final resting place, where he would join her eventually.[6]

After the provisional interment, Roger wanted only to be alone: "I felt the most urgent need of solitude to confront this unbelievable reality and to regain my self-control." He sent his brother away immediately but let Christiane stay two more days to help him go through Hélène's papers. The last page of her final testament, added not quite a year earlier on December 15, 1948, brought him to his knees: "To those whom I have loved in this world and who have kept their faith, I ask them to pray that God may grant me His mercy. To those whom I have loved who no longer believe in God, I ask them to keep me in their loyal and generous thoughts. If I have not loved them well and if I have made them suffer, may He pardon me as I pardon them myself from the depth of my heart for all the sufferings they brought to my life and which I have offered to God that He may return them as benedictions." Alone, he picked his way through the apartment, finding everywhere "her impression, her passing, her perfume, her writing. . . . I do not suffer from solitude but from *absence*. . . . Hélène was present in even the least of my thoughts. I thought *with* or *against*—but never *without*. Now I have a void that compromises the equilibrium of my life, leaving me distraught, anxious, uncertain, and maimed." Yet when a mutual friend suggested that he imagine Hélène looking down on him from above and their souls reuniting in eternity, Roger replied gently but with plaintive courage, "I have no need for that hope. *Peace through suffering*, to which I aspire and to which I shall arrive through my own strength and solitude, is, to the contrary, the clear consciousness that everything is irremediably finished."[7]

If Roger dared believe such consolation sufficient for himself, he knew well that he owed Hélène overt symbols of religious observance. He arranged a Mass in her behalf at the church in Bellême, the closest to Le Tertre, but because he had never bothered to meet the priest, he had to have Mathilde intercede on his behalf: "Explain to him Madame's desire for simplicity and my wish that the service be soigné, and I am certain that he will propose a satisfactory solution." For the tomb in the Cimiez cemetery, he ordered a fine stone carved with her name and dates, but because he made mistakes with the Roman numerals—1807 for 1887 and 1909 for 1949—its delivery was delayed by more than a month. These stumbles were inconsequential because Roger planned to lay bare his debit ledgers through public penance. For the first anniversary of Hélène's death, he would send a copy of her testament plea to all their friends. Father Valensin, in whom he now placed trust without reserve, would compose a memento as an accompaniment, and upon reading his words, Roger admitted that he could never have written them himself. Although Valensin's memento was not profound, it was true, true because he shared the faith that burned so fiercely within Hélène. Roger never comprehended, could never comprehend that faith, because he did not believe and had not ever believed. For Valensin, Hélène was "Severe with herself, always seeking out a task or a duty as if any relaxation would be weakness. Firm and invincible in Faith, yet from tact, respect, and acquiescence forcing herself to suppress a profoundly combative spirit, she believed that her vocation was to live as an advance sentinel among the non-believing. She suffered from having to bear her witness silently, working from within through secret generosity. Her trial was an overwhelming sense of discontent with her efforts, and she reproached herself for not living sufficiently in Christ that through her He did not conquer. But those who have known this tormented and inaccessible soul at close hand are more inclined to admire her than she was to condemn herself."[8]

Roger had known instantly that Hélène aimed her plea directly at him and directly at Christiane. For the moment, he did not divulge even its existence to Christiane, but he could not conceal other elements of the testament. Hélène left Christiane her pearl necklace and the right to her furs and fine gowns. She left the rest of her jewels to others and specified that her sister, Manon, and Marie Rougier distribute the rest of her personal belongings without consulting Christiane. Roger recalled Hélène once saying, "'When I think that after me these things might fall into Christiane's hands, I want to burn all of them!'" Thus far, however, Christiane had been the definition of filial devotion as she assisted Roger in the doleful task of sorting through Hélène's papers and possessions in the Cimiez apartment. She seemed, he thought, to be seeking some reconciliation of her own. The future was open: "I know perfectly well," Roger wrote to Rougier, "that *anything is possible*, given time. I might finish my life at Le Tertre *with* Christiane. I might let Christiane take the apartment on the Rue du Dragon, some day. ... Equally possible, I might just stay in Nice and have nothing to do with Christiane or her life. You see her trying to restore her relations with me, and you find that touching. But what you do not see is that Christiane, having destroyed her marriage, senses in her mother's premature death a sudden, exceptional, *unexpected chance* to 'remake her life' by centering herself on my old age." Wary of Christiane's motives, Roger resisted her efforts to treat him as "unbalanced and obsessed by my grief. Your imagination persuades you that I am prey to some romantic sensibility and 'morbid.' Everyone would smile at that idea, even the housemaid! I am, to the contrary, in exceptional *health* emotionally and physically." He suggested that she "spend less time thinking about me," and when she persisted with the invitation to drive him from Nice to Paris, he wrote her sharply, "Don't force my hand." Eventually, she snapped back, "I wish that you would, *once and for all*, consider my DISTRESS."[9]

Both relented before the awful work of examining what had accumulated in so many bureaus, dressers, secretaries, armoires, and closets at Le Tertre. Despite Hélène's preoccupation with order, she had filled drawers with sealed envelopes in which she had saved, "pell-mell," agendas of daily expenses since 1906, the electricity and telephone bills for Le Tertre since 1925, rent receipts for the Cimiez apartment, medical records, letters from Roger, letters from Christiane, letters from friends, random photographs, notes from her reading, the documents for Christiane's marriage, notarial acts from the Foucault estates, the testament of Roger's mother. Everywhere, Hélène's presence seemed to linger: the chaise longue in the park pavilion revealed where she had lain down, the pile of books on her table what she had been reading, the trace of her writing on the blotter when she had sat at her desk—"a thousand little intimate unexpected details." Roger called himself a "gravedigger" of the past, but he was instead a cremator. At the end of August after six weeks of sifting, he built a bonfire in the courtyard, and with Daniel to help him—not Christiane—he cast into its "purifying flames" "armfuls" of everything that Hélène herself had marked "to be burned" and anything else he thought might possibly reflect poorly on her in the eyes of anyone coming after him. Then, before leaving Le Tertre, Roger finally introduced himself to the priest at Bellême, Canon Poulain, thanked him for the Mass he had celebrated the previous year for the intention of Hélène, and gave him "five thousand francs ($180.00 in 2015), two thousand ($72.00) for the collection of the clergy and three thousand ($108.00) to defray the cost of future masses to be celebrated for the intention of the Martin du Gard and Foucault families."[10]

Once returned to Nice, Roger made final preparations for the memorial he was having printed and would mail on December 15, a four-page leaflet with a photograph of Hélène on the first page, the excerpt from Hélène's testament on the second, the memento by Valensin on the third and fourth, below which a photograph of the stone surmounting Hélène's tomb. When he sent an early copy to Christiane in the last week of October, she declared herself "profoundly shocked." She called Valensin's memento "solemn and noble" and the photographs "excellent" but protested that Hélène would never have wanted her testamentary plea made public. Then, she revealed her true emotion, fear of embarrassment: "I would have liked, for my part, to have been made aware of it in November 1949, and not through this leaflet. I find its character so intimate, so familial, that apart from you, me, the Father [Valensin], and Marie [Rougier], *no one* in the world should know of it. I can only imagine the remarks, the comments, even from the most intimate of friends, that it will provoke, and I have a horror of them. Silence! Great God! Silence, as much as possible! The letter from the father would have sufficed amply. Why did you not consult me? Am I so incapable of judging, of understanding, of appreciating?" The tone of Roger's response by return mail was implacable—and should have given Christiane fair warning of future relations with her father: "Your reaction hardly surprises me, and I acted alone to avoid hearing it earlier. . . . Your mother suffered greatly, and silently, because of me and because of you. I believe that this suffering should be made known, and I would be ashamed to conceal it. Too many people around us believed her to be happy and are inclined to cast me in the role of a Jean Barois, married to an inexcusable bigot. The publication of these lines from her testament will put matters in proper perspective. . . . I am saddened that you fail to understand and see only an unpleasant indiscretion. Perhaps upon reflection, you will judge me less severely."[11]

What Roger meant as "expiation," Christiane recognized as "excoriation." By acting to assuage his sense of guilt through contrition, he was asking Christiane to have the courage of his convictions. Yet Roger was ambiguous about revelation after another grievous loss. In mid-February 1951, he received word that Gide was failing rapidly. He rushed to Paris and was present for his friend's "exemplary death" a few days later. The burial was at Cuverville, just inland from the Atlantic coast near Caen, and when some members of Gide's family sent a Protestant pastor from Le Havre to invoke "the peace of God," Roger and Jean Schlumberger protested angrily. Nine months afterward in late November, François Mauriac, the most Catholic of France's great novelists, claimed in *Le Figaro* that some of Gide's last words implied a desire for religious conversion. Although he had been at Gide's bedside—and Mauriac most certainly had not been—Roger initially refrained from replying in public. He did so only after another article, this time in the weekly *Le Figaro littéraire* at the end of December, repeated Mauriac's allegation. For its next issue on January 5, 1952, Roger contributed a short response, "Sur la mort d'André Gide" (On the Death of André Gide), which ran on the first page and in which he insisted that Gide's words had given "no hint of mystical meaning." Immediately after reading it, Father Valensin wrote to praise Roger's having provided "objective testimony. Your tone was perfect. . . . It is not bad, when one is able, to halt the rise of legends."[12]

Valensin added, "Your book has been a great success with my [Jesuit] confreres. It is a work of loyalty." He was referring to Roger's brief memoir, *Notes sur André Gide, 1913-1951* (*Recollections of André Gide*), which he had quickly assembled from correspondence and from entries in his journal. When he recounted a friendship of almost four decades, he carefully suppressed the most notorious of Gide's revelations to him, especially a confession "attributing his incapacity for heterosexual relations to a psychological peculiarity." But shielding Gide's memory from enemies who would attack him on moral grounds was made difficult because the five men Gide charged as his literary executors had differing motivations. Roger and Jean Schlumberger knew almost all the secrets, recognized that these secrets would eventually become public, but hoped to delay the moment when they would be divulged. Arnold Naville, a banker from Geneva and financial advisor to Gide for decades, would almost by nature take confidences to his grave. Jean Lambert had married Catherine, Gide's daughter, in 1942, and though Catherine openly despised her father, Lambert feared that any damning material about Gide would lead to unpleasant scrutiny of Catherine's background and thus himself. Pierre Herbart had married Elisabeth van Rysselberghe, Catherine's mother, in 1931, and his relationship since to Gide had been fraught: Gide paid his bills but won back Elisabeth to live in an adjoining apartment and care for him. Inevitably, Herbart was the one who stripped away the veil in his *A la recherche d'André Gide* (In Search of André Gide), an account that was stunningly caustic. Gide's supporters railed against Herbart, but Roger, acknowledging reality, judged the book "both *terrible* and *true*. Its readers will divide in two categories: the ones for whom truth matters more than fond indulgence or proprieties and the ones whose affection for Gide does not bear well the harshness of this clinical diagnosis." He could have been expressing his own contradictory attitude toward Gide. Notably, Roger had agreed to accept Herbart's dedication of this book to him because in the end, "what matters is the lucidity, the perception, and the exactitude of the analysis."[13]

By mid-summer 1951 when Roger had completed the manuscript for his Gide memoir, he left Nice for Le Tertre. When he got there, he discovered that a few days earlier on July 14, Bastille Day, his rank in the Legion of Honor had been elevated from "Knight" (*Chevalier*) to "Commander" (*Commandeur*). No one had consulted him for fear that he would refuse, as he had in 1937. At Le Tertre, he tried to pick up his work on *Maumort* for the first time since just before Hélène's death two years before: tried and failed. Although he wrote

Valensin, "I am attacking my roman-fleuve with a fresh eye," he accomplished little. Le Tertre was his creation, now his recreation, but "what is this sense of suffocation, this slowing of all activity, this physical and moral aging that strikes me down as soon as I am in this house, a house which is so much mine but where each object evokes the *past*, is linked to the memory of my wife, my parents, my childhood, the joy of living that once lit up every moment, but where now death speaks to me without respite, as if it feared that I might forget for a single second the brevity of existence, the void of all life?" After a winter consumed with quarrels about Gide's memory—Mauriac's allegations coming in November and Herbart's vitriol published in February—Roger returned to Le Tertre in May 1952 determined to banish the ghosts that had haunted him the year before. He invited rounds of guests, held discussions with them and read from his *Maumort* fragments.[14]

Still seeking to insinuate herself, Christiane joined him at Le Tertre and quickly encountered his disdain. In mid-July, Roger was having a literary discussion with Jean Schlumberger and her son, Daniel, who was preparing to take the competitive examination for the Ecole Normale Supérieure. When Christiane tried to join them, Roger dismissed her, "Go back to your jellies and jams." A week later in a state of high dudgeon—the letter is marked "1 a.m."—she wrote to Marie Rougier: "*A serving girl*, that's what he wants of me . . . running the house, knitting, embroidering, *in the kitchen*, absent from all conversation. HE OPPOSES ALL MY ASPIRATIONS. . . . For my whole life, I have been dominated by men of iron, the sensualist Coppet, who exhausted me, and the misogynist father who tolerates women only if they resemble his mother." When Rougier tried to intervene, Roger adopted a harsh tone: "I have put up with these scenes, with this readiness to take offense, during forty years of my life, but I will not put up with their poisoning my last days. For the past two years, I have granted Christiane a large place in my life and even let her encroach on me. But about some things, I am absolutely intransigent: I want to talk with my friends and to give readings if I like without the obligation to keep her informed or to invite her participation. My house remains open to her, and I will welcome her for as long as she would like, but there is a limit to intimacy that I shall never breach. If she believes the place I have given her at Le Tertre or Paris is insufficient, she can return to her marriage."[15]

At the end of this letter to Rougier, Roger mentioned that a principal reason for his low tolerance of Christiane's moods was a new "preoccupation with my work. I am making considerable modifications to the beginning of my book, and that's a significant amount to imagine differently and then rewrite." What he was planning was yet another conception—the third—for *Maumort*. Despite the praise from Gide for the fragments he had finished,

Roger could not shake his fear of miring his novel in the recapitulation of historical events. To escape them and to add contingency to the specific recollections, he proposed recasting almost the entire novel as a series of letters from
Maumort to his best friend, Dr. Gévresin. Roger would be able to manipulate
this correspondence in various ways. He could leave gaps, for when one or
the other was out of contact or when letters were lost. He could use historical
events to trigger particular memories, and through them a more general and
profound exploration of the past. The events of Maumort's life would remain
the same, but their recapitulation would be freer in letter form than in a diary.
At least Roger hoped so, writing to Maria van Rysselberghe: "Sudden illumination! Or, more modestly, light at the end of my tunnel." He described the
epistolary structure and declared that "this modification would smooth over
most of the formidable obstacles that barred my path and would offer as well
valuable opportunities and shortcuts. But I have great work of recasting and
readjustment, about which I am more than a little anxious." During the next
weeks he immersed himself in "the complete revision of all the work for these
last years," "to demolish and begin again," because "I must reconstruct or otherwise renounce everything." Was a compendium of letters the resolution to
Roger's quandary about *Maumort*? Or was it just another false start—or worse,
more "incoherent meditation"? The question is without an answer because
before he could recast more than the material about Maumort's reaction to
the end of the war, Christiane's imperious quest for autonomy interrupted and
caused him grievous emotional turmoil.[16]

The new crisis arose after a difficult winter and spring for Roger in Nice.
He had new contention with Mauriac, who had won the 1952 Nobel Prize
for Literature a few months earlier. He was again pressuring Roger to seek
election to the Académie française and was criticizing the role played by
Gaston Gallimard during the war, especially his failure to denounce the collaboration of Drieu La Rochelle. Roger finally wrote him, "You are much to
be pitied, Mauriac, for you must suffer greatly from being unable to control
your worst instincts! I think of you with infinitely more sorrow than bitterness." Roger's physical woes also returned in force. Some were uncomfortable but not serious: three weeks in bed with influenza during January
and February, then rheumatism in his lower back. Others were painful and
dangerous: edema in both legs and prostatitis. By the time he went up to Le
Tertre in the late spring, his mood was dark. He had conceived a new analogy for dying and death, which he explained to Marie Rougier and Father
Valensin: "I would like to write the interior monologue of a traveler who
is leaving his town forever and is sitting in the waiting room of the station
before the arrival of his train. His fellow citizens have come to keep him

company and, believing that he will be interested, tell him what is happening in the town. Although the traveler listens to them politely, *these matters no longer concern him.*"[17]

But certain matters did concern Roger, and directly. In the early fall, he added this entry to his journal: "We spend our lives wanting to know who we are, seeking ourselves tirelessly. Sometimes we even imagine having arrived at a true vision of ourselves. But only at the threshold of old age can we *begin* to discover, appraise, and judge, when ... we finally have an overview of our lives. We humbly note the gross errors of judgment that we have committed, and nothing is left of the comforting illusions by which we deceived ourselves for so long." He was writing in dejection and mortification from a sense of having failed so abjectly as a father. For Christiane had announced to him that she intended to seek a divorce from Marcel and to live openly as the mistress of Raymond-Théodore Barthelmess, known as Henri Calet, who had a minor reputation as a journalist and novelist but a dubious reputation as a man.[18]

Born illegitimate in 1904, his father attracted to anarchism and his mother a sometime prostitute, Barthelmess showed no great promise in school or during his required military service or at a string of jobs. He did have a fascination with fast women and fast horses, and by 1930 he had acquired a married Russian café singer as a mistress and heavy debts at the race track. For the next step in his career, he took two hundred fifty thousand francs ($184,000 in 2015) from his employer's safe and fled with the Russian songstress, first to Great Britain, where he left her behind, and then to South America, finally taking refuge in Montevideo, Uruguay. There, he acquired a false passport under the name "Henri Calet" and posed as a Nicaraguan businessman. Within a year, he had spent almost everything. He returned to Europe furtively and lived under the name Calet because he had been convicted in absentia for theft and sentenced to five years in prison. As Calet, he published a well-received novel, *La Belle Lurette*, in 1935 with Editions Gallimard that attracted notice from both Gide and Herbart. He also continued a personal life of great disorder, taking a series of new mistresses and marrying two of them. During the war, he was an active member of the Resistance and after the Liberation in 1944, began writing for *Combat*, when Albert Camus turned his clandestine newspaper into a daily. He could thereby claim to be the colleague of Jean-Paul Sartre and André Malraux. His conviction erased by a judicial amnesty, Calet attained a certain renown through more novels and through becoming a radio journalist, though less from these accomplishments than from his connections.[19] In the summer of 1953, he was between mistresses when he met Christiane. She represented the opportunity for him to vault even higher.

He was everything that Marcel was not. They could never have resisted each other.

Roger could only wait until Christiane approached him. When she finally did so in early October, she coyly admitted, "Since this summer, I have not been alone in my life." Roger replied carefully, "If I may permit myself this counsel, it is that you be careful to preserve intact the esteem and affection of your children." Privately, he was appalled at her conduct. She had made matters much worse by telling her uncle an ugly lie, that Roger intercepted and destroyed a letter she wrote to Hélène explaining in detail her intention to divorce Marcel. "Mama would have aided me in divorcing," she had continued, "I know it, and today, she would approve of my liaison, and I would have an ally against my father." She had also accused him of homosexuality—to explain his "notorious misogyny." How could Christiane have imagined that Roger's brother would side with her? This treachery left Roger *stupefied*, because, as he wrote to Rougier, "Hélène and I were never so entirely and profoundly in accord than at this moment when Christiane's failings and stupidities toward her husband became clear to us!" And almost broken: "I have never felt so miserable! In the face of events about which I can do nothing but that threaten to disorganize my existence utterly and to increase still more my solitude. . . . I am placed in a situation that requires of me a lucid mind, a decisive spirit, and a firm will to execute the necessary recovery—but my strength fails me, and I no longer have the physical and emotional resources indispensable to do so! When my wife died, I could still sustain a brutal shock. Today, no."[20]

What was Roger to do? He began by revising his will, "dispossessing Christiane as much as possible to the benefit of Daniel and Annique" and taking the first steps "to ensure that my archives and notes will be placed *under seal* immediately after my death, to prevent any intrusion by an outsider." During the almost four years since Hélène's death, Roger had let Christiane have free run of the apartment on the Rue du Dragon, and she had given up the one on the Rue Villaret-de-Joyeuse. Should he reverse his decision and bar her from the Rue du Dragon, and from Le Tertre as well? Perhaps he should have sold both of them after Hélène's death, but he had not, and now "*I no longer have the strength for great decisions*, for courageous reorganizations. All that is left for me is to *flee*." Because Calet had only a modest apartment, about two miles away in the neighboring and far less grand fourteenth arrondissement, Christiane was letting him live with her at the Rue du Dragon: "She sleeps with him *in Hélène's bed*, she has given him Hélène's desk for his work; they make love beneath Hélène's photograph, in the midst of Hélène's painted flowers, in front of Hélène's little Directoire clock and in front of grandmother

Adrienne's portrait. And why not? She has no shame." Too late, he thought that after Hélène's death he should have told Christiane, "You have arranged your life to your liking, and so shall I mine. Leave now, for we have nothing in common. Manage to take your things from [the Rue du] Dragon without making a scene. You may come to Le Tertre occasionally for a few days, but you will no longer pass the summers there, and in my absence, you may not come at all." Roger worried especially about his papers falling into the hands of "*two strangers*, the woman bewitched by the man, the man *hostile to every-thing I represent, in literature as well as my life. . . . I* can imagine that on the day after my death, they would arrive *together*—finally free and 'rich!'—to empty my filing cabinets, to inventory my archives, to make decisions about using my notes and *my manuscripts.* . . . Simple prudence would be to safe-guard everything in advance, and doing so would be simple. I would have only to fill ten trunks with my papers and deposit them with the Bibliothèque nationale. Yes, so easy to say, and doing it is equivalent to renouncing not only my present work but all possible future work."[21]

Roger was all alone and sometimes descended to despair, as in this note on an index card that he headed, "*Written in the midst of crisis, at the height of distress. To destroy before my death*: "The day comes when you discover that the person in whose qualities you once believed is only a poor thing of mediocre and miserable character with whom you have nothing in common, a person whose faults are suddenly revealed to be so apparent, so base, so intolerably exasperating that no affection, no reasonable indulgence can blind you to them anymore, a person for whom you must make an exhausting effort merely to tolerate her presence! And this torture, unimaginable to anyone who has never endured it, is not, like death, a dreadful trial 'without a morrow.' No, the trial is renewed inexhaustibly." He was referring, of course, to Christiane.[22]

Yes, Roger did have allies, not just against Christiane but for him, in his brother and sister-in-law, Marcel and Marie-Louise, and in Marie Rougier. He had drawn them more tightly to him since Hélène's death, but they were not close to hand, and he did not see them often. He hoped to add Marcel de Coppet, whose company and especially whose comradeship in correspon-dence he sorely missed, but nearly a quarter-century of rancor remained between them. When Roger wrote him in November deploring Christiane's conduct, Marcel replied with reserve, "I retain for her a profound affection that I do not believe she has ever comprehended. No matter now, anyway. I see no reason why this divorce would change anything about our relations." The most surprising friendship of Roger's middle age and likely his surest guide was lost to him. Father Valensin suffered a severe myocardial infarction on

December 13, and died five days later. Through Rougier, he sent these last words: "'Tell Roger that I am dying with as much *dignity* as Gide. And in joy.'" Roger took them to heart, "At the fatal moment, may his example help us, *force* us, to be worthy of this great friend." On that very day, he placed a photograph of Valensin at the foot of his bed, next to the photograph of Gide, "to help me die well." He also composed this entry, with the title "Tolerance": *"One can be an unbeliever, even an anticlerical, without being a deicide."*[23]

With Christiane in his old apartment at the Rue du Dragon, Roger had taken a smaller one above it in the same building as a pied-à-terre. He planned to spend the Christmas holidays there and insisted to her in advance that if they were to see each other, "certain subjects" had to be avoided for fear that they might "gravely compromise the future of our relations." She understood and had Calet leave, but wrote back insolently, "I really don't understand your attitude; I would act differently with my children. Of course, I am not naturally inclined toward heavy secrets and dissimulation." Their visits were a wary truce during which Roger learned that Calet, though only forty-nine years old, suffered from serious heart disease and had experienced a dangerous attack of angina the previous October while working at the offices of *Marie Claire* magazine. After Roger left for Nice, Christiane began campaigning for him to meet Calet the following spring or summer. Her letters were relentless, and by March, Roger reacted: "Don't you understand how exasperating you are?" But she had worn him down to the point that he would consider receiving Calet for "a tête-à-tête, man to man." Even this concession was insufficient for her. She wrote saying that she wanted to spend the Easter holidays at Le Tertre, "But I do not want to leave my invalid"—meaning to bring Calet along. Roger refused, recognizing that to grant her request once meant "further offensives would follow until he is spending the summer, at my house!" Christiane did go alone to Le Tertre on Ascension Sunday, but when she returned to the Rue du Dragon, she found Calet in cardiac distress and blamed this new bout of angina on his not having been able to accompany her.[24]

The implacable quality of Christiane's malice generated its power. Some three weeks later, Roger himself arrived in Paris for his annual change of climates. Once settled at his pied-à-terre, his first act was writing Calet to arrange a private interview on June 21. For Calet, discretion and reserve could allay Roger's worst fears; for Roger, acceptance of the obvious could establish boundaries. The measure of their success came when Roger, denying he was "an old bourgeois conformist" and proclaiming Calet "a man of compassion, sensible and loyal," declared that he was resisting any association with his daughter's liaison only because "I am old, I am tired, I have certain habits of life, I need calm and peace, and I do not want to reorganize my life." And thus: "If we can part with a truly cordial handshake, without any mental reservations, I believe that we will have avoided misunderstandings, that we will have established our relations on a level worthy of you and worthy of me, and that we will, both of us, retain a good memory of this first encounter."[25]

Of course, Christiane was dissatisfied with the exterior form of the meeting, Calet made to seem a supplicant and herself excluded, and indignant at the implication that her liaison cut her off from her father's world. In late August, she wrote Roger asking to spend the beginning of September at Le Tertre and thereby give "Henri a few days in the country." When he did not reply, she tried enlisting Marie Rougier to persuade him. Rougier's direct refusal incited a tirade from Christiane—despite the certainty of its falling into Roger's hands: "'If Calet is not invited to Le Tertre in September, I will not come alone, ... and the day that Le Tertre is mine, I will take vengeance on Father Thibault *by making Henri its master.*'" Roger pretended to know nothing of her bitterness, and in October he unwisely accepted an invitation to come downstairs at the Rue du Dragon and have dinner with her and Annique. Soon after he sat down, his asking whether Calet was in Paris triggered Christiane's wrath: repeating every grievance since her childhood and especially since she met Calet, sobbing, yelling, threatening to sever all relations with Roger, threatening to commit suicide, threatening to remarry. After three hours—by Roger's watch—of this "pure madness," Annique, who was now almost nineteen years old, got up and prepared to leave. Roger joined her, and at the door, she told him, "Mama is completely crazy." The following morning, he found an envelope leaning against his door, and because he could not distinguish the handwriting of his daughter from that of his granddaughter, he wrote the following to Christiane: "If this letter is yours, take it back: pardon me, but I do not have the courage to open it. Perhaps I would have found a happy surprise? And if so, I would regret my prudence. But after what I had to hear yesterday, I am in no state to risk taking more."[26]

Such emotional stress almost certainly contributed to Roger's increasing medical problems while he was Paris. Soon after the meeting with Calet, he had a recurrence of phlebitis, this time accompanied by an infection that briefly caused a fever of 103 degrees Fahrenheit. The result was confinement to bed for twenty-five days, two penicillin injections a day, and frequent venipuncture. He appeared to recover, but three months later he had a new attack, this one so serious that his physicians sent him to the Pasteur Hospital for a month. Always before, the swelling in his left leg had been localized, but now it extended from his toes up to his knee. He had the additional complication of an effusion in the knee joint ("water on the knee"). "You can do nothing against old age," he complained, "you must accept the wearing out of organs and all these miseries." He had a visit from the chaplain, a priest in his fifties who had spent many years as a missionary and had a goatee "like a Tibetan high priest." Roger told him, "If you have come to convert me, you're too late! ... If you've come to administer last rites, you're too early! But if you've come to talk a bit, you're welcome!" For a moment, the chaplain was dumbfounded but then began to laugh and sat down.[27]

The experience of spending so long in a hospital bed unable to walk, one leg elevated, his body injected and prodded, had a curiously malicious effect on Roger. As soon as he was back to his pied-à-terre, he telephoned Calet and asked him to visit. The conversation lasted two hours and was far different from their initial awkwardness and posing in June. Roger reaffirmed—perhaps truthfully this time—that he was not in any way hostile to Calet or to his presence at the Rue du Dragon. Calet revealed that he had told Christiane "a hundred times *I will never go to Le Tertre because I would have nothing to do there.*" Roger sensed that Calet was tiring of Christiane but would not leave her because "he is gentle, weak, careless, a man who says 'yes' easily to preserve the peace." Christiane knew of their meeting, though not the substance, almost immediately, and if Roger had meant to roust her, he could not have done better. Just before meeting Calet, Roger left Christiane a substantial check for forty thousand francs ($11,185 in 2015) "to help you finish the year." She usually sent him an affectionate note right away in response for such gifts, but this time two and a half days passed without a word. Then, he found a thick envelope propped at his door, "like a 'time bomb,' and I did not have the courage to open it." Two more days later, when Christiane encountered Roger outside their building, she told him that she had indeed written to thank him for the check—"a happy surprise"—but had added "things *that I want you to know!* ... *You must cease meeting Henri above me!*"—a superb pun—"I have had enough of it!" Roger turned his back and walked away without a word: "I congratulated myself on having not opened the letter."[28]

For a month, father and daughter did their best to avoid each other. Roger placed some small Christmas gifts in her mailbox, for which Christiane expressed not the slightest gratitude: "Perhaps she was expecting more? But I just gave her a generous check." Her gift arrived in the form of a new letter at the end of the year, and this one Roger opened. Christiane demanded that he cease all contact with Calet: "I cannot accept these private conversations. They put me in a state of *internal* rage that pushes me toward the most *violent impulses. . . .* Eventually, through good sense and affection for you, I will perhaps accept your refusal to welcome Calet to your home, with me. *But I swear to you that I am capable of tearing down everything—everything!—if you persist in luring him behind my back!*" Before such vehemence, Roger agreed not to invite Calet again, but, "If we meet by accident, I will explain to him the reasons for my change in attitude."[29]

Roger had lost Hélène. He had lost Gide. He had lost Valensin. He was close to losing Christiane. He was becoming that traveler he had imagined, who has left everything behind and is waiting at the station for his appointed train.

Chapter 10

~

ESTRANGEMENT

BUT ROGER WAS NOT yet the traveler of the train-station analogy because he was not yet willing to leave everything behind. At the beginning of December 1954, he had a letter from Henry de Montherlant, who wrote, "I believe that among the men of French letters, you alone have dignity, and I say so often." Roger had last seen Montherlant fourteen years earlier in Nice during the Vichy days and had judged him disgustingly solipsistic. Still, because Montherlant was one of France's literary elite and his opinion counted, Roger admitted having "savored" this compliment, "sucked on it like a piece of candy all morning." He understood that for a man of Montherlant's aristocratic heritage, "dignity" meant "eminence of character and spirit," exactly what he thought Christiane lacked. His reaction also showed that though he talked of being forgotten and passé as a writer, his heart and soul were glad that he was not. Six weeks later he had dramatic proof when Editions Gallimard announced that it would add him to the authors in its "Bibliothèque de la Pléiade" (Pleiades Library) series, the complete works of France's most distinguished authors published in small, leather-bound volumes of lightweight offset "Bible" paper. Previously, only Gide had been so honored while alive. To his great pleasure, Albert Camus asked to write the introduction.[1]

Roger had only to compose his "Souvenirs littéraires," a kind of literary autobiography—"only," because he regarded any public disclosure about himself with horror. Then, just as he prepared to grapple with these details, his left leg once again became a serious medical problem. This time, he developed an acute streptococcal infection of the skin, leading to a week of fever ranging as high as 104 degrees Fahrenheit. He called the first half of May "infernal," for the daily administration of three different antibiotics, one intravenous, the other two through injection. Although beaten back, the streptococcus survived in some reservoir because the infection suddenly flared up in August, again with high fever. By multiplying the antibiotics and adding injections of camphor oil (then used to control nerve pain), his physicians finally managed a cure. Roger was capable of gallows humor: "*Complete Works* has a sinister obituary sound. . . . Perhaps they believe me done for." Because he was so unwell, he invited Marie Rougier to spend the summer with him at Le Tertre in the role of chatelaine, saying of her acceptance, "Alleluia!" Certainly, Christiane had disqualified herself for that role. And he asked Daniel, his grandson, now at the Ecole Normale Supérieure and the very opposite of his mother, to join him as much as possible, because Daniel had come to know the library at Le Tertre even better than Roger and was the perfect assistant. So at Le Tertre in the summer of 1955, he began his literary memoirs.[2]

As he drew his materials together, Roger wrote himself an admonition: "In the end, any autobiography, however sincere, however severe, however composed with the honorable plan of hiding nothing and granting no indulgence to grave failings, always reflects a certain self-acceptance that remains permeated with the intimate, secret, and unalterable *sympathy* that one has for oneself. . . . And thus, the title of any autobiography should be *Hagiography*." Of course, he ignored his own warning because he was writing for posterity—he understood the importance and permanence of the Bibliothèque de la Pléiade—and because, as he told Jean Schlumberger, who was the overall editor for the two volumes, "this autobiography is written through *the lens of death*."[3]

With discretion and economy, Roger sketched out his youthful formation. Louis Mellerio taught him that everything he wrote "must rest on a solid foundation, . . . that the work of a writer—especially during the preliminary period when he conceives the project in its entirety and calculates its proportions—has profound analogies to the work of an architect or an engineer." Abbé Marcel Hébert gave him *War and Peace* to read, from which he learned that a novelist could discover in even minor characters "the private and secret nature that lies hidden behind public and open appearance." At the Ecole des Chartes, he acquired such a passion for history that "it became impossible for me to imagine a character detached from his times" and "a certain moral and intellectual discipline that became second nature to me. I learned, not only to respect but to consider as indispensable to preparing a work worthy of confidence and esteem, the *rigor* that impartial historians applied to their research."[4]

When Roger turned to his books, he described how in 1913, *Jean Barois* was rejected by Bernard Grasset, accepted by Gaston Gallimard, and then became a best seller. After the war, he had the idea for a roman-fleuve based on the lives of brothers, Antoine and Jacques Thibault, sensing that through them he could "express simultaneously two contradictory tendencies in my nature, the instinct for independence, escape, revolt, and refusal to conform, and that instinct for order, measure, and the refusal of extremes that I owe to my heredity." He lavished praise on his longtime, his only, publisher, Editions Gallimard, declaring that with Gaston Gallimard, André Gide, and Jean Schlumberger, he always found "lucid counsel and hearty cheer." He praised the influence of the retreats at Pontigny for cultivating within him new ideas and noted the irony that these sessions were held in buildings that once housed a community of Cistercian monks. Paul Desjardins, the organizer of these "*décades*," once called himself the "laic successor to a long line of Grand Priors."[5]

Of anything after *Les Thibault*, of anything about the war or of *Maumort*, Roger wrote nothing. Instead, he sent this truncated memoir to Schlumberger in mid-September with the—perhaps—facetious comment, "You will surely be shocked by the tone of my 'Souvenirs,' by this belated exhibitionism that is so unlike me." Schlumberger replied, "There is not a trace of exhibitionism in this sober *curriculum vitae*." About ten days later, Pierre Herbart and Léon Steindecker, known as Léon Pierre-Quint, the prominent editor of Editions du Sagittaire and a friend of Gide, came to Le Tertre for a brief visit. Roger read to them and to Marie Rougier pages from these "Souvenirs littéraires," and all three protested at his having excluded the fifteen years of work on *Maumort*. Roger exclaimed that *Maumort* was a "*failure*," "nothing but a pathetic human adventure left *unfinished*." And yet he could not truly have believed so, because with the deadline for final submission looming, he immediately added material on *Maumort*, excerpts from correspondence with Gide about his early efforts, and a caution: "The enterprise was not, in fact, suitable either to my age or to my capacity for work. After years of persistent efforts, too often interrupted (whether by outside events, by circumstances in my private life, and most recently by frequent problems of health), I have had to accept the possibility of a renunciation that risks being definitive."[6]

Camus had already prepared his "introduction." He offered many sagacious comments about Roger's work and especially about *Les Thibault*: "Jacques and Antoine help us to understand that two sorts of men exist, the ones who will die having always been adolescents and the others who are born already adults. But the adults risk supposing that their equilibrium is the law of the world and that misfortune is therefore a failing." Camus had lived his life far more like Jacques than like Antoine, but for him, Antoine was "the true hero" of the roman-fleuve: "From the moment that Antoine reads his death sentence in the eyes of his mentor Philip until his final solitude, his stature never ceases to increase, in exact proportion to his recognition, one by one, of his doubts and weaknesses." When Camus turned to Martin du Gard the man, the tenor of his praise can be taken from this single sentence: "The last word is the one about which it is difficult to say of any other writer since the death of Tolstoy: kindness." The Pléiade edition appeared in November 1955, but Camus' introduction was published separately at the beginning of October in the *Nouvelle Nouvelle Revue française* (as the journal was calling itself since 1953). In thanking him, Roger claimed to have read it "nine times" and that "it enchanted him more with each reading, not only because it fills me with esteem for this R. M. G. whom you present to the public but because it is an *excellent piece by A. Camus*, and I am proud of having inspired it." In February 1956, André Malraux wrote Roger warmly that Camus had "said what ought to be said and said it well, though in place of 'kindness,' I would have preferred 'generosity.'" So thought two titans of modern French literature, men who were themselves considered to be of exemplary virtue.[7]

But for Christiane, "kindness" and "generosity" were utterly foreign to Roger's character. In October 1955, she sent him a letter—he quoted it to Marie Rougier—that began, "'You reproach me for living beyond my means. That is true, but you forget one thing, that you did nothing to give me a profession. You are *entirely* responsible for everything!'" And as a solution, she suggested that he might begin selling the "'pretty bibelots'" at Le Tertre, and by giving her the receipts, permit her to live more easily. In refusing a reply to this suggestion, Roger imagined that she would begin with the bibelots, then move on to the manuscripts and the library until everything was sold. In February 1956, never imagining that she might not be welcome, Christiane blamed him that she had not received an invitation to the party for Maria van Rysselberghe's ninetieth birthday and claimed, "You have within you a TERRIBLE destructive force!" Despite these bitter words, Roger could not resist an overwhelming sympathy for his daughter because Henri Calet, for whom she had compromised her present and in whom she had invested her future, was dying. His condition deteriorated seriously during the winter, and the two of them went to Saint-Paul-de-Vence, where Gide had recuperated, seeking warmer weather. They were short of money, and he was short of time. Once he learned of their plight in January, Roger began sending Christiane checks to pay their rent, never less than ten thousand francs a month ($265.00 in 2015) and often more. He feared the effect on her of this deathwatch, "this daily menace, this certainty of inevitable calamity."[8]

Because of Christiane's torment with Calet, Roger was determined not to reveal that he had serious medical problems of his own. Since the end of 1955, he had suffered grievously from prostatitis and was convinced that his prostate gland was cancerous. He arranged for Dr. Jean Cibert, a celebrated urologist in Lyon, to perform a prostatectomy that July. But three months beforehand, on April 16, Roger had a sudden attack of vertigo and digestive distress. For several days, he remained in a darkened room attended only by Daniel and unable to move his head without renewing the sense of nausea. Some ten days later he was feeling better and had the reassurance of his physicians that nothing serious had happened, but he had likely suffered another transient ischemic attack, similar to what he experienced in December 1921. Roger feared that if Christiane learned about either his vertigo or his prostatectomy, she might rush to his side when her place was surely with Calet: "Not at any price am I willing to alarm Christiane, who knows nothing and endures difficult hours beside her companion, whose life is in danger every night from violent cardiac crises." Because she might learn of his travel to Lyon, he contrived a simple ruse. Rougier had been in Paris to see Roger but would be going back to Nice and could stop in Saint-Paul-de-Vence to see Christiane, telling her that his physicians had arranged for Roger to consult with the famous Dr. Cibert, a consultation, nothing more.[9]

Roger's operation and recovery during the first days of July did not go smoothly: complications required reopening the incision with significant additional bleeding. He had planned to spend only a week at Cibert's clinic before shifting his recovery to the Hôtel Carlton in Lyon, but the setback delayed his doing so until the middle of the month. He was "groggy from fever and loss of blood. This operation—it's not nothing! I will need several months to be truly like new." But to his brother, he could write flippantly, "What a relief to leave my prostate in the garbage barrels of Lyon!" Just beforehand, early in the morning of July 14, Calet had died at Saint-Paul-de-Vence in Christiane's arms. Roger telegraphed, "Profoundly distressed, thinking of you with tenderness and infinite compassion." She replied, "I thank you for your message. No one can do anything for me. I will have known three years of gentleness and sweetness in my life, that's all. The rest will have been only brutality and constraint and incomprehension by everyone. . . . I'm going to stay here until his tomb is ready—our tombs. I have purchased a cemetery plot for the two of us, side by side." She cut herself off completely, insisting to Daniel and Annique that they leave her alone in Saint-Paul-de-Vence "for several weeks." Then, she learned that while friends of Calet agreed to pay half the cost of the plot, she would have to pay the other half herself. She did not have the money and had to ask Roger for help. Of course, he did. She ended this letter, "I am nothing but an old, old woman."[10]

As Roger had suspected, his recovery was slow, first in the hotel at Lyon for a week, then back to Paris by train with Rougier toward the end of July, and finally to Le Tertre with Daniel. He was, after all, seventy-five years old. Even in mid-August, he was not rising until noon and returning to bed in the early evening, "fighting constantly against fatigue." He had worried that Christiane would seek "some manner of reconciliation," which could only be false, but she had instead, whether because of her grief or in spite of it, increased "her calumnies, her demands, her threats." Her new favorite accusation was that he had fallen under the control of "shameless gangsters, Marie [Rougier] and Pierre [Herbart], who imposed on his hospitality and plotted to take control of his estate." He called her "more vehement, more absurd, more 'impossible' than ever, . . . the only solution, a frigid courtesy." But Christiane no longer practiced courtesy of any temperature. When she finally returned to Paris, Roger credited her checking account with twenty-five thousand francs ($665.00 in 2015), "thinking naively that it would be a happy surprise." Her only response was, "And thank you for the deposit." He should not have been disappointed, but he was, and furiously so. Writing out his frustration in a journal entry, he wondered whether Christiane had simply come to expect that he would pay her bills, or perhaps that she had expected more. Clearly, she had forgotten that he had given her more than half a million francs ($13,285 in 2015) since the beginning of the year to help care for Calet. "She is impossible. She insults, she rails, and the next day she is always ready to stop long enough to say, 'And thank you for the deposit.'"[11]

Worse, and then far worse followed. Christiane called the well-meaning deception about Roger's prostatectomy "inimical toward me" and Maria van Rysselberghe's failure to send condolences after Calet's death "heartless." She blamed Roger, blamed his "terrible *rancor*" against her. Now, "you have killed EVERYTHING between us. I shall never speak of it again, but know well, once and for always, that his death has sealed forever this rupture between us." Yet she added, "the day when you *need* me, when you ask for my aid, I will be there." Roger annotated the letter: "seems to burn the bridges yet proposes to take charge of my affairs—with me limited to signing big checks." Christiane's aggressive tone led him to reply in a manner that could not fail to aggravate her further: "Knowing how alone you are in the midst of your ruins, with no other guide than your ill will and your incommensurable pride, I fear that you are condemning yourself to grow old frightfully isolated." In a postscript, he thanked her for promising help in case of need, because "I am certain that in this new role you will neglect nothing to demonstrate your devotion and authority." And indeed he had goaded her into sending a four-page denunciation. She had friends, just no longer his; she had her children, despite his efforts to turn them against her; she would not have him: "'in three years, you never received Henri and me either at [the Rue du] Dragon or Le Tertre! *Your attitude toward Henri and me has consummated the definitive rupture between us!* . . . From now on—and I regret not having done so earlier—I shall fiercely protect myself against your poisoned arrows, for I have decided *never again to open a letter from you.*"[12]

After a day of reflection, Roger attempted conciliation. He proposed that they "'coexist' peacefully" by "maintaining prudent distance and resolute courtesy." On the envelope, he wrote, "*URGENT.*" In return, Christiane sent a telegram: "Letter not opened and given to Daniel"—who then wrote to Roger. "My dear Dad," he began, using the name he and Annique had chosen for him, "Mama is 'irreconcilable' in every way. Trying to have any relationship with her, *especially* that of father to daughter or *son to mother* is useless. ... Today, she is caught in her own trap: *she is frustrated by all reality*, she lives imprisoned by the impossible. With Calet dead, she takes on the role of widow charged with upholding his literary heritage. ... Her letters are as malicious as possible, as wounding as diabolical. You have succumbed to the temptation of responding, and that is exactly what Mama wants." He then described how he and Annique blithely disregarded angry complaints from Christiane until she finally stopped making them. "Against the furious, you can either attack or ignore." Roger was delighted, but more for the "witness" against Christiane than for the suggestion of tactics. He soon owed a far greater debt to Daniel, who convinced Christiane to read Roger's conciliation letter and to write in reply, "'So be it. Let us maintain appearances.'" For Roger, that meant "polite neutrality."[13]

History—and Roger knew his history both national and personal—taught that neutrality however polite requires constant vigilance. He could recall from his classical studies the injunction of Vegetius, "igitur qui desiderat pacem, praeparet bellum—he who desires peace prepares for war." Because he could not trust Christiane, he hastened the plan to deposit his manuscripts, journals, correspondence, and working papers at the Bibliothèque nationale. He would place them in the care of Julien Cain, its administrator, with this revealing stipulation: "These documents must remain sealed and not inventoried *until after the death of my daughter and at least twenty years after my death.*" What remained was to collect and to organize them, an enormous task. He would ask Marie Rougier and Daniel to assist, but the most important work would fall on his shoulders.[14]

The autumn of 1956 also brought grave international tension. At the end of October, France, Great Britain, and Israel attacked Egypt in what came to be called the Suez crisis. They were seeking the overthrow of Egypt's Arab nationalist president, Gamal Abdel Nasser, who was supplying arms to the Algerian liberation movement against the French, had seized the Suez Canal from the British, and was supporting terrorist attacks into Israel. Lack of support for the attack from the United States and threats from the Soviet Union caused its failure. The Soviet Union then used the furor over the Suez crisis as a cover for its own invasion of Hungary, which was seeking greater autonomy and perhaps even escape from the Eastern Bloc. In the more than a decade since the end of the second world war, Roger had occasionally recorded moments when belligerence threatened the peace: at the end of 1947, as the Soviet Union consolidated its hold on Eastern Europe, in late 1950 when the People's Republic of China entered the Korean War, in May 1954, with the collapse of French rule throughout Indochina following the disastrous defeat at Dien Bien Phu, and earlier in 1956, when the progress of the National Liberation Front in Algeria brought rumors that the French government would call for a "general mobilization." The Suez crisis and invasion of Hungary raised his worst fears. He wrote Rougier that "if war comes," he would take refuge at Le Tertre, where she was welcome to join him. They could use the fireplaces to stay warm. They could raise chickens and rabbits to eat. And they could stock up boxes of corydrane (a mixture of amphetamine and aspirin), "with which we could sustain a siege!" When tensions subsided—Nasser remained president in Egypt, the Hungarian Freedom Fighters were massacred—Roger went to Nice for the winter. But not by train this time, for Daniel convinced him to take a commercial air flight, his first since flying from Martinique to the Dominican Republic in November 1939, and went along with him for reassurance. Roger described having been conveyed from Paris to Nice "like a big Christmas present. . . . one hour forty-seven minutes from Orly to the airport at Nice! Just enough time to take tea."[15]

Roger was at Nice working through his papers there when Christiane provoked their final break. By the terms of "polite neutrality," Roger had continued to give her gifts of money and let her live in the large apartment on the Rue du Dragon but denied her access to Le Tertre and sometimes used Daniel as intermediary between them. In late February, she wrote proposing that he grant her the right to establish a personal and independent residence, including kitchen, in one of Le Tertre's two wings, where she could live at her pleasure whether he was there or not. Because he spent about half of the year in Nice, she would, in effect, gain its control. She asked Daniel to intervene with Roger, but she sent an insulting letter to Rougier, whom she knew would not support her. Daniel did write Roger, but with this injunction: "*I cannot advise you to make the slightest concession.*" And Roger thought: "If Hélène had not died in 1949, she would be dead of chagrin since because of Christiane. She could not have borne the thought of divorce, the abandonment of her children, Calet at the Rue du Dragon. Christiane believed, naively, that she could, with impunity, multiply scenes for years on end, shower me with blame and abuse, spread the most untrue, absurd, and vile rumors about me, without my withdrawing from her. . . . For the last thirty years, she has accumulated ruins around her, and she continues, with the same recklessness, persuaded that she is the victim of misfortune, persecuted by everyone, unjustly doomed to hardship." So Roger refused, but offered occasional contributions for her to take trips outside Paris elsewhere. Christiane tried a desperate telegram: "Profound nervous depression, beg you to reconsider." Roger's reaction: "What good responding? Everything has been written, clearly, *definitively*." He did ask a promise of his brother, not to let him, "perhaps paralyzed and without defense, fall into the hands of this triumphant shrew!"[16]

At the end of March, Roger received a new letter from Christiane and sent it unopened to Daniel, who reported that she was asking for sixty thousand francs ($1,550 in 2015) to pay additional fees at the Saint-Paul-de-Vence cemetery. Roger immediately wrote her that he would place one hundred fifty thousand francs ($3,870 in 2015) in her account, leaving her ninety thousand francs ($2,320) after she paid the fees. He concluded, "I embrace you." Thinking the trouble over for a while, he joked that despite Christiane's recurrent threats of suicide, "she now appeals for money, so perhaps she has renounced turning on the gas!" He could not have been more wrong. Almost the next day, he had a four-page letter from her with a key to Le Tertre enclosed. She had gone there on March 31 and spent three days "'looking after my affairs. I have taken a few things, a mattress, chaise longue, night table, some toilet articles.'" While she did not mention the money Roger had just given her, she did write, "'No financial payment will erase the emotional harm inflicted.'"[17]

For Roger, Christiane had not just broken the rules of their polite neutrality, she had flouted every standard of familial behavior. He was convinced that she had boasted to her children of the "burglary escapade" and then pressured them not to tell him. He quickly wrote Daniel that he understood the bind in which he and Annique had been placed: "I do not forget that you are unlucky to have been caught in painful circumstances of discouraging complexity." Christiane's trip to Le Tertre at the end of March was only the first of four, one of them lasting a week. That first time, she had no key and broke a window to gain entrance. The following day, she had several duplicate keys made: sending one of them to Roger was her way of taunting him. She lied to Baptiste and Mathilde that she had Roger's permission, and when they appeared suspicious, she threatened them with dismissal if they wrote him. To everyone, she exclaimed, "Nothing will ever prevent me from coming to Le Tertre whenever I care to and as often as I care to! When I want something, I always get it!" In the library, on a page of the register where Roger recorded to whom he loaned books, she wrote, first in pencil and then again in ink, "Christiane, *the expelled,* has taken no book. March 31, 57." For Roger, "to assess her exemplary life," she should have written, "Christiane, held apart by her mother, repudiated by her husband, regarded as reckless by her children, disowned and expelled by her father." He meant to impose an extreme sanction.[18]

Roger returned to Le Tertre on June 7, and spent two days measuring "the scope and the gravity" of Christiane's conduct. He reassured Baptiste and Mathilde. He had the locks changed. He traced with his finger the defiling of his register. Then he wrote his daughter: "*You had no right to come to my house against my will. And I formally forbid you to come back. . . .* If you have believed that you are able to do whatever you want and always force my hand and always demand more, without exhausting my patience, you are mistaken. Your unqualifiable conduct deserves no moderation." A few days later, he had Christiane's room at Le Tertre stripped to the bare walls: furnishings, linens, curtains, decorations taken away to storage. Until the day he died, she was to be told, if she did dare come to the door, "Monsieur has said that he does not wish to receive Madame, not today, not tomorrow, not ever." Roger wrote out instructions for his physicians, at Nice, at Paris, and at nearby Bellême, that in case of emergency, they were to notify only his brother and his grandchildren, and that "*If I become gravely ill, I forbid my daughter to visit.*" Then, he wrote the letter he had wanted to write for a long time, to Marcel: "I believe that despite our differences, accentuated by old age, and despite everything that has divided us, our grounds for agreement are infinitely more numerous and more important than any causes that might keep us apart." Marcel replied with tenuous generosity: "Your letter brings me great pleasure and does not surprise me. For I too have thought frequently of you and regret that life divided us to the point of making any reconciliation impossible for long years. I believe that we can end our lives together and that we have far more reasons to agree than to disagree. Of course, that is a theoretical view, a position of principle that reality may not confirm."[19]

For Roger, Christiane's trespassing at Le Tertre made all the more vital sheltering his papers from her reach. Despite his intention of the previous fall, he had made little progress because most of them were at Le Tertre and he had been in Nice since just before Christmas. Even there, he had accomplished little, before her sending him the duplicate key disrupted his focus entirely. But now, back at Le Tertre, he set to work with powerful concentration. He was determined to keep together not only the final manuscripts of his books but all the many drafts, to demonstrate his method of composition. For the correspondence, he hoped to add annotations, something he had begun in Nice. He also left explanations to guide the librarians and archivists who would eventually inventory and classify these papers for access. He worried about dying in the midst of this work, before he could turn everything over to Julien Cain, and if so, he directed Rougier to put anything left into a trunk, "*destroy* the key," and so prevent any intrusion until it could join the rest of the material in the storerooms of the Bibliothèque nationale. Once the time limit had passed, twenty years after his death, and assuming that Christiane was also dead, these trunks could, with his blessing, become the treasure trove of "archive rats"—he meant historians—"if their race is not extinct." What Roger thought less important, notes and correspondence about trivial matters, he destroyed. On October 16, assisted only by his brother, he spent two hours in the courtyard of Le Tertre burning what he estimated to be about sixty pounds of paper—like Hélène, he had kept everything: "Two painful hours. . . . But rather the fire and annihilation than the risk of shameless profanation."[20]

For the *Maumort* materials, Roger made an exception to the rule of lock away or eliminate. He kept the drafts and files beside his desk to retain at least the possibility of working with them further, though he never did do so. As early as 1951, he had decided to entrust a small number of friends with the responsibility of publishing the novel after his death. He chose Albert Camus and André Malraux, who regarded him as an elder guide, Gaston Gallimard, who was his longtime publisher, Jean Schlumberger, who was his longtime editor, Elisabeth Herbart, who was his link to Gide and Maria van Rysselberghe, Pierre Herbart, who had proved his integrity through the book about Gide, and Marie Rougier, who was as close to a confidante as he now had. They were to advise Daniel, who would be the executor of the estate. Roger understood that he was leaving the *Maumort* materials in highly disorganized condition, with a few chapters in finished form, some others in rough draft, and almost half not even sketched out. He admitted so in his instructions to these friends: "If I were to disappear now, drawing together the fragments of 'Maumort' would obviously not be easy. But not impossible." He urged them to read carefully through the dossiers he had prepared and through the notes he was leaving behind to conjure the personality of Maumort and of the various characters around him. He would trust them to do what they could.[21]

During the last ten months of his life, Roger made a good display of continuing an interest in what happened around him. He was indeed overjoyed when Camus won the Nobel Prize for Literature in 1957 and praised his having declared, in his acceptance speech, that the two great commitments of a writer must be "the refusal to lie about what we know and the resistance to oppression." Although he had always avoided taking public political positions, he made an exception in April 1958. He joined Camus, Malraux, and Jean-Paul Sartre in signing a petition, addressed to René Coty, president of the Republic, and published in three major French newspapers, *L'Express*, *L'Humanité*, and *Le Monde*, denouncing the alleged use of torture by the French army in Algeria against the National Liberation Front. He wrote Camus that he did so because "we will be side by side" and because "for once, silence and isolation weighed on me intolerably." At the end of May, the Fourth Republic, frequently hapless since its creation in 1946, collapsed over the question of retaining Algeria as a French possession. In desperation, its leaders granted Charles de Gaulle the power to prepare a revision of the constitution—which became the Fifth Republic—and to rule by decree for six months with the hope that he could resolve the crisis. One of de Gaulle's early decisions was creating a committee of distinguished Frenchmen to investigate the claims of torture, which had been documented in a book by Henri Alleg, *La Question*. He chose Roger, Camus, Malraux, Sartre, and Mauriac. Roger, Camus, and Mauriac were already Nobel laureates, Sartre would win, then refuse the Nobel Prize in 1964, and Malraux would forever deserve winning it. Roger was, of course, too ill and frail to serve, but de Gaulle had made clear his stature.[22]

And Roger had one last experience with his daughter's duplicity. Determined to be recognized as the keeper of Calet's memory—other former mistresses were competing against her—Christiane pulled together notes from his journal and correspondence to generate a posthumous book, *Peau d'ours, Notes pour un roman* (Skin of the Bear, Notes for a Novel), which Editions Gallimard published in April 1958, and as its editor, adopted the pseudonym "M. W." Roger immediately recognized that she had taken these initials from her paternal grandmother, Madeleine Wimy. He exclaimed, "Incredible, no? You must admit she is diabolical!" in a letter to his brother, who replied that Christiane's writing under the name "Martin du Gard" would have been even worse. Four months earlier, Roger had confessed sadly to Rougier, "Paternal fondness, which for long years was a fundamental part of my interior life, has ended by dying and disappearing *entirely*, leaving not even a wound, not a painful regret, instead, nothing, indifference, obliteration."[23]

But the true preoccupation for Roger of these last months was the death that he knew was coming soon. He had new warnings: an electrocardiogram taken when he returned to Nice in December 1957 gravely concerned his physician; he had neither energy nor appetite: "I let everything go"; more and more, he found himself half-awake in a "*no man's land* of gentle and tender melancholy." Like his Maumort, he ruminated about the past, fixating on the Belle Epoque, those golden years before the civilization of nineteenth-century Europe blew itself up in the Great War. Everything had changed after the Agadir crisis in 1911: "People felt the ground tremble beneath them: invasion by the Huns seemed possible, even menacing; Poincaré and military preparations; the poker game in the Balkans, the war of 1914, the odious twentieth century."

But beforehand, during that long period of peace, "Naturally, I hated violence, considered no country the enemy, believed the time of conquest over and the return of war unthinkable to the civilized world in which we lived, as unthinkable as the return of wigs, candles, carriages, or surgical operations without anesthesia." He wrote to himself, "In the evening of a man's life comes a moment of revelation when he realizes that he is tired of living. More or less confusedly, he is conscious of having had his time. Not that he wishes to die immediately, but he has had enough, he would prefer to be finished with himself and return to nothingness. From that moment of having experienced *this regret of being*, the man is no longer the same. He begins the last step, the distinctive weariness of approaching death." Later, he added, "If I have always dreaded the sufferings of old age and the pangs of death, I have truly never had *fear of oblivion*, which I have always believed to be the inevitable end to life."[24]

In March, Roger sent an elaboration of his waiting-room analogy to Marcel: "Late, past midnight in the deserted train station of a little town sleeping in the snow, a traveler, aged, *without baggage*, huddled in his overcoat, dozing, alone, in the semidarkness, in the silence.... He is waiting for the night train, which does not come at a fixed hour but *which always passes through* before the end of the night." The traveler had been a commanding figure in the town, which owed to him its new schools, stadium, sewers, and water distribution, but "that was over. He had resigned, he was leaving discreetly, his work was done, his accomplishments were of *absolutely no interest* to him anymore, the page was turned, and he was nothing but an anonymous traveler awaiting the hour of his departure to disappear into the night." Suddenly, the waiting room is filled with townspeople praising his success and beseeching him not to leave. "But none of that interests him anymore, and he hardly comprehends what they are saying to him. ... He is frightfully and irreparably detached from all of it, and the insistence of these important men in their fur coats, their briefcases stuffed with dossiers, seems inconceivable, stupefying, and pathetic. All that matters to him is this railroad, this inexorable timetable, this train which is going to take him away forever. All the rest is merely the games of children or the obsessions of lunatics. In vain, the men become more pressing. In vain, they seek to relight extinguished fires. The traveler smiles, surprised and distracted, barely recalling their names while listening for the bell that announces the arrival of the train. And he moves away from them on the platform. Without baggage."[25]

Roger revealed that he had written this extended version of the analogy "having already left this world where men exhaust themselves living their pathetic lives." Marcel was supposed to understand that Roger was the traveler and that he had taken leave of everything, that *nothing any more concerned him*. But when Marcel replied more than a week later after having "read and reread the fine pages you sent me," he saw in them not his friend's renunciation of life but "the elements of an extraordinary and gripping short story," which he urged Roger to write. Certainly, Roger had no such intention. On July 31, he wrote Marcel again, and when noting the unexpected death of Pierre-Quint six days earlier explained, "Before the new tomb of a friend, I experience a sense of calm in thinking of the deceased, 'That fortunate man has finished waiting, ... *he no longer has to die!*' I believe that you still love life so much that you cannot understand such a cowardly reaction, such an abdication, but I would be surprised if thoughts like these have never crossed your mind."[26]

Roger's waiting came to an end three weeks later. He was staying at Le Tertre as usual during the summer. Marie Rougier was there to look after him, and Daniel came out frequently from Paris, where he was preparing for a degree in sociology. During the night of August 15–16, Roger suffered two attacks of angina, which an electrocardiogram on August 16 revealed to have been a minor myocardial infarction. He was cautioned to remain in bed for two or three weeks. During the next days, he declared, "I would like to get better—and live," but also, "Indifference overtakes me, even about my end," and ominously, "I seem to have lost dominion over myself." On August 22, in the late afternoon, his heart rate became irregular and his breathing labored. He lay down, but his symptoms worsened in the next hours. About 8:30 p.m., as a new and sharp attack of angina seized him, he called out, "My pain is upon me, give me an injection." This time, the myocardial infarction was massive and acute, like Hélène's. A physician was at his bedside but could do nothing. Roger lapsed into unconsciousness and died a few minutes later. He was seventy-seven years old.[27]

Not long before he died, Roger wrote in his journal: "Happy are those who are dead. Happy are those who die while sleeping, without suffering. Happy are those who die while dreaming of the future. Happy are those who die without ever seeing themselves age. Happy are those who are dead: *they no longer have to die*." In writing these lines, Roger must have been thinking of Charles Péguy, mystical nationalist, though also a Dreyfusard, and mystical Catholic, though a convert only in 1908 at the age of thirty-five. In 1913, Péguy published what remains the longest poem in the French language, "Eve," and in one stanza declared famously, "Happy are those who have died in great battles, / Laid out on the ground before the face of God." Hardly a year later at the onset of the Great War, he volunteered for an infantry unit despite his age and despite being the father of four young children. He died in battle on September 5, 1914, exemplifying his words. And yet in an extended essay, "Clio: Dialogue of History and the Pagan Soul," written between 1909 and 1912 but published only posthumously in 1917, Péguy wrote of the "great secret: that since there have been men, no man has been happy."[28]

Which Péguy was the truer? Roger took note of both, and in the litany that he made his final journal entry, he adopted both the stanza form of "Eve" and the pessimism of "Clio" for his own version of happiness, the release and extinction of death—as in his analogy of the traveler, without baggage, at the station. Roger had boarded that night train. Five days afterward on the morning of August 27, 1958, he rejoined Hélène when his casket was placed next to hers in their tomb at the Cimiez cemetery. By his request, no one accompanied his mortal remains, honored him with a farewell, or placed flowers in remembrance. To ensure so, his friends circulated a false date and time. The sky was gloriously clear, the sun shining.[29]

Chapter 11

AFTERLIFE

"*DE MALE MORT DIEU me garde!*" (May God save me from a bad death!) is the motto Roger gave the fictional Maumort family. But for André Daspre, his *Maumort* might well have had such a "bad death." The two literary figures who were supposed to take the lead in publishing the fragments Roger left behind were never able to play their role. Albert Camus was killed in an automobile accident on January 4, 1960. André Malraux was always preoccupied by his responsibilities as minister of culture under Charles de Gaulle. The other five were old and either busy or ill-prepared. Gaston Gallimard, whose nephew Michel died with Camus in the crash, and Jean Schlumberger were running Editions Gallimard and the *Nouvelle Revue française*. The Herbarts, Pierre and Elisabeth, had no experience writing fiction. Marie Rougier was a confidante and secretary, but no more. A decade and a half slipped by until Rougier had an inquiry from Daspre, who was preparing a dissertation, "Roger Martin du Gard, romancier d'après *Jean Barois*" (Roger Martin du Gard as the author of *Jean Barois*), which he defended in 1976. Although not especially intuitive or creative, he was ambitious, industrious, and determined, and he had credibility as a professor of literature at the University of Nice. Rougier proposed to the others that he be given the chance to work on *Maumort*, and for the lack of any alternative, they agreed.[1]

Just as Roger had asked of her, Rougier put all the papers and correspondence still at Le Tertre when he died into chests and footlockers, destroyed the keys, and sent them to the Bibliothèque nationale as soon as possible. She separated out the *Maumort* materials for storage in one special iron trunk, and this key she kept. Over time, she went through the contents and organized them into various folders, using the knowledge she had gained from working with Roger as she typed up his manuscripts. She carefully preserved a brief memorandum from him requesting that the novel, if published, be dedicated to "the memory of André Gide, whose exceptional friendship has sustained me, guided me, and wonderfully enriched me during the second half of my life." When Daspre opened the trunk, he found the various drafts or sketches for chapters and episodes in chronological order, notes for characters, locations, and plot, clippings from newspapers and periodicals establishing context, and, in a separate black cardboard box, a set of reflections, some brief, some extended, that characterized the theme and philosophy of the novel.[2]

For five years, Daspre methodically combed through these papers, pulled the fragments together, added nearly two hundred and fifty pages of critical apparatus, and so created what appeared as *Lieutenant-Colonel de Maumort* in 1983 as Martin du Gard's third volume in the Pléiade Library.[3] His working principles were straightforward. Where Roger had left multiple versions of a chapter or episode, he used the latest one. When that latest one had gaps or inconsistencies, he relied on Roger's background notes as a guide in appropriating material from the earlier drafts to resolve the discrepancies. From them, he assembled the beginnings of a novel, the memoirs of Bertrand de Maumort that run from his childhood in the 1870s through the German invasion in 1940—but are radically incomplete. He set aside as an appendage the epistolary experiment Roger attempted in the fall of 1952 because incorporating these letters from Bertrand to Dr. Gévresin into the memoir would have required severe distortions. He also let the "Black Box" entries stand alone, Bertrand's mental kaleidoscope, but sometimes a glimpse at Roger's unfettered opinions.[4]

The novel opens with Bertrand at his modest château, Le Saillant, west of Paris in the Perche region not far from Normandy. Seventy years old and retired from the army at the rank of lieutenant colonel, he is contemplating the disaster that has overtaken France in 1940. He draws up the balance sheet of his country—the accounting made sharper because German officers have occupied his estate. Memory compels him to consider as well the course of his own life. These reminiscences become a history, of France, of French sensibilities, of genteel existence, of a life now disappeared. In their analysis of anxieties, hesitations, shame, remorse, courage, and honor, they are a judgment on that past and on himself. First tutored at home, then trained at a local Jesuit academy, Bertrand moves to Paris at seventeen to live with his uncle and aunt, who have a commanding position in the academic world of the Latin Quarter. Here, he studies both for his degree in the liberal arts and for admission to the military academy at Saint-Cyr. He has adventures and love affairs. He marries and has two sons. He serves in North Africa under the legendary General Hubert Lyautey. His wife dies young. He and his sons fight in the Great War: they are killed in battle; he is wounded but survives. Alone, he retires to Le

Saillant and watches the world he knew fall apart in the 1920s and 1930s. And then the Germans overrun France.[5]

In a working note, Roger described Bertrand's character as: "... rough. An old soldier, intelligent and philosophical, ... inflexible, slightly aggressive: *a difficult character*. All of his setbacks are explained in part by this *ornery attitude*, and also his isolation, his having few friends. He always frightened the circles in which he lived with his violent judgments, his blunt frankness, his natural, somewhat contemptuous severity, his haughtiness. *A quarrelsome wisdom*. Has always fallen out with everyone. Upright, rigid, understanding, and tolerant through effort and reflection, but abrupt in his relations, intransigent, surly, difficult to handle. He has never been loved except by very rare friends. His peers, as a whole, hated him. They felt judged. The respect he inspired was usually not accompanied by affection. *The opposite of easygoingness*." His character was not formed by accident. In old age, he recalled a moment at school when he learned that an "esoteric" philosophy was "reserved for the rare initiates" and had "this intuitive conviction in me that certain beings—of whom I felt myself indubitably to be one—had, from the quality of their nature, the right to live and to think according to their own directives, that is to say as outlaws, legitimately excused from submitting to the traditional rules."[6]

Bertrand was born at the beginning of July 1870 and grew up at Le Saillant with his sister, Henriette, who at nine years older regarded him as a play toy sent by God. His father, Hippolyte, a retired artillery officer educated at the Ecole Polytechnique (Institute for Science and Engineering), blamed himself that his wife died while giving birth to their son, and took on the cold and detached exterior that brought a dismal atmosphere to the country house. Bertrand believed "it was probably in the course of those first years that I acquired, if not a tendency to melancholy, at least this ability to get along easily without gaiety." A retired schoolteacher, Mlle Fromentot, already tutoring Henriette at Le Saillant, taught Bertrand his first lessons, but everything changed in the fall of 1882, when his sickly cousin, Guy Chambost-Lévadé, came from Paris to live with them. His parents, Eric, a founder of the Ecole des Sciences politiques (Institute for Political Studies), and his mother, Madeleine, who presided over a salon attracting important figures from the Parisian intellectual world, hoped that a year or two of country air would improve his health.[7]

A year older than Bertrand, Guy was not well, but he was well enough to be naughty. Of their first months together, Bertrand recalled, "it is to Guy that I owe having learned to lie," and that "imagination was his ruling faculty, and it was almost exclusively directed toward eroticism." He cheated at games, he nicknamed the dean of the local church "Old Punch" (*le vieux Guignol*), and he taught Bertrand to spy on girls as they bathed in a pond. Worse followed when Guy's father sent one of his best students, Xavier de Balcourt, to be the new tutor for the boys. For at the age of twenty-four, Xavier already had about him a sense of desperation: wearing "his destiny as a failure, a man without luck," poor but vain, slight and short, from a ruined family. Cruel and casually wanton, Guy sensed that he could "conquer" Xavier and did: by the spring of 1883, they were engaging in lascivious games. Far less precocious, Bertrand did not comprehend what was happening until much later. By then, Guy's health had so deteriorated that his parents sent him to a sanatorium in Switzerland, where he died not long after. Bertrand went off to a Jesuit boarding school, Saint-Léonard, in nearby Gevrésy, where all of the boys engaged in frequent masturbation, and occasionally in mutual masturbation. The priests regarded this concupiscence as a venial sin and intervened only when the school's secret vice might be revealed beyond its walls.[8]

Bertrand excelled in Latin, Greek, and French literature, but he stumbled in mathematics and German. To recover the German, he took special classes with one of the Jesuits at Saint-Léonard and made such rapid progress that "Goethe always had a place next to Montaigne in my officer's trunk." For the mathematics, his father had more ambitious measures in mind because he hoped that his son would seek entry to Saint-Cyr, where their mastery was fundamental. For the better part of a summer, Bertrand boarded with a local scholar and teacher, a M. Nacquot, who not only made up the deficiency in mathematics but instilled rigor, "taught me to bend my whim to the demands of the task, to begin at the beginning, to make a good start, to attack a problem the right way, ... to draw up a plan that was complete, well-balanced, and satisfying for the mind." In consequence, when he took the written and oral examinations for the baccalaureate degree, he passed with high honors. His father rewarded him with a fine hunting rifle from the best gunsmith in Le Mans, but more important, "began taking an interest in me because I was no longer a child." In more ways than one: during his stay with Nacquot, Bertrand had a brief but intense infatuation for his younger wife. In the dark silence of the dormitories at Saint-Léonard, "the naked bodies that haunted me were usually male. From the time of my stay with the Nacquots onwards, they were quite exclusively female." As an old man, Bertrand would insist on "the primordial role that these first curiosities, these first experiences, play in the maturing of the personality. ... Tell me what your puberty was like, and I will tell you who you are."[9]

Puberty over, what was Bertrand's future to be? He proposed to study for a degree in literature (*license ès lettres*) at the Sorbonne. His father asked what he would do afterward other than return to Le Saillant as a gentleman farmer. Instead, he proposed again Saint-Cyr. The resolution came from the Chambost-Lévadés. Lonely after the death of Guy, they invited Bertrand to live with them in their apartment on the Rue de Fleurus, a few steps from the Luxembourg Gardens and in the heart of the Latin Quarter. He would pursue two degrees at the same time, studying literature at the Sorbonne and preparing for the examination to Saint-Cyr at the Lycée Saint-Louis. When all agreed, Bertrand moved to Paris in October 1887: "I went straight from my backwater into the most cultivated, the most intellectual circle of the capital." Eric had by then ascended from the Ecole des Sciences politiques to the Institut de France (French Institute), the summit of the French intellectual world. In his studies of history, "he had arrived at the conviction that there was no moral Truth, that the source of all moral concepts was purely *emotional*, that moral judgment has no other foundation than moral emotion, and that, in consequence, morality was identical with ethics and that its only purpose was to control the behavior of people in society." On Sundays, Madeleine—Aunt Ma—held her salon, and so Bertrand, only seventeen, was introduced to such towering intellectuals as Ernest Renan (specialist in ancient Middle Eastern civilizations and languages), Albert Sorel (historian of diplomacy and the French Revolution), Emile Boutmy (historian of constitutional law), Charles-Marie-René Leconte de Lisle (celebrated Parnassian poet), Marcelin Berthelot (founder of modern organic chemistry), and Ferdinand Brunetière (critic and historian of literature). "Reason enough," he recalled, "to be a bit disoriented!"[10]

Eric passed his days discoursing on the evolution of moral conceptions, consulting rare books at the Bibliothèque nationale, and carrying out research among the many volumes of his own library. For all of these tasks but especially ferreting through the apartment library, he depended on Xavier de Balcourt, who had returned to his studies after Bertrand left for Saint-Léonard. Yet despite his diligent inquiries and the brilliant insights of his lectures, Eric wrote little. Anxious to impress, he "talked his books instead of writing them." Aunt Ma encouraged this tendency because she valued connections and social influence above all. If she had instead devoted herself to "protecting his solitude and his work as a writer, he would have left behind one of the great oeuvres of the nineteenth century." But her "prodigious vitality" and "insatiable appetite for life" made any idea of seclusion uncongenial. Bertrand delighted in telling stories of her mirth: once when she and a friend were confronted by a man exposing himself to passersby, she exclaimed, "Thanks, my good man, but we've got better at home."[11]

The Ecole des Sciences politiques produced an educated elite—as opposed to the hereditary elite of previous monarchical regimes—that would govern a republican France. Eric taught his students what he now taught Bertrand, that nothing was "more essential than a lucid vision of what can be undertaken and of what exceeds our abilities." Once that lesson was learned, a new maturity was possible: "He gave me faith in myself, in my strength, which is to say the courage to strive. He taught me to correct my faults and not to be satisfied with concealing them. To feel at ease with myself; to be frank without either presumption or insolence; to know men and myself in such a way as to take others into account while not fearing, in certain areas, to pit myself against others." An important manifestation of this confidence for the republican elite of the "Sciences Po" was that among them, "Catholic faith, and practice, had no place." In the Perche region, "right-minded society" attended religious services, even when many of its members were more indifferent than devout, and regarded anyone who did not as "the dregs of the populace, a local disgrace, lawless people, a hotbed of rioters and agitators, capable of any crime." Bertrand realized that he "had completely changed atmospheres." Eric had no use for religion at all, and Aunt Ma, who had at least gone to Easter Mass until Guy's death, never forgave "God the dreadful blow He had dealt her."[12]

Reflecting on the decade from 1880 to 1890, Bertrand considered these republican elites practically demigods. His encomium is worth quoting at length: "that enlightened, liberal, reasonable, hardworking French intellectual society played a predominant role in Europe ... something like the light of the world. . . . It seems to me, though, that when I think of Uncle Eric's circle, that all the rest of my life has been spent in a world that failed to measure up, a world disrupted, incoherent, credulous, sectarian, passion-driven, and lacking in grandeur. By that decade, it seems to me, all beliefs had collapsed. Every problem posed by philosophy, science, religion, art, and sociology was again up for discussion. All those thinkers liked to point this out. Rightly or wrongly, they imagined themselves as part of the vanguard of a new, privileged humanity which was suddenly awakening, after centuries of trial and error, and which had at last arrived at the threshold of Truth. They believed in the progress of civilization, through knowledge and reason. Because, though they doubted everything, they still had their dogmas. They respected moral consciousness. They debated everything but in fact accepted as imperative those elementary rules of right and wrong that dictate our natural conscience, provided we are born with one." This elite was bourgeois, but rentier-bourgeois: "that upper level of the nineteenth-century bourgeoisie that had more respect for conscience and things of the mind than for money. . . . Most of them were neither poor nor rich; they generally scorned wealth but were much attached to their modest incomes, which freed them from material worries, provided they contented themselves with a restricted and orderly existence in which their only luxuries were those of the mind." Of course "disgruntled folk complained about the political mess, favoritism in high places, the waste of public funds, general slackness. . . . In reality, the Third Republic inspired trust and a sense of security. . . . Between 1875 and 1905, France lived under the freest regime, by far, that it has ever known—that any country, I believe, has ever known."[13]

But freedom expands the realm of license, and Bertrand illustrated this effect by interjecting an account of the pathetic end to Xavier de Balcourt. They could hardly avoid each other in the Chambost-Lévadé library, and soon enough Xavier confided, "You know, every man has two very distinct and often contradictory lives: his social life, that is to say his life in front of others, with his family, in the world; and then his secret life, or to put it bluntly, his sexual life, about which no one around him generally has the slightest inkling." About that secret life, from Le Saillant, Bertrand strongly suspected Xavier's homosexuality. And about that social life, Bertrand quickly recognized Xavier's manifold failings: "he knew enough about genius to realize that he had none, and also to be inconsolable about it"; "he criticized everything and everyone"; "he had a diabolical ingenuity for explaining away what had happened, for showing himself to be the victim, and finally, for extracting from those unfortunate circumstances the maximum of self-justification and self-esteem." Xavier was stalking his own doom—and he caught up with it while participating in a training exercise for his army reserve unit during the summer of 1888, about nine months after Bertrand had arrived in Paris. The soldiers were bivouacking in a village, Aunay-sur-Marne, and Xavier, a noncommissioned officer, found himself attracted to a baker's apprentice, seventeen, an orphan and ward of the state, an impressionable boy. Because one of the other bakery workers noticed and roughly threatened Xavier, he arranged to meet the boy secretly along the nearby river. When they mixed up their directions and wound up on opposite banks, the boy tried to swim across and drowned. Xavier thought nothing would come of this episode, but in September, a police inspector interrogated him based on a report by the boy's fellow worker. Terrified by what might happen—"my nights are simply a series of nightmares"—he committed suicide two months later.[14]

Having revealed Xavier's life, Bertrand revealed his own. Because he was a well-born, well-connected, financially secure young man about Paris, his contemporaries assumed that he had a certain level of sexual experience. He encouraged that supposition: "through veiled hints, knowing smiles, I did everything necessary to make people think that I had mistresses, and that it was due to my discretion that nobody could name any of them." In fact, Bertrand remained a virgin. He might have courted the "girls of the Latin

Quarter," but "to go to bed with one of them, I would have had to tell her that I loved her, and to prove it with a modicum of preliminary involvement. . . . But I had nothing but distaste for that romantic shamming. What I wanted was the initiatory possession, with no frills." At the same time, the example of so many literary heroes left him with an allure for a grand passion, and he almost succumbed. He felt strongly attracted to Pauline, the young wife of Eric's brother, Hector—as he had been to the wife of Nacquot—and because she was taken, let himself believe that he was falling in love with their daughter Eva. Although she was "silly and utterly devoid of any special gifts," "what I loved or thought I loved in her was not so much the child of sixteen that she was as the young woman, the fiancée, the bride she was to become. At the time I had this idea . . . of the malleable, teachable woman in her first bloom, whom the man marries for her charming freshness and of whom he makes, through the miracle of love, the ideal companion."[15]

Bertrand saved himself from this ethereal involvement by falling for its opposite, an intensely physical affair with an exotic woman from the French Antilles, Célie, called "Doudou" (Darling), and then later with her niece, Zabette. They lived in a crowded, rickety house on the Rue Mouffetard at the poor end of the Latin Quarter that was home to many in Paris's Martiniquais community. That first time for Bertrand was revelatory: "Although one may know everything about love in theory, how, without having experienced it, can one form an idea of what that burning penetration is, and that unknown sensation of two people becoming a single merged being." Célie was in her late twenties, another older woman, and she so captivated him that he did not at first have "to separate lovemaking from affection." And indeed, Bertrand's affair with aunt and niece ran on for nearly two years. But with time, he could not resist imposing bourgeois, white, European judgments: "Their faults and virtues are those of children. . . . The child's incapacity for steady application, prolonged effort, the fickleness of mood, the involuntary lack of concentration." And with this stricture, he eliminated even the possibility of respect: "The girls, as soon as they were nubile, were all willing to lose their virginity, and appeared to attach only a very relative price to it." As if to punctuate the end to his adolescence, Bertrand turned from the Rue Mouffetard and its easy delights to the rigors of Saint-Cyr and the preparation for a military career.[16]

That moment came in the autumn of 1889. By then Bertrand had completed his literature degree, but he never resolved the "deep duality" of his nature that left him "neither an officer with a great future nor a talented man of letters. Pulled in opposite direction, I spread myself thin. In the army as in literature, I was only an ambitious amateur." Always the outsider, he sensed the need for some form of incorporation and found it in the Saint-Gall family, which he came to know through friendship with its heir-in-waiting, Blaise, his fellow student in Greek at the Sorbonne. They met translating *The Bacchae* of Euripides and continued their studies first at the Chambost-Lévadé apartment and then at the Saint-Gall house nearby on the Rue Saint-Guillaume. For Bertrand, the initial attraction was the sense of ease that Blaise had and that he had not: "a supremely discreet elegance ... due, in part, to the naturalness of his manners, to that air he had of being perfectly, intrinsically comfortable with himself." But almost immediately, he was even more drawn to Blaise's large family, "where there was no spare time for withdrawing into oneself, for nursing one's selfishness, for becoming the center of the world ... I could not help comparing my childhood, my life at Le Saillant, the mood of my father's house, with what I had glimpsed of the Saint-Galls's existence. And all of a sudden I realized the austerity of my youth." When Blaise brought him to La Popelière, the Saint-Galls's rambling country retreat at Melun, to the southeast of Paris, Bertrand found "an atmosphere of noisy cheerfulness, like a perpetual party ... people who were happy simply to be reunited in a setting that they loved, and who had no mistrust of one another." Of course, he fell in love with Blaise's twin sister, the devoutly Catholic Laure. And of course, Laure had already accepted her vocation to become a nun.[17]

While a cadet at Saint-Cyr and then an officer at Versailles, Bertrand had a "tortured relationship" with a young married woman, Raphaële Dancenis. When the affair was over in the fall of 1892, he was drawn back to the Saint-Gall family when Blaise contracted typhoid fever. He found his friend's younger sister, Claire, deeply apprehensive and comforted her. And so began a courtship. Claire was now eighteen and lovely: "her Nordic fairness, her baby's complexion, her smooth skin, her pale, gray-blue, astonishingly limpid gaze, her frail and graceful body, her little hands, her brisk and mischievous movements, her smile like a beaming child's, her dazzling teeth." Foolishly, Bertrand thought her docile: "She was always easy to live with, even-tempered, smiling, accepting me as I was without appearing to suffer from it." And so he married her. The following year, in 1895, she gave birth to a son, Didier, and in 1898, to a second, Alain. By then, he had learned that she was "headstrong, unswerving, and of rocklike solidity. No influence, no argument, no amount of shared living, of common interest or thought, had the slightest effect on that gemstone."[18]

This realization came three years into their marriage, in 1897, with Claire expecting their second child. Bertrand was stationed in northeastern Algeria. Claire had undergone her first pregnancy and delivery there in conditions that were primitive compared to Paris. She was unwilling to do so again and did not hesitate to go home. When Bertrand joined her just before Alain was born, he realized that the "months of separation had allowed us to reassume our own personalities, I as a bachelor officer in an African garrison, she by returning to the fold and plunging back into her origins, putting herself once again under the collective tutelage of the clan." He began to resent the "family yoke" he had once admired because he recognized that Claire could "bloom and be happy" only when she was surrounded by the Saint-Galls and that the most he could ever offer her would be "the trials of a kind of exile." After Alain's birth in 1898, Claire remained in Paris, and Bertrand returned to North Africa: "We never loved each other so well as with the Mediterranean between us." Claire died suddenly in 1904, when she was barely thirty, from a pulmonary infection. Didier and Alain each met death during the Great War, Didier at nineteen, Alain at twenty. Alone in his old age, Bertrand pondered his choices and his fate. Blaise, from whom he had grown distant, lived long enough to see several of his grandchildren married and to preside over a family dinner for seventy guests, forty-six of them born Saint-Gall. By contrast, Bertrand knew for certain, "I shall take to my grave the last trace of the Maumorts on this earth . . . I shall take with me everything I know of my kin, everything I know of myself, all my memories, all my experience. Nothing will remain of the Maumorts."[19]

Nothing would remain of the Maumorts not because Claire, Didier, and Alain were dead but because Henriette, his sister, also died during the Great War, in June 1917 after a series of heart attacks. She was the only person in Bertrand's life for whom he truly felt "exceptional intimacy." When their father died in 1894 after years of torment from a bladder disease, Henriette hoped that Bertrand would resign his commission and return to Le Saillant, where they could manage the estate together. Instead, he married Claire Saint-Gall and went off to Algeria. Some four years later, when his Dreyfusard opinions made him enemies among his fellow officers and offended the piously conservative Saint-Galls, he did come back to Le Saillant. Where else could he go? To be rid of him, the army granted Bertrand a leave for two years. The Saint-Galls, other than Claire and his sons, refused to see him at all. Initially, he thought he had left the army forever, but by 1900, the pardon granted Alfred Dreyfus and new leadership among the high command who purged the worst of the bigots and reactionaries drew him back. Even so, the choice was hard because he and Henriette had together restored Le Saillant after their father's neglect. During "those two years of daily closeness, of collaboration, of shared responsibility," they had discovered such a "deep-seated communion" that until she died, their "dearest dream was one day to resume our sibling partnership."[20]

The year after their father's death, the year after Bertrand had married Claire and taken up an assignment in Algeria, Henriette startled him with the news that she was going to marry a neighbor, Viscount Adolphe de

Pontbrun. Bertrand thought the choice incomprehensible: despite the noble title, the Pontbrun family lived in penury nearby on a dilapidated property, and Adolphe, three years older than Henriette at thirty-seven, was thin, sickly, and possessed of an ugliness that was "certainly remarkable but not without a certain distinction." Yes, he was a pious Catholic, as was Henriette, and his almost pathetic weakness made her want to nurse him, as she had Bertrand as a child and their father during his painful sickness. But Bertrand eventually suspected that the marriage was an act "of disappointment and perhaps of pique" at his refusal to remain with her at Le Saillant. She quickly conceived a child, a daughter, Anna, who was born prematurely in the spring of 1896 and lived only two months. Adolphe died the following November. Was Bertrand thinking of himself or his sister when he reacted to this news with "tremendous joy. . . . I took it as a gesture of courteousness, of tact. His presence in the family had poisoned my thoughts, but when you came right down to it, he really hadn't overstayed his welcome, and he withdrew like a perfect gentleman."[21]

When Bertrand returned to the army in 1900 after two years with Henriette, he was deserting her for a second time. Just before he was to go, they let themselves be caught up in a complicated situation. About five years before, one of their tenant farmers had taken in a baby girl, Emma, given up to the Bureau of Social Assistance by an unwed mother. Now, with the foster mother dead, Henriette agreed to care for Emma temporarily. But fearing the isolation of living alone at Le Saillant, she soon thought of doing much more, of becoming Emma's guardian, perhaps even of adopting her. Believing that he could go off "with a lighter heart if I had left Henriette with a daughter to raise," Bertrand supported leaving Emma in her hands but won a formal promise that any adoption should be delayed until ten years had passed. Once Bertrand took up his assignment—with the 14th Hussars, light cavalry, not far away at Alençon—Henriette began to treat her like "the young lady of the château," not just as the daughter she had lost, but as a kind of fancy doll. When Bertrand saw Emma again some months later while on leave, he found her unrecognizable: new clothes, new manners, "a sort of ludicrous self-consciousness," and "concerned with what was due her." He learned from Henriette herself that local opinion was unanimously against her having transformed this "fruit of some illicit affair." Everyone, whether gentry, petty bourgeois, or common folk, agreed that it was "an act of revolt against the sacred laws of the family, against the laws of nature, against custom."[22]

Bertrand was embarrassed for himself, as a Maumort, but more so for Henriette, whose "beautiful clear-sightedness which never spared anything or anyone" now seemed clouded. He worried that "she was no longer my

Henriette." He should not have, because when he came back to Le Saillant fifteen months later, he found her fixation had abated. Had she been influenced by the ugly gossip? Had she realized that her interest in Emma was a reaction, almost a whim, to Bertrand's leaving? Or had Emma simply failed to meet her expectations? The girl had not so much "grown" as "thickened." She could not keep up with her class at school. She seemed happiest doing simple chores and helping out in the kitchen. Henriette had replaced her fine clothes with plain cotton shifts. Bertrand was relieved: "my sister had recovered her balance." To maintain that balance, Henriette pushed Emma further away, took her out of school and gave her increasingly menial tasks. She was not quite a servant, but she was Henriette's special chambermaid. Bertrand was not there to see what was happening because he spent the years from 1904 to 1914 in the military campaigns for control of Morocco, with only brief leaves in 1909 and 1913. He did note that more than ten years had passed since Emma had entered Le Saillant and that Henriette no longer had any interest in adoption.[23]

When the Great War began in 1914, Henriette helped establish an auxiliary hospital for wounded soldiers in nearby Menneville and took charge of running it herself. Emma went with her and became a nurse. For the next thirty months, Henriette hardly left the hospital except twice to meet Bertrand, when he had leave to Paris in the fall of 1915 and the summer of 1916. This overtaxing devotion broke her health. In April 1917, she suffered a serious heart attack and was transported to a clinic at Le Mans. More faithful than Henriette deserved, Emma followed and cared for her. Despite all efforts to stabilize her condition, she had a series of new minor attacks leading to a second acute one in mid-June that took her life. The state of the war eliminated any possibility that Bertrand could go to Le Mans earlier, and he did not even realize the gravity of her condition because Henriette insisted that Emma send only optimistic news. He learned of her death while his regiment was on the front line: "The brigadier-general ... offered to let me quit my post for three days. I refused. The men were worn out from six weeks of combat without any real replacements. The onslaughts kept coming constantly. Our positions were shelled every night.... Perhaps I would have hesitated if it had been a matter of seeing my sister alive one last time." In his place, Emma notified Aunt Ma, a widow since Eric had died in 1905. She brought Henriette's body back to Le Saillant and arranged for the funeral.[24]

Bertrand learned all these details in a letter from Aunt Ma, who added that Emma was beginning a novitiate with a nursing order of nuns in Le Mans. Bertrand never saw either of them again, Aunt Ma because she died in 1918 before the Armistice, Emma because the order sent her to Lyon after she took her vows. He had good reason not to seek contact. When he went through

Henriette's desk, he found a notebook in which she had carefully recorded every expenditure for Emma, not just for her education and clothing or the added cost of food but even for "bars of soap and the resoling of a pair of shoes." On the first page, she had written, "*To be given to Emma after my death.*" If Bertrand had obeyed this injunction, Emma would have learned that Henriette had calculated the price of taking her in for sixteen years at approximately one hundred twenty thousand francs ($518,200 in 2015). Bertrand felt a chill as he turned the pages, realizing that Henriette must have harbored "an obscure desire for some sort of revenge, a wish to humiliate her ward." Because he loved his sister, he absolved her through this casuistry: she had never revealed her antipathy while alive. But of course, he did not send the notebook to Emma.[25]

By then, Bertrand's military career was over. Half a year after Henriette's death, a serious shrapnel wound to his knee required treatment for two months at the hospital in Compiègne. Left lame, he was assigned to an office at the Ministry of War in Paris and there would learn that his younger son, Alain, died in battle near the end of September 1918, just ten weeks before the Armistice. A year later in 1919, Bertrand retired as a lieutenant colonel, the rank he had attained in 1916. He was only forty-nine years old.

Roger never prepared even drafts of the chapters that would have covered Bertrand's years as an officer. He did leave substantial notes for the years in North Africa, 1894 to 1914, with a gap from 1898 to 1904. For the Great War, he left barely an outline, not even a sketch. Based on these notes, Bertrand chose his military career as "a way to live usefully, within an established order," combining the notion of duty from his father and admiration for the Third Republic from Uncle Eric and his colleagues. He had a soldier's devotion: "disciplined, full of abnegation, virtue, humility, dedicated to the point of totally renouncing his own will, mystically accepting the hardest sacrifice for the sake of his ideal." But in the Dreyfus Affair, the army betrayed everything that he, as a Dreyfusard, wished to defend. Understanding that "his homeland was represented by justice rather than the army," he asked for and received the two years of leave from 1898 to 1900 and planned to resign without returning. The political triumph of the Dreyfusard cause that led to a thorough purge of the high command tempted him back. What confirmed him in his decision was serving at Alençon as a captain of the hussars under then-Colonel Lyautey, who combined aesthetic sensibilities with military and organizational skill. From 1894 to 1897, Lyautey had destroyed the threat of piracy off the coast of Indochina. From 1897 to 1902, he had suppressed a revolt in the northern and western parts of Madagascar. But beforehand in the late 1880s and early 1890s, Lyautey had a reputation in Paris salons for exquisite taste and literary ambitions. He was also a friend of Pierre Desjardins, who would later organize the Pontigny retreats. At Alençon, not long after Bertrand joined him with the hussars, he received promotion to brigadier-general.[26]

Lyautey knew well that he was soon to receive a new colonial assignment and saw in Bertrand exactly the kind of cultured yet disciplined officer he wanted for his staff. And in August 1904, when he assumed command of the Algerian-Moroccan Division at Aïn-Sefra, the center for military operations along the border with Morocco, he requested that Bertrand accompany him. In turn, Bertrand admired Lyautey because "he never let himself be mastered by circumstances. They were for him what cards are for the gambler: external factors, unmodifiable, which life flung at him and which he seized upon immediately without vain recriminations." He was, in this fashion, the "implementer only of the 'possible,'" a tactician rather than a strategist. But he did have one strategy to which he clung throughout his many years of securing the French empire: "the aim was not to destroy the enemy but to pacify him. . . . Military action was only a way to commence political action." From the moment Lyautey took command at Aïn-Sefra, he pushed the limits of his authority. Ostensibly defending the rail line from the southwestern interior to the coast, he sent his troops into formally independent Morocco and occupied the border town of Béchar. When the Moroccan sultan protested, the French government backed Lyautey, promoted him to major-general, and made him military governor at Oran. Beginning in 1907, he launched new attacks, compelled trade concessions, and imposed a large measure of French control throughout much of Morocco. His reward this time was the title high commissioner of these territories, with his headquarters in Casablanca. Because military tensions were rising in Europe, he was brought back to France in 1909 as an army corps commander at Rennes. Three years later when a new sultan led an insurrection against French control, Lyautey returned to Morocco to crush it and impose a formal protectorate under his rule as resident-general.[27]

Always at Lyautey's side except for the two years at Rennes, Bertrand was in North Africa from 1904 to 1914 and was promoted to major. Based on Roger's notes, he "took part in the Moroccan campaigns with the youthful ardor of a crusader, convincing myself that our conquering armies were bringing peace, justice, and order and that we were missionaries of civilization." As a leader, "I cultivated in myself that secret strength of assurance, that energy, will, decisiveness, unbending perseverance in execution, which has a hold on others and compels their immediate trust. . . . I don't know if I had courage, but I *displayed* it, and that is all that is required." As a soldier, he believed in the "fraternity of arms": "it is something other than love, friendship, camaraderie, something different from family feeling or the bond among schoolmates. It exists only after danger has been faced together." Yet Bertrand was a soldier on his own terms: "I passed for a dissident, though I never showed any hostile resistance to my superiors. But they felt that I could do without them, that I was not 'part of the family,' and they did not forgive me for it." And in a note Daspre found with the account of Xavier de Balcourt and the baker's apprentice, Roger has Bertrand declare, "*Personally, I have no inclination toward homosexuality,*" but then confess, "My rare homosexual adventures were always due to the hazards of life in North Africa ... isolated at his post for many weeks, an officer in his thirties may succumb to the temptation offered by a young boy passing through on a caravan."[28]

When the Great War began in August 1914, Bertrand returned to France and joined the staff of the First Cavalry Corps at Saint-Quentin. These forces protected the French retreat from Charleroi in the last week of August and then were heavily engaged in the Battle of the Marne during the first and second weeks of September, when the German advance was halted. Shortly afterward, Bertrand learned that his elder son, Didier, had died in the military hospital at Meaux after being wounded on patrol. Only nineteen years old, he had not waited to be drafted and had volunteered for a combat unit. For the next three years, until Henriette's death in June 1917, Roger left only a brief chronology. Bertrand spent from late 1914 until early 1915 in the Woëvre and the Eparges region, the site of terrible fighting in Lorraine. That summer, he took command of a dragoon squadron, mounted infantry, and was fortunate that his sector remained quiet. A year later in 1916, with the uselessness of cavalry in trench warfare finally apparent, they were reassigned to simple infantry regiments. Promoted to lieutenant colonel, Bertrand led one of them to the front and had just endured a horrific six weeks of combat when he learned that his sister was dead.[29]

Roger prepared no drafts of the chapters that would have covered Bertrand for the next twenty-one years, the 1920s and 1930s. As with the Great War, he left only an outline, but some references from the material about the Second World War offer hints. When Bertrand returned to Le Saillant in the spring of 1919, he had a solitary life: "He is alone in the world: he has lost his wife, his two sons, his sister; he has neither relatives nor friends." Although lame, he could still ride a horse and oversee the estate. He spent most of his time reading, Aunt Ma having left him Eric's library of eighteen thousand books. The experience of the Great War excited a fascination for changing tactics and technology. Over time, he published several articles in military journals such as the *Bulletin des questions stratégiques* (Bulletin of Strategic Questions) criticizing the "inferiority" of France's air force, the "insufficiency" of its armored units, and "the conventional notions" of the high command. In early 1935, when he was sixty-four, his horse slipped on black ice, and he was thrown, breaking his pelvis. Even after months of recovery at a clinic in Le Mans, he had difficulty walking and could never again mount a horse. He gave oversight of the estate to the longtime tenant farm families and became evermore reclusive.[30]

Beginning with the disaster of 1940, the finished, even polished, chapters of *Maumort* resume. From that moment in the middle of a sleepless night when Roger conceived the novel, he knew that it had to begin with the Germans occupying Le Saillant and Bertrand retreating to his library and recollecting his past. Roger had always granted Bertrand clarity of vision while burdening him with a judgmental temperament. Inevitably, Bertrand could draw from the illusions of the 1920s and the disillusions of the 1930s only a severe pessimism. The rout of French forces did not surprise him. On June 14, he watched the flight before the German advance: "the wealthiest in cars, the others in carts, and then the dusty, exhausted pedestrians, limping along, pushing wheelbarrows or baby carriages loaded down with clothes ... mixed in with the civilians, soldiers of various divisions ... were wandering aimlessly, leaderless and orderless, and several had neither rifle nor gear ... it was upon seeing them that I truly understood how vain was all hope." The Germans could not be far behind, and Bertrand's valet, Bocca, who had followed him from military service, suggested, "If I were you, *mon colonel*, I certainly know what I would do. . . . I'd put on my uniform."[31]

Yes, Bertrand would. Three days later on the morning of June 17, when a German officer leading a large squadron of men knocked at the front door of Le Saillant, he opened it wearing a hussar's red breeches, frogged dolman, kepi circled with braid, and patent-leather boots. The Germans acted with respect toward this fellow soldier, but they made clear that they were taking possession of the château for a local command center. Although Bertrand was to remain in their custody, they graciously offered him the use of one wing, including the library, for his internment. Once he was alone, "a flood of impotent rage rose in my throat. . . . I remember I was standing over there, in front of the stove in the fireplace; I put my elbows on the marble, held my head between my fists, and squeezed my eyelids tight to keep from crying." That same night, Philippe Pétain, newly named prime minister, announced that he was seeking an armistice. During the next months, Bertrand stayed in his wing with the windows and curtains closed: he did not want to see the swastika flying above his courtyard. He could read and write and sleep, but he felt "like a wounded beast caught in a trap. . . . At my age, you get used to almost everything, I think, except humiliation." Then, near the end of the summer, Dr. Gévresin, one of the few friends Bertrand had made in retirement, managed to smuggle him a letter from the Vichy Zone. Now at Piérac, in the Lot region about two hundred and fifty miles away, Gévresin wrote that he was putting together a resistance group and hoped that Bertrand would join him.[32]

Even as Bertrand contemplated escape, he was betrayed by his seventy-year-old body. In mid-October, he fainted, fell hard, and was placed in a cast for three weeks as a precaution against unknown injuries. Obviously, he could no longer care for himself. Until then, he had refused all contact with his German captors, but as some of them assisted him, he could not avoid conversation. In this artificial manner, Roger contrived the discussions about Nazism that he believed necessary to demonstrate Bertrand's intellectual side. He began them with Gralt, a medical orderly, who defined Nazism as the antithesis to individualism: "For us, liberty is not, as here, the right of everyone to do whatever seems good to him; liberty is, for each of us, the sense of belonging, of feeling deeply that we are forming an integral part of a nation that is truly free because it is strong." And of Germany's atrocities in Poland, "a few injustices, a few cruelties, a few crimes even, are only incidental, and in no way alter the greatness and legitimacy of a heroic life." Roger wondered, "Is it by virtue of his 'will to power' that he deserves to reign over the planet? Is it in conquest and domination alone that he must find his reason for living, and is there no other happiness for him than in the 'heroic' life leading to success, to victory through daring and battle rather than through right?" Gralt at least offered an argument, while Kert, the commander's adjutant, merely sneered that "German hegemony is legitimate because Germany is the only great nation that is virile and young." And if Gralt felt the need to justify the horrors perpetrated in Eastern Europe, Kert smiled when Bertrand told him angrily that "all the injustices of history and the horrors of the barbarian invasions themselves would seem like peccadilloes to those who will study the campaign of the Nazi armies in Poland."[33]

Bertrand's longest discussions, and the ones that shocked him most, were with Dr. Frank Weissmüller, the physician who treated him after his fall. Weissmüller insisted that "the extinction of the weak is a natural law, of vital importance for humanity. ... The future will belong to the races that not only give free play to natural selection but also foster and hasten its effects by the deliberate, rational elimination of the mentally retarded and physically disabled. Insane asylums, homes for the incurable are social nonsense." Bertrand's answer would have made Uncle Eric proud: "the whole effort of civilization has consisted of a struggle of man against the brutal laws of nature and ... all the progress accomplished by intelligence and reason has been reached through fighting against natural instincts." Weissmüller made clear where he would have stood in the Dreyfus Affair: "In France you think all is lost if your famous *republican liberties* are compromised, or only muzzled by someone in power. As if authority and discipline were intolerable shackles! ... The German, on the other hand, not only is unafraid to submit to the orders of a just and enlightened chief, but wants to, because he is aware that he will find in him a prop against his weakness and a way of fulfilling his potential to the maximum." One day, Bertrand noticed him staring at the library shelves and later asked Gralt if Weissmüller might want to borrow some book. Gralt smirked, "You know the comment he made to me? He said: 'How can someone clutter up his house, and even his bedroom with all that printed trash?'"[34]

In an alternative version of *Maumort* that Roger prepared, Bertrand never had any of these discussions because he slipped away in late August to join Gévresin in the Lot when the rotation of occupying German units left Le Saillant temporarily "free of its locusts." Presumably, he helped to organize sabotage and guerrilla operations, but unfortunately, Roger left behind not even a note about them. Regarding the necessity for such "resistance," Bertrand had not a doubt: The Vichy government was "an irreparable political error; it ruled under the barely veiled supervision of the enemy ... 'collaboration' might have been favorably received by French minds more eager for concord than revenge if Germany had been prudent enough to hide its secrets better. But with such an onslaught of deliberate, organized, legalized cruelty, how would the French conscience, how would any human conscience, not have rebelled? ... Make no mistake about it: even more than patriotism or the call of liberty, it is *indignation* that aroused the whole of France against Nazi barbarity! The Resistance really was the kernel of France, the enduring heart of the motherland."[35]

In this alternative version, Bertrand returned to Le Saillant after the Liberation and between the end of December 1944 and the middle of January 1945 wrote Gévresin nine letters. Daspre let them stand alone in his reconstitution of the novel: in form and content, they do not fit the rest of Bertrand's recollections, but they provide precious information otherwise missing in the rest of the material. On several note cards attached to the manuscript of these letters, Roger finally offered a physical description of his protagonist: tall, lean, partially deaf, nearsighted and occasionally using a monocle, white hair, weathered complexion, and the face of "an old Punchinello"—high forehead, bushy brows, pale eyes, aquiline nose, thin lips, jutting chin, gaunt neck and prominent larynx. In one letter, Bertrand described the damage done to Le Saillant by the Germans and the effort to make preliminary repairs, an account remarkably similar to Roger's own experience at Le Tertre. In another, he described how he lost his diaries and letters: before the Germans arrived, he and Bocca carefully hid them in the wall of the wine cellar, but a clogged drain pipe caused seepage that reduced them to "a mucky mess, a shapeless and stinking amalgam."[36]

The last four letters revealed Bertrand disillusioned over the loss of a world that had been his and perfectly willing to accept a death that would spare his having to witness worse. He complained: "Mediocrity, even a certain baseness, has spread like an oil stain, laxly tolerated in the widespread lassitude. In every domain, spiritual values are in decline, weakened, unappreciated, yet never have they been more indispensable for holding in check those evil forces—violence, money—which triumph openly and divert mankind not only from a considered effort to recover its balance, but also from a valid conception of the future." He recognized inevitability: "Like it or not, our path is the one that history lays out for us. Well, for quite a while now, and especially for the last quarter of a century, the path has taken a turn; and I haven't wanted to see it, I haven't been willing to follow the turn." And he explained: "What have I been, my whole life, when you come right down to it? A sort of outcast. Without essential affinities, without ties. . . . And I have instinctively chosen most of my friends from among 'outcasts' like me: born, usually, into the well-to-do class but having rejected its prejudices and its faults, and kept nothing but certain rules of courtesy, a certain way of behaving in one's relations with oneself and others, a certain knack for humor, a certain notion of moral elegance and of honor, an aesthetic rather than an ethic." So: "Tomorrow no longer has any appeal for me. No use striving in vain. . . . I no longer have any desires, not even to die soon. I await my death in a barely conscious passivity."[37]

How Bertrand might have come to die in this alternative version is unknowable. Because he left the ninth letter unfinished, Luc Brébion and Timothy Crouse have imagined his suffering a fatal stroke as he slept, and for their English translation of *Maumort*, they composed "a tentative ending for the epistolary version of the novel." If so, Bertrand's death took place in January 1945, when he was seventy-four years old. Perhaps the darkness and pessimism of the Gévresin letters arose from their having been written when Roger himself was profoundly melancholic. His original plan, set forth in the outline of the novel more than a decade earlier, was for Bertrand to live until 1950, when he was eighty. This Bertrand would rage less and accept more even as he demanded to die not on death's terms but his own. The proof comes from two fragments that Daspre placed in a brief section entitled "Epilogue." Nearing the end of his life, Bertrand insists, "I have known painful griefs, hard ordeals. . . . I have lived in great solitude; nevertheless, if I look back I have no complaints about how fate has treated me; I even feel that I have everything I could have wished for. . . . Why should we be ashamed of our defeats? Nothing is more foolish, unless it is to glory in our successes." And having reached that end, having suffered a stroke from which he had made a slight recovery but fearful of another, "he prepares his suicide by gas. The note he leaves on his table, near the envelope containing his will: 'Why extend the reprieve? Tomorrow can only be worse. I am cutting short the wait. Farewell to all.'"[38]

Naturally enough, Roger's own experiences influenced his perception of Bertrand's, and he drew from them in many ways for *Maumort*. He turned Le Tertre into Le Saillant, the apartment building on the Rue du Dragon into the Saint-Gall house on the Rue Saint-Guillaume, and the Château de Roquefort where he and Hélène briefly took wartime shelter outside Figeac into the ruined manor occupied by the Pontbrun family. He certainly appears to have borrowed teaching principles from Louis Mellerio for Nacquot, adamantine conviction from Hélène for Claire Saint-Gall, predatory homosexuality from Gide for Xavier de Balcourt, and racial prejudice toward the Martiniquais from himself for Bertrand. According to Daspre, he based Eric Chambost-Lévadé on Paul Desjardins, and the fidelity of Bertrand's valet Bocca likely had its origin in the loyal service of Baptiste at Le Tertre. When Roger conceived the structure of the Maumort family, he all but duplicated that of the Thibaults: siblings, Henriette and Bertrand, nine years apart like Antoine and Jacques, growing up with an overbearing father guilt-ridden because his wife died from the birth of their second child. Finally, for Bertrand's military career, he had the model of his friend Emile Mayer, who was an outspoken artillery officer and Dreyfusard, lost both his sons at the beginning of the Great War, retired afterward as a lieutenant colonel, and protested, without much effect, the failures of French military preparations during the 1930s.[39]

For the inner Bertrand, Roger had himself, however much he sometimes appeared to resist. In his life and in his novels, the fundamental problem was the derivation of meaning in a world without God. He had abandoned religion as an adolescent, and his disdain for its imperatives distorted his marriage to Hélène. Yet two of his closest friends were priests: when young, Abbé Marcel Hébert, and when old, Jesuit Father Auguste Valensin. In *Jean Barois* and in *Les Thibault*, Abbé Lévys and Abbé Vécard, respectively, play notable, even noble, roles. At the height of his powers, in 1928, before the calamities of Christiane's marriage, the Great Depression, and the New Year's Day crash, Roger wrote his friend Félix Sartiaux, "I sense the terrible fragility of moral customs, moral appearances, this thin moral mask, and I deny with despair that morality can be founded on anything other than religion. Anyone who claims to do so is uttering hollow phrases." So how was Bertrand, who had also lost his faith as an adolescent, to find meaning when not just lives but an entire civilization would be wrecked before his eyes on the shoals of history?[40]

Roger left no definitive answer, but in the Black Box reflections, he asserted the imperative of the individual conscience against the vagaries of fate. He had Bertrand meditate on the role of contingency: "The most crucial events leading to irrevocable decisions almost always arise from some insignificant chance circumstances, from a fortuitous encounter. ... The most cautious, the most deliberate life is still a blind walk." And in reaction, he encouraged Bertrand's "fundamental tendency to withdraw into myself, to be concerned with my development; to question myself and to observe myself living; to be sufficient unto myself; to be more interested in myself than in anything else." And because he was "*self-centered*," he could suffer his losses—the failure of his marriage, the lack of distinction either as a soldier or as an intellectual, the early deaths of his wife, sons, and sister, his long years of loneliness—"with a minimum of inner torment and despair ... because, losing everything, I was still left with myself." This radical individualism risked becoming solipsistic: "all agreement between two people is, to a greater or lesser degree, but always, always *the result of a misunderstanding*. One of the bitterest, most indigestible, most difficult truths to accept." Or selfish: "The best of marriages is a purgatory. Definition of a purgatory: a hell that is not eternal." Above all, solitary: "I was only at ease when withdrawn and alone in my shell, like a snail."[41]

From that desperate isolation, Roger granted Bertrand the right to decide: "One has to accept oneself, ... Everything is allowed, on the condition that one can, in everything that one allows oneself, keep one's self-esteem and feel that, in doing so, one remains true to oneself and to one's real nature. What do the rules dictated by standard morality matter? ... At bottom, I have always obeyed *my* law, defended *my* truth, followed *my* morality, without, however, openly infringing *the* accepted law, truth, morality." Yes, "the contradiction is to love life, instinctively to judge it precious, and yet be forced, by one's reason, to deem it bad, incoherent, absurd. It may be in this contradiction that the whole force of life resides, and life itself."[42] Secure in that mystery, neither Bertrand nor Roger had need of ultimate truth and could die without expectation.

Notes

To provide dollar values for francs, I have adopted the following procedure. Using the table from the Institut national de la Statistique et des etudes économiques: Pouvoir d'achat de l'euro et de franc (February 1, 2011), available at www.insee.fr, I have first converted francs to euros. Then, I have converted euros to dollars using the coefficient 1.36, which is higher than the current conversion ratio but comes closer to the true values of the past.

Whenever I have quoted Martin du Gard from his journal or his correspondence, the translation from French to English is mine. Whenever I have quoted Martin du Gard from his literary works, the translation is from the English-language edition.

CHAPTER I

1. Horst Frenz, ed., *Literature 1901–1967*, Nobel Lectures (Amsterdam: Elsevier, 1969), 343, 349.

2. Roger Martin du Gard (hereafter cited as RMdG), *Le Lieutenant-Colonel de Maumort*, edition établie par André Daspre (Paris: Gallimard, 1983), 32; translated by Luc Brébion and Timothy Crouse as *Lieutenant-Colonel de Maumort* (New York: Alfred A. Knopf, 2000), 27. Citations from the novel are for both the French and English versions, as in this instance: 32/27.

3. Roger Martin du Gard, *Journal*, ed. Claude Sicard, 3 vols. (Paris: Gallimard, 1992–1993), 1:16.

4. RMdG, *Journal*, 1:19–38, quotations from 1:27, 37, 38.

5. RMdG, *Journal*, 1:38–42, quotations from 1:41, 42–43.

6. The relationship between RMdG and Abbé Marcel Hébert was one of those enduring friendships between mentor and student much encouraged by nineteenth-century French Catholic schools: see Carol E. Harrison, *Romantic Catholics: France's Postrevolutionary Generation in Search of a Modern Faith* (Ithaca, NY: Cornell University Press, 2014), the chapter titled "The Education of Maurice de Guérin," especially 79–88; RMdG, *Journal*, 1:57–58, quotation from 1:57.

7. RMdG, *Journal*, 1:59–65, quotation from 1:64.

8. RMdG, *Journal*, 1:66–67, quotations from 1:112–13, RMdG to Gustave Valmont, March 29, 1902.

9. RMdG, *Journal*, 1:69–118, quotations from 1:72, RMdG to Valmont, August 14, 1900; 1:90–91, RMdG to Valmont, September 26, 1990; 1:118, Valmont to RMdG, August 12, 1902; of the 591 letters in their correspondence, RMdG wrote 309, Valmont 282.

10. RMdG, *Journal*, 1:99–123, quotations from 1:99, RMdG to Valmont, July 23, 1901; 1:102, RMdG to Valmont, August 18, 1901; 1:123, RMdG to Valmont, September 1, 1902.

11. RMdG, *Journal*, 1:129–39, quotation from 1:137, RMdG to Madeleine Martin du Gard, August 30, 1903; Roger Martin du Gard, *Correspondance générale*, ed.

Maurice Rieuneau, Jean-Claude Airal, et al., 10 vols. (Paris: Gallimard, 1980–2006), 1:21, from the introduction by Rieuneau.

12. RMdG, *Journal*, 1:116–17, 140–45, quotations from 1:116, RMdG to Valmont, May 18, 1902; 1:142, statement by Marcel Martin du Gard to Marie Rougier in June 1960; 1:141, RMdG to Valmont, September 23, 1903; 1:142, Valmont to RMdG, September 24, 1903; 1:143, Marcel de Coppet to RMdG, end of September 1903.

13. RMdG, *Journal*, 1:157–72, quotations from 1:167, RMdG to Valmont, October 6, 1904; 1:172, note by Sicard; 1:159, statement by Marcel Martin du Gard to Sicard in April 1965; 1:162, statement by Marcel Martin du Gard to Marie Rougier in June 1960.

14. RMdG, *Journal*, 1:173–77, quotations from 1:175, RMdG to Valmont, September 5, 1905; 1:177, RMdG to Valmont, September 20, 1905.

15. RMdG, *Journal*, 1:181, diary of Hélène Foucault, February 18, 1906.

16. RMdG, *Journal*, 1:186–25, quotations from 1:186, RMdG to Valmont, March 8, 1906; 1:187, RMdG to Valmont, April 16, 1906, for "Une vie de saint"; 1:189–93, RMdG to Coppet, June 21, 1906, on "Une vie de saint"; 1:208–09, Valmont to RMdG, February 15, 1907, for negative reading; 1:195, RMdG to Valmont, July 18, 1906; 1:208, RMdG to Valmont, February 11, 1907; 1:214–15, RMdG to Coppet, April 15, 1907; 1:221–22, RMdG to Valmont, July 12, 1907; 1:224–25, RMdG to Coppet, July 24, 1907.

17. RMdG, *Journal*, 1:236–38, quotations from 1:237–238, RMdG to Coppet, February 11, 1908.

18. RMdG, *Journal*, 1:191–94, 245–47, quotations from 1:194, RMdG to Valmont, June 30, 1906; 1:247, RMdG to Coppet, April 28, 1908.

19. RMdG, *Journal*, 1:248–81, quotations from 1:248–49, RMdG to Coppet, May 23, 1908; 1:250, Coppet to RMdG, June 9, 1908; 1:281 for the strain between RMdG and Valmont.

20. RMdG, *Journal*, 1:265–66, quotations from 1:266, RMdG to Madeleine Martin du Gard, June 12, 1909; 1:265, RMdG to Coppet, June 9, 1909.

21. On "Marise," see RMdG, *Journal*, 1:272–74, RMdG to Coppet, September 4, 1909; *L'une de nous* appeared in 1910; for *Jean Barois*, RMdG, *Journal*, 1:296, quotations from 1:296, RMdG to Coppet, March 15, 1910; 1:296, RMdG to Coppet, February 27, 1910.

22. RMdG, *Journal*, 1:300–301, RMdG to Valmont, May 8, 1910; 1:337–38, RMdG to Coppet, May 10, 1911.

23. RMdG, *Journal*, 1:338, 339, 341, RMdG to Coppet, May 10, 1911; 1:304, RMdG to Coppet, May 16, 1910.

24. RMdG, *Journal*, 1:352–53, RMdG to Coppet, September 19, 1911; 1:362, entry dated February 1912, "A la Bibliothèque nationale" (At the National Library); 1:361, RMdG to Coppet, April 25, 1912.

25. RMdG, *Journal*, 1:405–6, entry for April 12, 1912; 1:403, entry for March 10, 1913; 1:409, entry for June 15, 1913.

26. RMdG, *Journal*, 1:410–26, quotations from 1:410–12, RMdG to Pierre Margaritis, July 3, 1913, citing Grasset to RMdG, June 17, 1913, Schlumberger to RMdG, July 1, 1913, and André Gide to Schlumberger, July 3, 1913. Proust's *Swann's Way* was the first volume of his *A la recherche du temps perdu* (*In search of Lost Time*), the seven volumes published between 1913 and 1927.

27. This verbatim recapitulation of *Jean Barois* is taken, with permission, from Benjamin Franklin Martin, *Years of Plenty, Years of Want: France and the Legacy of the Great War* (DeKalb: Northern Illinois University Press, 2013), 78–81; the quotations

from *Jean Barois* (Paris: Gallimard, 1913) are from the English translation by Stuart Gilbert (New York: Viking Press, 1949), 272, 252, 255, 279, 287, 307, 313, 317, 333, 334, 335, 336, 352–53, 354–55, 357.

28. RMdG, *Jean Barois*, 3; RMdG, *Journal*, 1:409, RMdG to Madeleine Martin du Gard, June 17, 1913; 1:428, 430, Valmont to RMdG, November 15, 1913; 1:432, RMdG to Valmont, November 17, 1913; 1:433, RMdG to Coppet, November 18, 1913.

29. RMdG, *Journal*, 1:456, RMdG to Valmont, February 1, 1914; 1:457, Valmont to RMdG, February 2, 1914; 1:460, RMdG to Valmont, February 17, 1914; 1:462, Valmont to RMdG, February 26, 1914; 1:497, Coppet to RMdG, June 21, 1914, RMdG to Coppet, July 6, 1914; RMdG to Valmont, July 14, 1914, Valmont to RMdG, July 19, 1914.

30. RMdG, *Journal*, 1:364, RMdG to Coppet, April 25, 1912; 1:398, journal entry, "La Tolérance!" (Toleration!)

31. RMdG, *Journal*, 1:485, RMdG to Coppet, April 29, 1914, from Sorrento; 1:490, RMdG to Coppet, May 20, 1914, from the steamship Equateur, off Elba; 1:494, journal entry, "Le Mariage" (Marriage).

CHAPTER 2

1. RMdG, *Journal*, 1:525–30, quotations from 1:525, 526, journal entries for July 31, August 1, August 3, 1914; 1:529–30, RMdG to Hélène Martin du Gard, August 10, 1914; 1:532, RMdG to Hélène Martin du Gard, August 13, 1914; both Roger and Marcel held the rank of *maréchal de logis* (sergeant).

2. RMdG, *Journal*, 1:534–58, quotations from 1:540, 541, journal entry for August 30, 1914; 1:543, journal entry for September 4, 1914; 1:545, journal entry for September 7, 1914; 1:547, journal entry for September 9, 1914; 1:555, journal entry for October 2, 1914. For the early battles of the war, see Holger H. Herwig, *The Marne, 1914: The Opening of World War I and the Battle that Changed the World* (New York: Random House, 2009); here and elsewhere, the totals for casualties are approximate because of differences in calculation.

3. RMdG, *Journal*, 1:556–58, 569, 583, quotation from 1:556–58, RMdG to Coppet, October 9, 1914; RMdG, *Correspondance générale*, 2:34, 35, RMdG to Marcel Hébert, November 3, 1914.

4. RMdG, *Journal*, 1:564, 565, 573, quotation from 1:573, journal entry of December 18, 1914; 1:575, 576, RMdG to Hélène Martin du Gard, December 18, 1914; 1:580, RMdG to Hélène Martin du Gard, December 20, 1914; 1:586, RMdG to Hélène Martin du Gard, January 1, 1915. Coppet's money order was for 300 francs, $1,238.00 in 2015. From personal experience during military service, I consider waterproof boots a godsend.

5. RMdG, *Journal*, quotations from 1:669, RMdG to Paul Martin du Gard; 1:645, RMdG to Coppet, July 26, 1915; 1:642, RMdG to Hélène Martin du Gard.

6. RMdG, *Journal*, 1:619–26, quotations from 1:619, RMdG to Hélène Martin du Gard, April 7, 1915; 1:621, RMdG to Hélène Martin du Gard, April 8, 1915; 1:620, RMdG to Albert Foucault, April 8, 1915; 1:622, RMdG to Paul and Madeleine Martin du Gard, April 8, 1915; 1:622, journal entry, April 9, 1915; 1:626, RMdG to Mme Albert Foucault, April 22, 1915.

7. Ernest Hemingway, *Ernest Hemingway: Selected Letters, 1917–1961*, ed. Carlos Baker (New York: Scribner, 1981), 199–201, Hemingway to F. Scott Fitzgerald,

April 20, 1926; RMdG, *Journal*, 1:700, RMdG to Hélène Martin du Gard for the Croix de Guerre; 1:718, journal entry, September 1, 1916, for chef de section; 1:752, journal entry, January 20, 1917, and 1:752, RMdG to Hélène Martin du Gard, January 22, 1917, for adjutant; quotations from 1:627, RMdG to Hélène Martin du Gard, April 22, 1915; 1:638, RMdG to Hélène Martin du Gard, June 10, 1915; 1:635, RMdG to Coppet, May 24, 1915; 1:662, RMdG to Coppet, September 19, 1915.

8. RMdG, *Journal*, 1:683, RMdG to Margaritis, February 18, 1916; 1:707, journal entry July 17, 1916; 1:725, 726, RMdG to Hélène Martin du Gard, October 18, 1916, and November 1, 1916; RMdG, *Correspondance générale*, 2:286, André Fernet to RMdG, April 13, 1916; 2:157, RMdG to Maurice Ray; see also Martin, *Years of Plenty*, 82–83.

9. RMdG, *Journal*, 1:734, RMdG to Hélène Martin du Gard, November 1, 1916, for the poilus; 1:744, 745, journal entry, November 29, 1916, for Montenard; 1:769, RMdG to Margaritis, March 5, 1917, for *Le Feu* (Paris: Flammarion, 1916); 1:751, RMdG to Hélène Martin du Gard, January 14, 1917, mentioning "many letters from Antoinette."

10. RMdG, *Journal*, 1:649, journal entry, "Monday, August 16, to Sunday, August 22"; 1:682, RMdG to Coppet, February 14, 1916; 1:640, RMdG to Hélène Martin du Gard, June 21, 1915; 1:698, journal entry, "May 22, 1916"; 1:658, RMdG to Margaritis, September 7, 1915; for *Le Testament du Père Leleu*, see 1:413–14, RMdG to Valmont, August 30, 1913; 1:415–16, RMdG to Margaritis, September 12, 1913; 1:416–19, RMdG to Coppet, September 12, 1913.

11. RMdG, *Journal*, 1:683, RMdG to Coppet, February 14, 1916; 1:680, RMdG to Christiane Martin du Gard, February 9, 1916; 1:782, 783, 784, RMdG to Hélène Martin du Gard, April 16, 1917; 1:785, Hélène Martin du Gard to RMdG, April 20, 1917; 1:779, Hélène Martin du Gard to RMdG, April 11, 1917.

12. RMdG, *Journal*, 1:821, RMdG to Hélène Martin du Gard, July 19, 1917; 1:758, RMdG to Margaritis, February 17, 1917; 1:754, RMdG to Hélène Martin du Gard, January 27, 1917; 1:778, Coppet to RMdG, April 8, 1917.

13. RMdG, *Journal*, 1:787, 788, 790, RMdG to Coppet, May 8, 1917; 1:790, 791, RMdG to Hélène Martin du Gard, May 8, 1917.

14. RMdG, *Journal*, 1:792–93, Hélène Martin du Gard to RMdG, May 10, 1917; 1:795, RMdG to Hélène Martin du Gard, May 12, 1917.

15. RMdG, *Correspondance générale*, 2:191, RMdG to Ray, August 1, 1917; RMdG, *Journal*, 1:829, RMdG to Coppet, July 31, 1917; 1:863, RMdG to Hélène Martin du Gard, December 18, 1917.

16. See Martin, *Years of Plenty*, 62–66.

17. RMdG, *Correspondance générale*, 2:164, RMdG to Pierre Rain, December 17, 1916; 2:167, RMdG to Henriette Charasson, December 20, 1916; 2:182–83, RMdG to Ray, June 14, 1917; 2:205, RMdG to Ray, November 24, 1917; 2:213, RMdG to Gaston Gallimard, December 25, 1917; 2:231, RMdG to Ray, April 19, 1918; RMdG, *Journal*, 1:837, RMdG to Margaritis, September 10, 1917; 1:858, RMdG to Margaritis, November 22, 1917. On the issues of wartime sentiment, see Nicolas Mariot, *Tous unis dans la tranchée? 1914–1918, les intellectuels rencontrent le peuple* (Paris: Editions du Seuil, 2013).

18. RMdG, *Journal*, 1:899, RMdG to Hélène Martin du Gard, January 25, 1918; 1:864, RMdG to Hélène Martin du Gard, December 24, 1917; RMdG, *Correspondance générale*, 2:247, RMdG to Ray, October 19, 1918.

19. RMdG, *Journal*, 1:846, RMdG to Coppet, October 20, 1917; 1:851, RMdG to Hélène Martin du Gard, November 9, 1917; 1:1057, Margaritis to RMdG, November 8, 1917; 1:852, RMdG to Margaritis, November 10, 1917. Pierre and Noël Margaritis also had two sons, Gilles and Florent.

20. RMdG, *Journal*, 1:983, RMdG to Margaritis, October 13, 1917; 1:990, RMdG to Hélène Martin du Gard; 1:992, Margaritis to RMdG, October 29, 1918; 1:1069, journal entry, "Dossier: La Mort de Pierre Margaritis" (File: The Death of Pierre Magaritis), based on Noël Margaritis to RMdG, November 29, 1918.

21. RMdG, *Journal*, 1:994–99, journal entry, "November 1918: Death of Pierre," quotations from 997, 999; 1:993, RMdG to Madeleine Martin du Gard, November 2, 1918; 1:1001, RMdG to Alfred Brumeau, November 6, 1918.

22. RMdG, *Journal*, 1:1002, RMdG to Hélène Martin du Gard, November 11, 1918; 1:1005, RMdG to Hélène Martin du Gard, November 12, 1918; 1:1007, RMdG to Hélène Martin du Gard, November 26, 1918; 1:009, journal entry, "Anniversaires" (Anniversaries) Of course, the correct date for Pierre Margaritis's death was October 30, 1918.

23. Félix Le Dantec, *Le Conflit: Entretiens philosophiques* (Paris: A. Colin, 1913); Le Dantec, *L'Athéisme* (Paris: E. Flammarion, 1907); Le Dantec, *Le Problème de la mort et la conscience Universelle* (Paris: E. Flammarion, 1917).

24. RMdG, *Journal*, 1:814, RMdG to Hélène Martin du Gard, June 11, 1917; 1:819, RMdG to Margaritis, June 27, 1917.

25. RMdG, *Journal*, 1:238, RMdG to Coppet, February 11, 1908.

26. RMdG, *Journal*, 1:809, RMdG to Hélène Martin du Gard, June 3, 1917; 1:1018, note by Sicard on Hélène's mother, who was born Marie Tournadre de Noaillat; she died March 23, 1919, at the age of fifty-seven; she had four children: a son, Henry, and three daughters, Hélène, Suzanne (Suzon), and Manon. Suzon entered the Dominican convent at Montrouge in October 1918, taking the name Marie du Cénacle.

27. RMdG, *Journal*, 1:970, RMdG to Hélène Martin du Gard, September 27, 1918; 1:901, Hélène Martin du Gard to RMdG, December 1, 1917; 1:915, RMdG to Coppet, May 15, 1918; 1:922, Hélène Martin du Gard to RMdG, May 29, 1918; 1:927, Coppet to RMdG, June 7, 1918.

28. RMdG, *Journal*, 1:938, RMdG to Hélène Martin du Gard, July 10, 1918; 1:939, Hélène Martin du Gard to RMdG, July 13, 1918; 1:941, Hélène Martin du Gard to RMdG, July 29, 1918; 1:943–44, RMdG to Christiane Martin du Gard, August 5, 1918.

29. RMdG, *Journal*, 1:948–49, RMdG to Hélène Martin du Gard, August 20, 1918; 1:949–51, Hélène Martin du Gard to RMdG, August 23, 1918.

30. RMdG, *Journal*, 1:962, RMdG to Hélène Martin du Gard, September 12, 1918; 1:978, RMdG to Suzanne Foucault, October 4, 1918; 1:965, Hélène Martin du Gard to RMdG, September 4, 1918.

31. RMdG, *Journal*, 1:976–77, RMdG to Paul Martin du Gard, October 2, 1918.

32. RMdG, *Journal*, 1:1019–20, RMdG to Hélène Martin du Gard, January 25, 1919.

33. RMdG, *Journal*, 1:1050, RMdG to Marcel Martin du Gard, May 14, 1919.

34. RMdG, *Journal*, 1:1052, RMdG to Hélène Martin du Gard, May 24, 1919; 1:1053, note by Sicard; 1:1053–54, Coppet to RMdG, June 14, 1919.

CHAPTER 3

1. Sophocles, *The Antigone: An English Version*, ed. and trans. Dudley Fitts and Robert Fitzgerald (New York: Harcourt Brace, 1939), l.484; *Holy Bible*, King James Version, Proverbs 16:18.

2. RMdG, *Journal*, 2:18–19, Hélène Martin du Gard to RMdG, July 18, 1919; Hélène's mother died on March 23, 1919; 2:20, journal entry, "July 18, 1919"; 2:62, Hélène Martin du Gard to RMdG, November 18, 1919; 2:63, RMdG to Hélène Martin du Gard, November 19, 1919.

3. RMdG, *Journal*, 2:36, Coppet to RMdG, July 29, 1919.

4. RMdG, *Correspondance générale*, 3:70, RMdG to Verdier, May 16, 1920, for the plan of *Les Thibault*; 3:85, RMdG to Verdier, September 23, 1920, for disappointment at progress; RMdG, *Journal*, 2:118, RMdG to Coppet, April 7, 1920; 2:147, journal entry, "July 18, 1920."

5. RMdG, *Journal*, 2:115, journal entry, "March 22, 1920," for the luncheon with Gide; 2:132, RMdG to Coppet, May 20, 1920; 2:127, Hélène Martin du Gard to RMdG, May 18, 1920; 2:141, journal entry, "June 17, 1920," on Christiane's tonsillectomy; 2:143, journal entry, "June 26, 1920," on Hélène's condition; 2:145, RMdG to Coppet, July 15, 1920.

6. RMdG, *Correspondance générale*, 3:107–8, RMdG to Félix Sartiaux, February 3, 1921; 3:117, RMdG to Georges Duhamel, March 28, 1921; RMdG, *Journal*, 2:189, journal entry, "December 3, 1920"; 2:154, journal entry, "August 21, 1920"; 2:163, journal entry, "August 30, 1920"; 2:202–3, journal entry, "January 18, 1921."

7. RMdG, *Journal*, 2:212–13, journal entry, "February 20, 1921"; 2:217, Hélène Martin du Gard to RMdG, March 11, 1921; 2:227–28, journal entry, "April 11, 1921."

8. RMdG, *Journal*, 2:249–50, journal entry, "July 17, 1921."

9. RMdG, *Journal*, 2:251, journal entry, "July 18, 1921"; 2:253, Coppet to RMdG, June 18, 1921; 2:255, RMdG to Coppet, August 19, 1921; 2:269, Suzanne Foucault to RMdG, October 22, 1921; 2:260–61, journal entry, "September 10, 1921"; 2:277, journal entry, "December 30, 1921."

10. RMdG, *Correspondance générale*, 3:127, RMdG to Gallimard, July 28, 1921; 3:468, Romain Rolland to RMdG, June 10, 1922; 3:177, RMdG to Verdier, August 31, 1922.

11. This verbatim recapitulation of *Les Thibault*, parts 1–2, is taken, with permission, from Martin's *Years of Plenty*, 89–92, the quotations from Roger Martin du Gard, *Les Thibault* (parts 1–6) (Paris: Gallimard, 1922–1929), translated by Stuart Gilbert as *The Thibaults* (New York: Viking Press, 1939), 20, 8, 97, 110, 112, 167, 189, 191, 238.

12. RMdG, *Journal*, 2:289, RMdG to Coppet, February 5, 1922; RMdG, *Correspondance générale*, 3:153, RMdG to Verdier, February 15, 1922.

13. RMdG, *Journal*, 2:218, journal entry, "April 5, 1922"; 2:347, journal entry, "November 25, 1922"; 2:274–75, journal entry, "December 22, 1922."

14. RMdG, *Journal*, 2:1231, RMdG to Coppet, December 21, 1920; 2:294, journal entry, "March 11, 1922"; 2:296, journal entry, "March 14, 1922."

15. RMdG, *Journal*, 2:348, journal entry for "November 28, 1922," for the royalties; 2:315, journal entry, "July 3, 1922."

16. RMdG, *Journal*, 2:298, journal entry, "April 2, 1922"; 2:302, 303, journal entry, "April 21, 1922."

17. RMdG, *Journal*, 2:315, journal entry, "July 3, 1922"; 2:1255, 1256, Hélène Martin du Gard to RMdG, August 20, 1922; 2:323–28, journal entry, "September 1, 1922," about the Pontigny retreat, August 14–24, 1922, with quotations from 327 and 328; 2:333, RMdG to Coppet, September 23, 1922; 2:345, journal entry, "November 3, 1922."

18. RMdG, *Journal*, 2:363, journal entry, "February 6, 1923"; 2:365–66, journal entry, "February 28, 1923"; 2:367, Hélène Martin du Gard to RMdG, March 7, 1923; 2:1261, 1262; Hélène Martin du Gard to RMdG, May 24, 1923; 2:1263, RMdG to Hélène Martin du Gard, May 25, 1923; 2:376, journal entry, "July 26, 1923."

19. This verbatim recapitulation of *Les Thibault*, part 3, is taken, with permission, from Martin's *Years of Plenty*, 92–93, the quotations from Martin du Gard, *The Thibaults*, 263, 334, 341, 404, 419, 455, 456.

20. RMdG, *Journal*, 2:385, journal entry, "September 12, 1923"; 2:395, journal entry, "October 4, 1923"; 2:404, journal entry, "December 23, 1923."

21. RMdG, *Journal*, 2:405, journal entry, "December 31, 1923"; 2:415, journal entry, "April 5, 1924, Mort de mon père"; 2:415–22, journal entry, "June 10, 1924," account of father's death and mother's diagnosis; 2:435, journal entry, "August 10, 1924," no hope for remission; 2:443, journal entry, "September 20, 1924," Hélène's self-sacrifice; 2:437, journal entry, "August 12, 1924," Roger on mother's death; 2:458, journal entry, "December 31, 1924"; 2:461, journal entry, "January 15, 1925"; 2:461, journal entry, "January 18, 1925"; RMdG, *Correspondance générale*, 3:333, RMdG to Berthe Lemarié, September 30, 1924; 3:345, RMdG to Lt. Col. Emile Mayer, December 31, 1924.

22. RMdG, *Journal*, 2:385, journal entry, "August 15, 1923"; 2:440, journal entry, "September 13, 1924"; 2:447, journal entry, "October 15, 1924"; 2:463–64, journal entry, "February 7, 1925."

23. RMdG, *Journal*, 2:389, Carnet d'Hélène (Hélène's Notebook), September 15, 1923; 2:408, Carnet d'Hélène, January 25, 1924; 2:414, journal entry, "March 29, 1924."

24. RMdG, *Journal*, 2:410–11, Coppet to RMdG, February 28, 1924; 2:423, RMdG to Hélène Martin du Gard, April 2, 1924; 2:427, journal entry, "June 22, 1924"; 2:448, journal entry, "November 2, 1924."

25. RMdG, *Journal*, 2:1298–99, RMdG to Coppet, March 5, 1925; 2:499, RMdG to Hélène Martin du Gard, January 20, 1926; 2:499, Hélène Martin du Gard to RMdG, January 21, 1926; 2:516, RMdG to Coppet, April 29, 1926; 2:506, Coppet to RMdG, July 6, 1926; RMdG, *Correspondance générale*, 4:151–52, RMdG to Verdier, April 9, 1927.

26. RMdG, *Journal*, 2:472, journal entry, "March 29, 1925"; 2:476, journal entry, "June 25, 1925."

27. RMdG, *Journal*, 2:478–80, journal entry, "July 10, 1925," discussing letters from Christiane; 2:482, Hélène Martin du Gard to RMdG, July 13, 1925; 2:483–84, Coppet to RMdG, August 16, 1925; 2:486–88, RMdG to Coppet, November 28, 1925; 2:472, journal entry, "March 29, 1925."

28. RMdG, *Journal*, 2:509, journal entry, "June 17, 1926"; 2:551, RMdG to Christiane Martin du Gard, January 19, 1927, quoting her; 2:524, journal entry, "September 8, 1926"; 2:526, RMdG to Coppet, September 9, 1926.

29. RMdG, *Journal*, 2:521, journal entry, "August 7, 1926"; 2:521, Hélène Martin du Gard to RMdG, August 15, 1926; 2:527, journal entry, "October 6, 1926"; 2:529, journal entry, "October 11, 1926"; 2:536, 538, journal entry, "December 26, 1926."

30. RMdG, *Journal*, 2:562, journal entry, "May 17, 1927"; 2:567, Hélène Martin du Gard to RMdG, June 9, 1927; 2:568, RMdG to Hélène Martin du Gard, June (9 or 10), 1927.

31. RMdG, *Correspondance générale*, 3:382, RMdG to Gallimard, May 19, 1925; 4:27, RMdG to Verdier, February 7, 1926; 4:126, RMdG to Verdier, January 18, 1927; 4:204, RMdG to Lucien Maury, September 11, 1927.

CHAPTER 4

1. Edith Hamilton, *Mythology* (New York: Little, Brown, 1940), 44.

2. RMdG, *Journal*, 2:569, journal entry, "July 9, 1927," for "Work"; 2:570, journal entry, "July 12, 1927"; 2:1312–13, RMdG to Hélène Martin du Gard, August 6, 1927, quotation from 1313. Based on the few details available, the original estate was worth approximately 9,000,000 francs ($7,110,000 in 2015), to be divided equally between the two sons. After deductions for taxes and court costs, Roger and Marcel would have had approximately 4,000,000 francs apiece ($3,160,000 in 2015). After purchasing and renovating Le Tertre, and allowing for market declines, RMdG would therefore have had left approximately 2,000,000 francs ($1,580,000 in 2015).

3. RMdG, *Journal*, 2:578, journal entry, "La décade de Pontigny" (The Pontigny Retreat); 2:581, journal entry, "September 29, 1928," for "glacial silence"; 2:582, Carnet d'Hélène, October 10, 1927; 2:593–94, RMdG to Christiane Martin du Gard, November 5, 1927.

4. RMdG, *Journal*, 2:597, journal entry, "November 11, 1927," for Christiane's accident; 2:599, journal entry, "November 23, 1927," and 2:601–2, journal entry, "December 16, 1927," for Hélène's cyst; 2:603, journal entry, "December 25, 1925," for Christmas; 2:622, journal entry, "February 17, 1928," for "Mystery"; 2:623, Carnet d'Hélène, February 28, 1928, for "sweetness of life"; 2:637, journal entry, "May 2, 1928," for "realizing yourself"; 2:651, journal entry, "July 2, 1928," for "false smiles." Abbé Maurice-Antoine Sudour was a highly trained theologian and had befriended Antoine de Saint-Exupéry.

5. RMdG, *Journal*, 2: 662, journal entry, "September 8, 1928: La décade de Pontigny"; 2:664–68, journal entry, "September 9, 1928," quotations from 665, 667, 668.

6. RMdG, *Journal*, 2:671, journal entry, "September 16, 1928," for "Thief"; 2:675, Carnet d'Hélène, October 8, 1928; 2:675–78, journal entry, "October 10, 1928," quotations from 676, 678.

7. RMdG, *Journal*, 2:679, journal entry, "October 14, 1928," for Christiane; 2:682, RMdG to Coppet, October 24, 1928; 2:686, Coppet to RMdG, November 30, 1928; 2:696, journal entry, "December 31, 1928"; 2:697, Carnet d'Hélène, January 6, 1929.

8. RMdG, *Correspondance générale*, 3:382, RMdG to Gallimard, May 19, 1925, for apology; 3:446, RMdG to Robert de Traz, December 22, 1925, for "eclipse"; 4:27, RMdG to Verdier, February 7, 1926, for "great work"; 4:126, RMdG to Verdier,

January 18, 1927, for "push further"; 4:274, RMdG to Mayer, February 14, 1928, for Thibauderie.

9. RMdG, *Correspondance générale*, 4:312, RMdG to Henri Ghéon (the pen name of Henri Vangeon), April 5, 1928; 4:567–69, Ghéon to RMdG, July 13, 1928; 4:357, RMdG to Ghéon, July 16, 1928.

10. This verbatim recapitulation of *Les Thibault*, parts 4, 5, 6, is taken, with permission, from Martin's *Years of Plenty*, 93–95, the quotations from Martin du Gard, *The Thibaults*, 585, 602, 618, 734, 780, 791, 869, 870.

11. RMdG, *Journal*, 2:620, Coppet to RMdG, January 23, 1928; 2:620, journal entry, "February 15, 1928," on Coppet's complaint; 2:635, journal entry, "April 28, 1928," on Coppet as a friend.

12. RMdG, *Journal*, 2:712, journal entry, "May 6, 1929," for Coppet's arrival; 2:707, RMdG to Christiane, May 6, 1929, for Marcel Martin du Gard's marriage; 2:714, journal entry, "May 30, 1929," describing the Verdé-Delisle family as parvenus and canaille; 2:715, journal entry, "June 14, 1929," describing his brother's marriage, the civil ceremony on June 3, and the religious ceremony on June 5. Over time, Roger came to like his sister-in-law, and she became one of his fiercest defenders.

13. RMdG, *Journal*, 2:716, journal entry, "June 14, 1929," for long-term friendship; 2:743, journal entry, "September 15, 1929," for his mistress, Lydie; 2:786, journal entry, "November 2, 1929," for the daughter of Coppet's cousin, Henry; 2:733, Christiane Martin du Gard to RMdG, September 6, 1929; 2:733, Christiane Martin du Gard, September 7, 1929; the subject of the Pontigny retreat was "the success of Classicism."

14. RMdG, *Journal*, 2:734–35, journal entry, "September 11, 1929," for Roger's thoughts; 2:737, journal entry, "September 12, 1929," for Christiane's soliloquy.

15. RMdG, *Journal*, 2:738–39, journal entry, "September 12, 1929."

16. RMdG, *Journal*, 2:739, 742, journal entry, "September 12, 1929"; 2:743, journal entry, "September 15, 1929," for the suitor, whose last name was Oboussier, his first name long forgotten.

17. RMdG, *Journal*, 2:743, journal entry, "September 15, 1929," for Roger on Marcel; 2:748–49, journal entry, "September 20, 1929," for Christiane and double treason; 2:750, journal entry, "September 21, 1929," for Marcel on Roger; 2:752–53, Hélène's indictment; 2:754, RMdG to Hélène Martin du Gard, September 21, 1929, for Roger's reply.

18. RMdG, *Journal*, 2:783, RMdG to Hélène Martin du Gard; 2:785–90, journal entry, "November 2, 1929," quotations from 787 and 790; 2:793–95, journal entry, "November 3, 1929," quotation from 793.

19. RMdG, *Journal*, 2:799, journal entry, "November 10, 1929," quoting Marcel; 2:766, journal entry, "October 8, 1929," quoting Christiane to RMdG, no date but early October 1929; 2:790, journal entry, "November 2, 1929"; 2:804, journal entry, "November 16," quoting Hélène to RMdG, November 9, 1929.

20. RMdG, *Journal*, 2:816, journal entry, "December 14, 1929"; 2:817–18, Christiane Martin du Gard to RMdG, December 13, 1929, quoting Manon Foucault Flicot to Christiane Martin du Gard, December 2, 1929; 2:818, RMdG to Christiane Martin du Gard, December 14, 1929; 2:821, journal entry, "December 19, 1929."

21. RMdG, *Journal*, 2:825, journal entry, "December 27, 1929"; 2:826–27, journal entry, "December 29, 1929," quotations from 827; 2:828–30, journal entry,

"December 30, 1929," quotation from 830; 2:832–34, journal entry, "December 31, 1929," quotations from 832, 833, 834.

22. RMdG, *Correspondance générale*, 4:515, RMdG to Jean Schlumberger, December 2, 1929; 4:517, RMdG to Mayer, undated but early December 1929; 4:525–26, RMdG to Duhamel, December 12, 1929; 4:531, RMdG to Verdier, December 17, 1929; 5:11, RMdG to Emilie Noulet, January 16, 1930; 5:15, RMdG to Ghéon, January 29, 1930; RMdG, *Journal*, 2:844, journal entry, "March 23, 1930."

23. RMdG, *Journal*, 2:843, journal entry, "March 23, 1930"; 2:849–51, journal entry, "May 1, 1930," quotations from 849, 850, 851; 2:854, RMdG to Christiane de Coppet, June 16, 1930.

24. RMdG, *Journal*, 2:853, RMdG to Maria van Rysselberghe, June 14, 1930; 2:860–61, RMdG to Maria van Rysselberghe, June 25, 1930; Roger Martin du Gard, *Confidence africaine* (Paris: Gallimard, 1931), translated by Austryn Wainhouse as *Confidence africaine* (Marlboro, VT: Marlboro Press, 1983).

25. RMdG, *Journal*, 2:857, journal entry, "June 21, 1930," for Christiane's dowry and reductions at Le Tertre; 2:872, journal entry, "October 13, 1930"; RMdG, *Correspondance générale*, 5:117, RMdG to Mayer, October 25, 1930.

26. RMdG, *Journal*, 2:872–74, journal entry, "November 24, 1930," quotation from 874.

27. RMdG, *Correspondance générale*, 5:58, RMdG to Jean Fernet, May 6, 1930; 5:109, RMdG to Eugène Dabit, September 28, 1930; 5:133, RMdG to Maury, December 5, 1930.

28. RMdG, *Correspondance générale*, 5:147, RMdG to Duhamel, January 7, 1931; 5:149, RMdG to Noël Margaritis, January 9, 1931; RMdG, *Journal*, 2:881–86, journal entry, "March 18, 1931."

29. RMdG, *Journal*, 2:886–90, journal entry, "March 18, 1931"; 2:891, journal entry, "March 23, 1931," for "same age"; 2:902–3, journal entry, "July 9, 1931," for Hélène's possible tumor; 2:906, journal entry, "August 10, 1931," for Hélène's operation; RMdG, *Correspondance générale*, 5:216, RMdG to Gilles Margaritis, April 9, 1931, "cold fog"; 5:525, RMdG to Jean-Richard Bloch, April 19, 1931, about Verdier's death on April 2, 1931; 5:260, RMdG to Sartiaux, June 22, 1931; 5:270, RMdG to Berthe Lemarié, July 8, 1931; 5:278, RMdG to Bloch, August 2, 1931, for "terribly afraid."

30. RMdG, *Journal*, 2:890, journal entry, "March 18, 1931," for genesis of *Un taciturne*; 2:902–5, journal entry, "July 9, 1931," for Hélène's assistance; 2:919–21, RMdG to Coppet, December 1, 1931, for details about the rehearsals, production, performance, and reviews; Roger Martin du Gard, *Un taciturne* (Paris: Gallimard, 1932).

31. RMdG, *Journal*, 2:821–22, journal entry, "December 19, 1929," quotation from 822; 2:908, journal entry, "August 18, 1931," for "instincts."

32. RMdG, *Journal*, 2:937–38, journal entry, "January 10, 1932," quotation from 937.

33. RMdG, *Journal*, 2:938–42, journal entry, "January 10, 1932," quotations from 938, 940–41. The changing exchange rate from year to year between the franc and the dollar produces different calculations for the same amount of money. For

example, in 1927, 2,000,000 francs was the equivalent of $1,580,000 in 2015; in 1931, 2,000,000 francs was the equivalent of $1,552,240 in 2015.

CHAPTER 5

1. RMdG, *Journal*, 2:922, journal entry, "December 1, 1931."

2. RMdG, *Journal*, 2:945, Hélène Martin du Gard to Jacques Copeau, January 30, 1932; 2:943–44, journal entry, "January 22, 1932."

3. RMdG, *Journal*, 2:954, journal entry, "April 24, 1932," in Sauveterre; 2:967, journal entry, "July 11, 1932," decision on Rue du Cherche-Midi; 2:976, journal entry, "September 28, 1932," for move to Rue du Dragon; RMdG, *Correspondance générale*, 5:415, RMdG to Schlumberger, May 27, 1932, on "material existence"; 5:435, RMdG to Duhamel, June 25, 1932, on both Rue du Cherche-Midi and Rue du Dragon.

4. RMdG, *Journal*, 2:945–46, journal entry, "February 5, 1932"; 2:950, RMdG to Coppet, March 10, 1932; 2:957, journal entry, "April 24, 1932," for "two years"; RMdG, *Correspondance générale*, 5:433–34, RMdG to Gallimard, June 20, 1932.

5. RMdG, *Journal*, 2:958, journal entry, "April 25, 1932," for decision to write *Vieille France*; 2:991, journal entry, "November 3, 1932, " for dedication; Roger Martin du Gard, *Vieille France* (Paris: Gallimard, 1933), translated by John Russell as *The Postman* (New York: Viking Press, 1955).

6. RMdG, *Journal*, 2:926, journal entry, "December 4, 1931," for "reconcile"; 2:959, journal entry, "April 25, 1932," for "not hesitate"; 2:963–66, journal entry, "June 1, 1932," 963 for "weak at the knees," 966 for Coppet's hair and face; 2:977, journal entry, "September 28, 1932," for "beyond my enduring" and "aging husbands"; RMdG, *Correspondance générale*, 5:479–80, RMdG to Marthe Lamy, October 19, 1932, for "killing four or five."

7. RMdG, *Journal*, 2:1018, journal entry, March 20, 1933, for "Daniel"; 2:1021–22, journal entry, "March 30, 1933," for "curse"; RMdG, *Correspondance générale*, 6:24, RMdG to Maurice Martin du Gard, February 11, 1933, for "mimosa"; 6:20, RMdG to Mme Bergmann (daughter of Lt. Col. Mayer), February 8, 1933, for "Parisian suburb."

8. RMdG, *Journal*, 2:1338, RMdG to Coppet, April 15, 1933, quoting Coppet to RMdG, no date given, for "hardness of heart"; 2:1343, Coppet to RMdG, April 28, 1933.

9. RMdG, *Journal*, 2:1345, Christiane de Coppet to RMdG, May 7, 1933; 2:1347, RMdG to Marcel Martin du Gard, May 10, 1933; 2:1028–29, journal entry, "June 7, 1933."

10. RMdG, *Journal*, 2:1015, journal entry, "March 14, 1933," for negotiations about the screenplay; 2:1034–35, journal entry, "July 16, 1933," for completion of screenplay; 2:1051, RMdG to Marcel Martin du Gard, November 29, 1933, for "strength declines"; 2:1047, journal entry, "October 15, 1933," for Daniel; RMdG, *Correspondance générale*, 6:101, RMdG to Eugène Dabit, July 30, 1933, for payment for screenplay; 6:100, RMdG to Mayer, July 17, 1933, for "not valiant."

11. RMdG, *Journal*, 2:1067–68, journal entry, "March 1, 1934," for royalties and third-class ticket; 2:1069–70, journal entry, "May 1, 1934," for the apartment, number thirty-four of the one hundred apartments at the Grand Palais de Nice, and for cooking; 2:1112, journal entry, "December 28, 1934," for details of their budget; 2:1120,

RMdG to Marcel Martin du Gard, February 1, 1935, for a small loan; RMdG, *Correspondance générale*, 6:315, RMdG to Fernet, November 9, 1934, for "chatelaine"; 6:117, RMdG to Schlumberger, August 24, 1933, for mortgage; 6:223, RMdG to Schlumberger, March 14, 1934, for loan.

12. RMdG, *Correspondance générale*, 6:383–84, RMdG to Lemarié, June 1, 1935, for the taxes, the Jongkind painting, and "not a penny"; 2:393, RMdG to Lemarié, July 6, 1935; 2:395–96, RMdG to Lemarié, July 11, 1935, for acceptance of sale; 2:409, RMdG to Lemarié, August 4, 1935, for commission rejected; 2:428–29, RMdG to Lemarié, September 28, 1935, for the Palizzi painting; RMdG, *Journal*, 2:1137, journal entry, "August 6, 1935," for the tax bill.

13. RMdG, *Correspondance générale*, 6:264, RMdG to Schlumberger, June 14, 1934, for Djibouti assignment; 6:289, RMdG to Mayer, May 24, 1935, Christiane's arrival; RMdG, *Journal*, 2:1106, RMdG to Coppet, November 24, 1934, for "sapped"; 2:1110, Coppet to RMdG, December 12, 1934, for the reply.

14. RMdG, *Journal*, 2:1003, journal entry, "January 1, 1933," for "solitude"; 2:1121, journal entry, "February 16, 1935," for fixation on death; 2:1123, journal entry, "June 22, 1935," for Mme Dalstein, whose first name is now unknown; 2:1076, journal entry, "May 1934," for Hélène to Corsica and Gide to Nice; RMdG, *Correspondance générale*, 6.66, RMdG to Schlumberger, April 25, 1933, for friendship.

15. RMdG, *Journal*, 2:1129–31, journal entry, "May 30, 1935," 1129, for "little Jesus"; 2:1138, journal entry, "August 6, 1935," for "stupid things."

16. RMdG, *Journal*, 2:1145–46, RMdG to Christiane de Coppet, referring to her letter to him, August 27, 1935; 2:1148, RMdG to Christiane de Coppet, September 7, 1935, for "refusing to baptize"; 2:1154, journal entry, "October 15, 1935," referring to Coppet to RMdG, October 11, 1935, for "daring"; 2:1157, Hélène Martin du Gard to RMdG, November 10, 1935; 2:1157–58, Christiane de Coppet to RMdG, November 12, 1935; 2:1161–63, RMdG to Coppet, November 16, 1935, referring to his letter to RMdG, November 13, 1935, for advice.

17. RMdG, *Journal*, 2:952, journal entry, "April 5, 1932," for "paganism"; 2:985, journal entry, "October 24, 1932," for "stupidity"; 2:1033, journal entry, "June 11, 1933," for "principles of 1789"; RMdG, *Correspondance générale*, 5:379, RMdG to Florent Margaritis, March 19, 1932, for "imbeciles"; 6:149, RMdG to Wladimir d'Ormesson, October 30, 1934; 6:158–59, RMdG to d'Ormesson, November 5, 1934; 6:170, RMdG to d'Ormesson, November 27, 1934; Wladimir d'Ormesson, *La Confiance dans l'Allemagne?* (Paris: Gallimard, 1928); 6:374, RMdG to Fernet, May 1, 1935, for "following spring"; 6:419, RMdG to Maurice Martin du Gard, his Catholic and nationalist cousin, for "monster"; 6:425, RMdG to Emilie Noulet, September 4, 1935, for "imposters."

18. RMdG, *Journal*, 2:1065, RMdG to Marcel Martin du Gard, February 11, 1934, for "incalculable"; RMdG, *Correspondance générale*, 6:202, RMdG to Jules Froment, a prominent neurologist, February 18, 1934, for "hours of violence"; 6:206, RMdG to Mayer, February 23, 1934, for "yaw"; 6:207, RMdG to Jean Paulhan, February 25, 1934, for "domain of civil war"; 6:216, RMdG to Raymond Aron, March 10, 1934, for "fourth French Revolution"; 2:1074, RMdG to Christiane de Coppet, April 6, 1934, for "barracks"; 2:1079, RMdG to Coppet, April 29, 1934, for "congratulate."

19. RMdG, *Journal*, 2:1174, RMdG to Coppet, March 16, 1935, for "hung on the radio"; 2:1208, RMdG to Maria van Rysselberghe, November 27, 1936, for "two

dictatorships"; RMdG, *Correspondance générale*, 6:414, RMdG to Mayer, August 14, 1935, for "capitalism is the cause"; 6:510–11, RMdG to Mayer, May 9, 1936, for "French fascism"; 6:567, RMdG to Marcel Lallemand, September 9, 1936, for "anything but war."

20. RMdG, *Journal*, 2:1165, journal entry, "December 28, 1935," for completion; 2:1111, journal entry, "December 28, 1934," for "six or seven hours"; 2:1127, journal entry, "May 17, 1935," for Hélène's judgment; RMdG, *Correspondance générale*, 6:321, RMdG to Sartiaux, November 15, 1934, for "return to the past"; 6:354, RMdG to Gallimard, February 2, 1935, "I assure"; 6:456–57, RMdG to Schlumberger, December 27, 1935, for manuscript; 6:36, RMdG to Pascal Copeau, February 25, 1933, for "leaves."

21. This verbatim recapitulation of *Les Thibault*, part 7, is taken, with permission, from Martin's, *Years of Plenty*, 102–7, the quotations are from Roger Martin du Gard, *L'Été 1914*, published as part 7 of *Les Thibault* in 1936 and translated by Stuart Gilbert as *Summer 1914* (New York: Viking Press, 1940), 26, 69–70, 75, 114, 144, 157, 259, 312, 342, 352, 360, 493, 506, 511–12, 522, 524, 526, 532, 534, 576, 607, 659–60, 670, 678, 703, 718, 756.

22. RMdG, *Journal*, 2:1186, RMdG to Coppet, May 14, 1936, for "prisoner"; 2:1179, journal entry, "May 15, 1936."

23. RMdG, *Journal*, 2:1179–83, journal entry, "May 15, 1936," 1180, for "perjure," 1181 for "louts," and "invective," 1182 for "broken."

24. RMdG, *Journal*, 2:1195, RMdG to Hélène Martin du Gard, August 23, 1936; 2:1196, Hélène Martin du Gard to RMdG; 2:1196, RMdG to Hélène Martin du Gard, August 31, 1936; 2:1196, Hélène Martin du Gard to RMdG, September 5, 1936.

25. RMdG, *Journal*, 2:1192, RMdG to Christiane de Coppet, August 9, 1936; RMdG, *Correspondance générale*, 6:559, RMdG to Mayer, August 13, 1936.

26. RMdG, *Journal*, 2:1210, journal entry, "December 14, 1936."

CHAPTER 6

1. RMdG, *Journal*, 3:4, journal entry, "January 1, 1937," for jetty and suicide; 3:19, journal entry, "February 25, 1937," for "tired of life."

2. RMdG, *Journal*, 3:14–15, RMdG to Christiane de Coppet, February 8, 1937, 14, for "Beneath a certain level," and 15, for the comparison of Roger to Hélène; 2:1205, RMdG to Maria van Rysselberghe, November 22, 1936, for the checks and purchases; 3:19, journal entry, "February 19, 1937," for "fragile" and "rock."

3. RMdG, *Journal*, 3:58, journal entry, "July 10, 1937," for Christiane as "mother hen"; 3:49, journal entry, "July 3, 1937," for Christiane as "queen"; 3:63, journal entry, "July 18, 1937," for Coppet; 3:20, journal entry, "February 27, 1937," for Gide, van Rysselberghe, and Schlumberger.

4. RMdG, *Journal*, 3:22, journal entry, "March 4, 1937," for the arrival of Maria van Rysselberghe; 3:25, journal entry, "March 11, 1937," for Hélène's anger; 3:29, journal entry, "March 15, 1937," for Hélène and Paris.

5. RMdG, *Journal*, 3:23, journal entry, "March 4, 1937," for Schlumberger; 3:1151–52, RMdG to Marcel Martin du Gard, March 12, 1937, for the condition of his marriage.

6. RMdG, *Journal*, 3:31, journal entry, "March 21, 1937," for the departure to Rome; 3:32, journal entry, "April 4, 1937," for sales of *L'Eté 1914*; 3:34, journal entry, "April 13, 1937," for Hélène as a friend; 3:35, journal entry, "April 19," for "monstrous."

7. RMdG, *Journal*, 3:45, journal entry, "June 8, 1937," for the decision to open Le Tertre; 3:46, journal entry, "June 11, 1937," for the arrival of Christiane and her children; 3:46–47, RMdG to Coppet, June 11, 1937; 3:47, journal entry, "June 25, 1937," for "anguish." RMdG, *Correspondance générale*, 7:103, RMdG to Schlumberger, June 7, 1936.

8. RMdG, *Journal*, 3:70, journal entry, "July 24, 1937," for "sort of convent"; 3:75, journal entry, "July 30, 1937," for "domain of the old"; 3:81–91, journal entry, "October 18, 1937," 82, for the Universal Exposition; 83, for Pontigny; 88, for Hélène's reaction; 88, for the literary prize.

9. RMdG, *Journal*, 3:90, journal entry, "October 18, 1937."

10. RMdG, *Correspondance générale*, 7:169, RMdG to Gallimard, October 24, 1937, for departure to Nice; RMdG, *Journal*, 2:1152, journal entry, "September 20, 1935," on desire for privacy; 3:1159, RMdG to Hélène Martin du Gard, November 12, 1937; 3:1158, Hélène Martin du Gard to RMdG, November 11, 1937; 3:1171, Hélène Martin du Gard to RMdG, November 17, 1937; 3:1163, Christiane de Coppet to RMdG, November 13, 1937; 3:1167, Coppet to RMdG, November 15, 1937.

11. RMdG, *Journal*, 3:1162, RMdG to Hélène Martin du Gard, November 13, 1937, for his lack of money; 3:1168–69, Schlumberger to RMdG, November 15, 1937, for suggestions; RMdG, *Correspondance générale*, 7:189, RMdG to Gallimard, November 14, 1937; 7:195, RMdG to Schlumberger, November 15, 1937.

12. RMdG, *Journal*, 3:1160, RMdG to Gide, November 12, 1937; 3:1164, Hélène Martin du Gard to RMdG, November 14, 1937; 3:1170, Gide to RMdG, November 16, 1937.

13. RMdG, *Journal*, 3:1175, RMdG to Hélène Martin du Gard, November 19, 1937, for the Legion of Honor; 3:1172–74, RMdG to Christiane de Coppet, 1173, for the messages and the translations; 1174, for the field and the dog; RMdG, *Correspondance générale*, 7:196–97, RMdG to Per Hallström, permanent secretary of the Swedish Royal Academy, November 16, 1937.

14. RMdG, *Journal*, 3:95–101, journal entry, "Prix Nobel" (Nobel Prize), composed at the beginning of April 1938, quotations from 95, for Jean Marx; 98, for "Italian"; 100, for daggers and smiles; for each couple, the cost of travel was approximately four thousand francs ($2,940 in 2015).

15. Frenz, *Literature 1901–1967*, 341–50, quotations from 347 for Hallström, 350 for Roger; RMdG, *Journal*, 3:102–9, journal entry, "Prix Nobel," composed at the beginning of April 1938, quotation from 107, for Gustaf Adolf.

16. RMdG, *Journal*, 3:107–16, journal entry, "Prix Nobel," composed at the beginning of April 1938.

17. RMdG, *Journal*, 3:117, journal entry, "Prix Nobel," composed at the beginning of April 1938.

18. RMdG, *Journal*, 3:118, journal entry, "Prix Nobel," composed at the beginning of April 1938; 3:1176–77, RMdG to Christiane de Coppet, December 26, 1937; RMdG, *Correspondance générale*, 7:224, RMdG to Mayer, December 31, 1937.

19. RMdG, *Journal*, 3:121–22, "Prix Nobel," composed at the beginning of April 1938, describes the trip to Copenhagen, but the portion of his journal about Berlin,

Dresden, Prague, and Vienna Roger burned on June 24, 1940, as the German invasion of France threatened his arrest; 3:124–26, RMdG to Christiane de Coppet, January 14, 1938, 125, for "madmen"; 3:127, RMdG to Marcel Martin du Gard, January 25, 1938, for Prague and Vienna; 3:131, RMdG to Coppet, February 21, 1938, for the vision of a new war; RMdG, *Correspondance générale*, 7:233, RMdG to Lemarié, January 13, 1938, for "appalling impression."

20. RMdG, *Correspondance générale*, 7:264, RMdG to Noulet, April 2, 1938, "world is insane"; RMdG, *Journal*, 3:141–44, journal entry, "April 16, 1938," quotations from 141 for "shadow," and 142 for "taste for accusation."

21. RMdG, *Correspondance générale*, 7:279, RMdG to Jean Rostand, May 14, 1938, for "tête-à-tête with death"; 7:284, RMdG to Jules and Lise Romains, May 25, 1938, for "go pipi"; RMdG, *Journal*, 3:146, journal entry, "April 16, 1938," for Guadeloupe; 3:146, RMdG to Hélène Martin du Gard, April 19, 1938, for death of Madeleine Gide; 3:151, journal entry, "May 16, 1938," for Hélène's urging and Gide's arrival; 3:152, journal entry, "May 24, 1938," for Gide's comment; 3:156–57, journal entry, "May 28, 1938," for Hélène's return; 3:158, journal entry, "June 11, 1938," for Christiane's arrival.

22. RMdG, *Journal*, 3:159, journal entry, "June 11, 1938," for impossible to work; 3:165, journal entry, "July 19, 1938," for Guadeloupe's death and Hélène's lament; 3:166, journal entry, "July 28, 1938," for the adoption proceedings; 3:167, journal entry, "August 26, 1938," for black horizon; 3:167, journal entry, "September 7, 1938," for Marcel to Dakar; RMdG, *Correspondance générale*, 7:305, RMdG to Anne Heurgon-Desjardins, June 16, 1938, for "greater application"; 7:329, RMdG to Lallemand, September 3, 1938, for "July 1914"; 7:331, RMdG to Lallemand, September 12, 1938, for "Summer 1938."

23. RMdG, *Journal*, 3:176, journal entry, "September 29, 1938," for Mussolini; 3:176, journal entry, "October 4, 1938," for "ashamed"; RMdG, *Correspondance générale*, 7:336, RMdG to Jean Blanzat, a journalist friend of Schlumberger, September 29, 1938, for "immediate danger"; 7:338–39, RMdG to Blanzat, October 8, 1938, for Munich.

24. RMdG, *Journal*, 3:187, journal entry, "November 21, 1938," for Ray; 3:188, journal entry, "November 26, 1938," for Mayer; 3:192–94, journal entry, "November 27, 1938," for Suzon's tuberculosis; 3:192–94, journal entry, "December 21, 1938," for Hélène's sister and father, 193, for Suzon's last words; 3:196, journal entry, "Christmas Day," for Hélène's physical condition; 3:199, journal entry, "January 14, 1939," for Hélène's spirit.

25. RMdG, *Journal*, 3:200, journal entry, "January 27, 1939," for flight and mail; 3:178, journal entry, "October 11, 1938," for the first attacks on Coppet; 3:180, journal entry, "October 17, 1938," for the succeeding attacks on Coppet; 3:184–85, journal entry, "November 1, 1938," for Coppet's reaction; 3:242, RMdG to Maria van Rysselberghe, May 8, 1939, for the reassignment; for the attacks themselves, see *L'Action française*, October 8, 9, 10, 11, 18, 1938, always on the front page; RMdG, *Correspondance générale*, February 6, 1939, RMdG to Elisabeth Herbart, February 6, 1939, for the Literary Guild; 7:449, RMdG to Simon Bussy, June 18, 1939, for "reign over the Malagasy."

26. RMdG, *Journal*, 3:218, RMdG to Christiane de Coppet, March 20, 1939, for conditions on Guadeloupe; 3:219, RMdG to Christiane de Coppet, March 27, 1939, for

"colonial hotel"; 3:228, journal entry, "April 6, 1939," for the villa; 3:243, journal entry, "May 25, 1939," for Hélène's blood pressure; RMdG, *Correspondance générale*, 7:423, RMdG to Félix Bertaux, May 6, 1939, for prospects of war; 7:425, RMdG to Lallemand, May 12, 1939, for Danzig, the Polish Corridor, and "anguish of Europe."

27. RMdG, *Journal*, 3:229, journal entry, "April 7, 1939," for "essentially natural"; 3:231, journal entry, "Easter [April 9, 1939]," for "savagery of the past"; 3:237–38, journal entry, "April 24, 1939," for "discovered"; 3:257, journal entry, "July 10, 1939," for "island."

28. RMdG, *Journal*, 3:244, journal entry, "May 26, 1939," for finished; 3:247–48, journal entry, "June 6, 1939," 247, for "phobia"; 248, for Hélène; RMdG, *Correspondance générale*, 7:433, RMdG to Schlumberger, June 5, 1939, for "whole and complete."

29. This verbatim recapitulation of *Les Thibault*, part 8, is taken, with permission, from Martin's *Years of Plenty*, 110–12, the quotations from Martin du Gard, *Summer 1914*, 785, 789, 844, 845, 875, 901, 902, 918, 954, 922, 931, 995, 929, 986–87, 1004, 1008.

30. RMdG, *Journal*, 3:255, journal entry, "June 27, 1939," and 3:262, journal entry for "July 29, 1939," for the improvement in Hélène's health; 3:263, RMdG to Christiane de Coppet, August 1, 1939, for the cruise plans; 3:267, journal entry, "August 9, 1939"; 3:269, journal entry, "August 15, 1939," and 3:270, journal entry, "August 17, 1939," for the cruise; 3:273–75, RMdG to Christiane de Coppet, August 30, 1939, for the captain's announcement and Roger's unwarranted optimism.

31. RMdG, *Journal*, 3:281, Coppet to RMdG, September 2, 1939.

32. RMdG, *Journal*, 3:282, RMdG to Marcel Martin du Gard, September 8, 1939, for "inconsolable"; 3:283, Hélène Martin du Gard to RMdG, September 10, 1939, for "first ship"; 3:285, RMdG to Hélène Martin du Gard, September 11, 1939, for "thousands, millions"; 3:290, RMdG to Marcel Martin du Gard, September 26, 1939, for "nervous state."

33. RMdG, *Journal*, 3:292–93, RMdG to Schlumberger, October 17, 1939, 293 for "testamentary" instructions; 3:296, RMdG to Marcel Martin du Gard, November 19, 1939, for travel from Martinique to New York and the autograph; 3:297, RMdG to Marcel Martin du Gard, November 21, 1939, for the Conte-di-Savoia.

34. RMdG, *Journal*, 3:301, RMdG to Christiane de Coppet, December 6, 1939, for arrival in Nice; 3:303, RMdG to Hélène Martin du Gard, December 22, 1939, for the puppy and frozen pipes; 3:306, RMdG to Maria van Rysselberghe, December 25, 1939, for the difficulties at Le Tertre; 3:309, RMdG to Hélène Martin du Gard, December 25, 1939, for trunks and cold and puppy.

Chapter 7

1. RMdG, *Journal*, 3:319–21, RMdG to Christiane de Coppet, January 24, 1940, 320, for the cold and Hélène in Nice, 319 for Christiane's discontents, 321 for the new project; 3:309, RMdG to Hélène Martin du Gard, December 25, 1939, for the trunks; 3:311, RMdG to Coppet, January 2, 1940, for Schlumberger; 3:316, RMdG to Maria van Rysselberghe, January 8, 1940, for the possible loss to Editions Gallimard.

2. RMdG, *Correspondance générale*, 8:56, RMdG to André Rousseaux, who wrote the March 2, 1940, review for *Le Figaro littéraire*; 8:69–70, RMdG to Fernand Gabilanez, March 17, 1940, and 8:80, RMdG to Duhamel, March 28, 1940, for reaction

to *Epilogue*; RMdG, *Journal*, 3:326, RMdG to Maria van Rysselberghe, March 8, 1940, for the tone of the reviews; 3:331–32, RMdG to Coppet, 331 for the letters from veterans, 332 for the "countryside around me"; 3:321, RMdG to Maria van Rysselberghe, for "truly sinister"; 3:324, RMdG to Hélène Martin du Gard, for "vitality lessens" and resignation.

3. RMdG, *Journal*, 3:333, RMdG to Hélène Martin du Gard, April 9, 1940, for "energetically"; 3:337, RMdG to Maria van Rysselberghe, May 23, 1940, for Hélène's arm and the refugees; RMdG, *Correspondance générale*, 8:105, RMdG to Dorothy Bussy, May 23, 1940, for "terrifying."

4. RMdG, *Journal*, 3:338, RMdG to Marcel Martin du Gard, June 7, 1940, for "tribulations"; 3:339–42, journal entry, "September 7, 1940," RMdG's account of their flight; RMdG, *Correspondance générale*, 8:111, RMdG to Pierre Herbart, June 14, 1940, for "profound distress."

5. RMdG, *Journal*, 3:342, journal entry, "September 7, 1940," for "appalling conditions" and "depth of despair."

6. RMdG, *Journal*, 3:342–46, journal entry, "September 7, 1940," 345 for "in disgrace"; 3:348, RMdG to Maria van Rysselberghe, July 22, 1940, for "New York"; RMdG, *Correspondance générale*, 8:112, RMdG to Schlumberger, July 22, 1940, for "overturning."

7. RMdG, *Journal*; 3:350, journal entry, "August 12, 1940," for Coppet; 3:351–52, journal entry, "News about Le Tertre"; RMdG, *Correspondance générale*, 8:121, RMdG to Noël Margaritis, August 16, 1940, for "paws"; 8:124–26, RMdG to Florent Margaritis, September 4, 1940, for sources of income.

8. RMdG, *Journal*, 3:354, journal entry, "October 10, 1940," for Henry de Montherlant; 3:361–62, journal entry, "November 9, 1940," for Gide, 361 for "odious," 362 for "abuses"; 3:403, journal entry, "May 16, 1941," for Catherine's avowal; 3:355–56, journal entry, "October 11, 1940," for Claudel.

9. RMdG, *Journal*, 3:367-68, journal entry, "Nice, Noël 1940," for the arrival; 3:371, journal entry, "December 31, 1940," for Daniel as "serious," Annique as "exquisite," and Marcel as "talking too loudly"; 3:391–96, journal entry, "March 29, 1941," 393, for Christiane and chatter, 392 for Daniel as "capricious" and Annique as docile, 395 for Marcel "bitterness"; 3:398, "April 19, 1941," for Hélène's work; RMdG, *Correspondance générale*, 8:157, RMdG to Florent Margaritis, December 27, 1940, for "worn out"; 8:168, RMdG to Heurgon-Desjardins, February 1, 1941, for the ration line.

10. RMdG, *Journal*, 3:367, journal entry, "December 15, 1940," for Munich; 3:370–72, journal entry, "December 31, 1940," 370 for the course of the war, 372 for individualism and America; 3:377, journal entry, "February 2, 1941," for Jean-Paul.

11. RMdG, *Journal*, 3:382–86, journal entry, "February 25, 1941," 384 for "localized infection," 383 for "death by hemorrhage"; 3:388–89, journal entry, "March 23, 1941," 388 for "old man," 389, for "certain days."

12. RMdG, *Journal*, 3:363, journal entry, "November 17, 1940" for "impose itself"; 3:399, journal entry, "May 2, 1941," for the plan of "Maumort."

13. RMdG, *Journal*, 3:401, journal entry, "May 11, 1941," for the planning; 3:409, RMdG to Christiane de Coppet, May 29, 1941, for the final preparations; 3:412–15, journal entry, "June 26, 1941," 412 for colibacillosis, 413 for abundant food, 414 for Maumort.

14. RMdG, *Journal*, 3:415, journal entry, "June 26, 1941," for the German invasion and its implications; 3:373–78, journal entry, "February 2, 1941," 374 for Pétain's character, 373 for his underlings, 378, for Pétain's accomplishments; 3:402, journal entry, "May 11, 1941," for "subjugation" and "liberator"; 3:407-08, journal entry, "May 24, 1941," 407 for "definitively suspect," 408 for his meditation; *La Gerbe* (weekly, published at Vichy), May 20, 1941, p. 7.

15. RMdG, *Journal*, 3:419–20, journal entry, "July 16, 1941," 419 for Maumort's characterization, 420 for the necessity of differentiation; 3:442, RMdG to Christiane de Coppet, October 4, 1941, for "great calm"; RMdG, *Correspondance générale*, 8:237, RMdG to Heurgon-Desjardins, July 25, 1941, for "posthumous."

16. RMdG, *Journal*, 3:421, RMdG to Christiane de Coppet, July 16, 1941, for the conditions and "life had not been so easy"; 3:453, journal entry, "November 5, 1941," for "calm atmosphere"; 3:452, journal entry, "October 28, 1941," for train reservations and frozen toothpaste; 3:453, journal entry, "November 9, 1941," "home from the pole"; RMdG, *Correspondance générale*, 8:255, RMdG to Heurgon-Desjardins, October 5, 1941, for "potatoes"; 8:263, RMdG to Jacques Heurgon, October 27, 1941, for "bundled"; 8:268, RMdG to Heurgon-Desjardins, November 10, 1941, for "marrow" and "paralyzed"; 8:264, RMdG to André Havas, October 28, 1941, for the problem of train reservations.

17. RMdG, *Journal*, 3:458–61, journal entry, "December 31, 1941," 458 for temperature in study; 459–60, for his sense of growing old, 460–61 for the course of the war; 3:493, journal entry, "May 20, 1942," for Roger's weight, from 206 to 169; RMdG, *Correspondance générale*, 8:277, RMdG to Mme Grunebaum-Ballin, December 31, 1941, for "epileptic"; 8:272, RMdG to Heurgon-Desjardins, December 7, 1941, for Hélène to Paris and Pearl Harbor; 8:287.

18. RMdG, *Journal*, 3:463, RMdG to Christiane de Coppet, January 1, 1942, for Roger's plaint; 3:464, journal entry, "January 8, 1942," for Christiane's arrival and appearance; 3:465, journal entry, "January 13, 1942," for Christiane's views; 3:465, journal entry, "January 19, 1942," for Hélène's return; RMdG, *Correspondance générale*, 8:287, RMdG to Heurgon-Desjardins, January 25, 1942, for mumps.

19. RMdG, *Journal*, 3:490–91, journal entry, "April 27, 1942," 491 for "last and ultimate"; RMdG, *Correspondance générale*, 8:297, RMdG to Froment, February 17, 1942, for "crisis of premature aging."

20. RMdG, *Journal*, 3:466, journal entry, "February 18, 1942," for "complete biography"; 3:482, journal entry, "March 17, 1942," for "jugged hare"; RMdG, *Correspondance générale*, 7:43, RMdG to René Lalou, for the Ecole des Chartes; 8:309, RMdG to Pierre Rain, March 23, 1942, for the information about Maumort's school; 8:329, RMdG to Jean Bruller, May 26, 1942, for "anguished world"; 8:321, RMdG to Elisabeth Herbart, May 12, 1942, for arrival in Cap d'Antibes, staying at the Villa Clémence Isaure; 8:327, RMdG to Simon and Dorothy Bussy, May 24, 1942, for "without lines."

21. RMdG, *Journal*, 3:486, journal entry, "April 15, 1942," for "all that I wish"; 3:491, journal entry, "May 15, 1942," for "never be completed."

22. RMdG, *Journal*, 3:495, journal entry, "June 12, 1942," for "characters take shape"; 3:498, journal entry, "July 16, 1942," for the "early childhood"; 3:504, journal entry, "August 18, 1942," for thick stack; 3:503, RMdG to Christiane de Coppet, August

1, 1942, for "alleluia"; 3:515, RMdG to Christiane de Coppet, October 5, 1942, for "stonemason."

23. RMdG, *Journal*, 3:504, journal entry, "August 18, 1942," 3:507, RMdG to Christiane de Coppet, August 20, 1942, and 3:505, Coppet to RMdG, September 9, 1942, for Hélène's trip to Figeac; 3:510–13, journal entry, "September 28, 1942," 510 for "God will have refused," 512 for "more and more indifferent," 513 for "curse"; 3:524, journal entry, "November 2, 1942," for "Hélène does not much like"; 3:520, journal entry, "October 28, 1942," for "Why bother?"

24. RMdG, *Journal*, 3:526-27, journal entry, "November 15, 1942," for Christiane's anxiety; 3:3:547, RMdG to Marcel Martin du Gard, March 1, 1943, for the blood pressure reading; 3:1180, RMdG to Copeau, February 28, 1943, for bitterness flooded; 3:534, journal entry, "December 30, 1942," for "emptiness around her" and "most unhappy"; RMdG, *Correspondance générale*, 8:433, RMdG to Sartiaux, March 20, 1943, for heating fuel; 8:360, RMdG to René Serre, August 1, 1942, for matches; 8: 355, RMdG to Lydia Garnier, undated but July 1942, for shoes.

25. RMdG, *Journal*, 3:545, Christiane de Coppet to RMdG, February 10, 1943, for "S. O. S." and "sad"; 3:542, RMdG to Christiane de Coppet, February 12, 1943, for "suffering in his solitude"; 3:545, Christiane de Coppet to RMdG, undated but likely February 15, 1943, for "fear for my older years"; 3:551, RMdG to Marie-Louise Martin du Gard, March 10, 1943, for Annique, Daniel, and Christiane's "nervous exhaustion"; 3:555, journal entry, "March 16, 1943," for Marcel's dogmatism, Puritanism, and "truth in his pocket," 352 for Christiane and "highly emotional"; 5:559, RMdG to Maria van Rysselberghe, March 21, 1943, for the summing up.

26. RMdG, *Journal*, 565–69, journal entry, "April 8, 1943," 565 for "characters in action," 566 for "reading the script" and new plan, 567 for "slices," 569 for the role of his preparatory work; RMdG, *Correspondance générale*, 8:467–69, RMdG to Jean Morand, May 3, 1943, 467 for "interior vision" and "recent memory," 469 for "imagination no longer."

27. RMdG, *Journal*, 3:598–99, Christiane de Coppet to RMdG, August 21, 1943, for Christiane's trip to Paris and La Bourboule; 3:600, RMdG to Coppet, August 22, 1943, for excuse; 3:602, RMdG to Christiane de Coppet, August 23, 1943, for "delivering yourself to the demons"; 5:606, Christiane de Coppet to RMdG, August 27, 1943, for "impossible"; 3:606-7, Coppet to RMdG, August 30, 1943, for "seeks out difficulties"; 3:608, Coppet to RMdG, August 31, 1943, for "nil"; RMdG to Christiane de Coppet, September 13, 1943, praising her decision to remain in Figeac.

28. RMdG, *Journal*, 3:577, journal entry, "May 15, 1943," for "fatigue"; 5:583, journal entry, "June 28, 1928," for Hélène's accepting the invitation; 3:587, journal entry, "July 20, 1938," for Hélène's new friendship; 3:594–96, journal entry, "August 11, 1943," 594, for "resuscitated" and "too much, perhaps," 595 for "swollen," 596 for "curses of heaven"; 3:612, RMdG to Marcel Martin du Gard, September 26, 1943, for "charming winter."

29. RMdG, *Journal*, 3:589, journal entry, "July 26, 1943," for fall of Mussolini; 3:607, Coppet to RMdG, August 30, 1943, for "think about it!"; 3:609, September 1, 1943, for trunk to Rue du Dragon; 3:617, journal entry, "October 4, 1943," for Gestapo and arrests; 3:614, RMdG to Marcel Martin du Gard, dated only October 1943, for "Aryan"; 3:631, RMdG to Christiane de Coppet, December 2, 1943, for

"world of slaves"; 3:632, journal entry, "December 4, 1943," for "young fanatics"; 3:634, journal entry, "December 8, 1943," for prostatitis.

30. RMdG, *Journal*, 3:593, journal entry, "August 6, 1943," for Maumort and the Germans; 3:609, journal entry, September 1, 1943, for Maumort and St. Cyr; 3:641, journal entry, "December 30, 1943," for "I have renounced nothing."

Chapter 8

1. RMdG, *Journal*, 3:706, journal entry, "October 6, 1944," for the Comité national des écrivains (National Committee of Writers); 3:662, journal entry "April 1945, Belated Note," for the family of Oscar von Wertheimer; Wertheimer died at Auschwitz; 3:672, journal entry, "May 20, 1944, Summary Recapitulation," for the warning from the Resistance; 3:655, journal entry, "February 1, 1944," for Figeac as a refuge; RMdG, *Correspondance générale*, 8:695, RMdG to Pierre Marois, December 7, 1944, for "learn afterward."

2. RMdG, *Journal*, 3:670–73, journal entry, "May 20, 1944, Summary Recapitulation," for leaving Nice and arriving at the Château de Roquefort; 3:673, RMdG to Marie-Louise Martin du Gard, May 25, 1944, for Gogol; 3:691, RMdG to Maria van Rysselberghe, July 19, 1944, for "sixteenth century"; 3:676, journal entry, "June 11, 1944," for the Resistance caves.

3. RMdG, *Journal*, 3:698–99, journal entry, "August 26, 1944," 698, for Hélène's fall and the hospital, 699 for "days"; 3:699, journal entry, "September 15, 1944," for Marcel to Paris.

4. RMdG, *Journal*, 3:1183, RMdG to Christiane de Coppet, January 4, 1944; 3:646–47, journal entry, "January 5, 1944"; 3:1184, Christiane de Coppet to RMdG, January 10, 1944; 3:1185, RMdG to Christiane de Coppet, January 13, 1944, for the origin of these bitter quarrels; 3:700, journal entry, "September 15, 1944," for "no longer the stranger" and "collisions"; 3:712, Christiane de Coppet to RMdG, November 3, 1944, for "no longer" and "marriage"; 3:713, Christiane de Coppet to RMdG, November 5, 1944, for "imbeciles."

5. RMdG, *Journal*, 3:714, RMdG to Christiane de Coppet, November 5, 1944, for "we have lived"; 3:715–16, Christiane de Coppet to RMdG, November 10, 1944, for "neither dowry nor trousseau."

6. RMdG, *Journal*, 3:717–19, RMdG to Christiane de Coppet, November 15, 1944, 717 for "you were not married," 719 for "ready to give you"; 3:721, Christiane de Coppet to RMdG, November 21, 1944, for apology.

7. RMdG, *Journal*, 3:1187, Hélène Martin du Gard to RMdG, March 4, 1944, for "support one another"; 3:1188, RMdG to Hélène Martin du Gard, March 7, 1944, for "sad wisdom."

8. RMdG, *Journal*, 3:686, journal entry, "July 7, 1944," for "most miserable"; 3:696, journal entry, "August 2, 1944," for "without descendants"; 3:701, journal entry, "September 15, 1944," for "forsake."

9. RMdG, *Journal*, 3:724, journal entry, "November 17, 1944"; 3:724, journal entry, "November 27, 1944"; 3:726, journal entry, "December 20, 1944," for the difficulty in obtaining a truck; 3:729, journal entry, "January 15, 1944," for the trip to Nice and "return to civilized life"; 3:702, journal entry, "October 3, 1944," for "while other parts."

10. RMdG, *Correspondance générale*, 9:22, RMdG to Gallimard, January 16, 1945, for Le Tertre, "without courage," and "I do not want"; 9:38, RMdG to Schlumberger, March 3, 1945, for "dishonored"; 8:695, RMdG to Marois, December 7, 1944, for "disposition"; 9:51, RMdG to Schlumberger, March 19, 1945, for Drieu La Rochelle, who committed suicide on March 16; RMdG, *Journal*, 3:746, journal entry, "May 24, 1945," for "serve French letters"; 3:732, RMdG to Marcel Martin du Gard, January 23, 1945, for Maurras; 3:735, RMdG to Gallimard, March 17, 1945, for Drieu La Rochelle.

11. RMdG, *Journal*, 3:441, journal entry, "September 16, 1941," for "indelible shame"; 3:482, journal entry, "March 24, 1942," for "forbidden"; 3:535, journal entry, "December 31, 1942," for justifying Vichy.

12. RMdG, *Journal*, 3:757–62, journal entry, "August 8, 1945," for the trial session, 757, for "unforgettable day," 758 for "courteous detachment," 760 for "canaille," 761 for "nobility"; RMdG, *Correspondance générale*, 9:85, RMdG to Dorothy Bussy, August 4, 1945, for "settling of scores"; 8:643, RMdG to Sartiaux, July 18, 1944, for "taste."

13. RMdG, *Journal*, 3:750–53, journal entry, "July 15, 1945," for Le Tertre, 752 for "recaptured."

14. RMdG, *Journal*, 3:766, journal entry, "October 27, 1945," for "a perfect understanding"; 3:774, Hélène Martin du Gard to RMdG, December 12, 1945, for the bitter griefs; 3:774–75, RMdG to Hélène Martin du Gard, December 16, 1945, for anodyne and frustrated.

15. RMdG, *Correspondance générale*, 9:20–22, RMdG to Gallimard, January 16, 1945, 20 for "getting under way," 22 for "more than ever"; 8:695, RMdG to Marois, December 7, 1944, for "aspiration"; RMdG, *Journal*, 3:691, RMdG to Maria van Rysselberghe, July 19, 1944, for "insanely vast"; 3:723, RMdG to Duhamel, November 14, 1944, for "misanthrope"; 3:741, journal entry, "May 5, 1945," for "so much detail."

16. RMdG, *Journal*, 3:783, 787, journal entry, "January 31, 1947," 787, for the changes to Maumort, "pending the passage," and "a complete revision," 783 for "perceptible."

17. RMdG, *Journal*, 3:789, journal entry, "March 6, 1946," for Hélène's condition; 3:784–86, journal entry, "January 31, 1947," 784 for travel to Paris, 785 for Roger's legs, 786 for "varicose," his pulmonary congestion, and "we will revive"; RMdG, *Correspondance générale*, RMdG to Rougier, December 27, 1946, for the condition of Roger and Hélène as they depart for Nice.

18. RMdG, *Journal*, 3:788, journal entry, "January 31, 1947."

19. RMdG, *Correspondance générale*, 9:457, RMdG to Dorothy Bussy, December 30, 1945, for Marcel's appointment as chief of staff; RMdG, *Journal*, 3:776, journal entry, "December 30, 1945," for the background to Marcel's appointment as chief of staff; 3:788–89, journal entry, "January 31, 1947," 788 for "revenge," 789 for the plans of divorce, and *gougandine*.

20. RMdG, *Journal*, 3:789–93, journal entry, "January 31, 1947," 789 for Roger's warning and attempt to reconcile, 790 for "Oscar Thibault," 791 for "after what they have," 793 for "I can do nothing."

21. RMdG, *Journal*, 3:790, note by Claude Sicard for the uprising in Madagascar; 3:835, journal entry, "February 1948," for the Banque d'Afrique-occidentale; 3:816, journal entry, "May 29, 1947," for Daniel's "measure and perspicacity"; RMdG,

Correspondance générale, 9:477, RMdG to Jean Roudié, February 8, 1948, for Coppet, Madagascar, and the Bank of West Africa.

22. RMdG, *Journal*, 3:803–5, journal entry, "April 10, 1947," 803 for "closeness," 803–4 for "of all the people," 805, for "to supplant"; 3:825, journal entry, "July 14, 1947," for "I suffer"; 3:826, journal entry, "July 15, 1947," for "with Christiane."

23. RMdG, *Journal*, 3:796, journal entry, "March 23, 1947," for "sixty-six"; 3:797–800, journal entry, "March 24, 1947," 797, for "I think," 798 for "civil service and cremation," 792–93, "when you think."

24. RMdG, *Journal*, 3:795, journal entry, "March 16, 1947," for "thankless," and "genealogy"; 3:800–802, journal entry, "April 4, 1947," 800 for the framework of cells, 801 for "to friends," 802 for "single nuance"; 3:828, journal entry, "August 31, 1947," for work on Maumort's childhood; 3:832, journal entry, "November 2, 1947," for "how deeply rooted."

25. RMdG, *Correspondance générale*, 8:448–49, RMdG to Serre, April 10, 1943, and 9:211, RMdG to Justin O'Brien, September 20, 1947, for Albert Camus; RMdG, *Journal*, 3:771, journal entry, "November 8, 1945," for Jean-Paul Sartre; 3:765, journal entry, "August 8, 1945," for André Malraux; 3:770, journal entry, "November 2, 1945," for "old-fashioned"; 3:832, journal entry, "September 15, 1947," for "partisans."

26. RMdG, *Journal*, journal entry, "June 15, 1947," for Jean Benoist-Méchin; RMdG, *Correspondance générale*, 9:193, RMdG to François Mauriac, June 10, 1947, for "your role"; *Le Figaro*, June 12, 1947, 10; on July 30, 1947, the president of the Republic, Vincent Auriol, reduced Benoist-Méchin's sentence from death to twenty years in prison, of which he would serve seven and a half until released on parole in November 1954; for war and occupation literature, see Gisèle Sapiro, *La Guerre des écrivains: 1940–1953* (Paris: Fayard, 1999), translated by Vanessa Doriott Anderson and Dorrit Cohn as *The French Writers' War, 1940–1953* (Durham, NC: Duke University Press, 2014).

27. RMdG, *Correspondance générale*, 9:227, RMdG to Hélène du Bois, January 3, 1948, for conditions in Paris, Hélène's blood pressure, and conditions in Nice; 9:248, Hélène du Bois, April 24, 1948, for Hélène's condition; RMdG, *Journal*, 3:834–35, journal entry, "December 28, 1947," for Christiane's calls.

28. RMdG, *Journal*, 3:850, journal entry, "June 15, 1948."

29. RMdG, *Journal*, 3:462, RMdG to Christiane de Coppet, January 1, 1942, for New Year's Eve dinner; 3:754–57, journal entry, "August 8, 1945," 574 for "millions," 575 for "repent," 576 for "my testament"; 3:851–52, journal entry, "June 15, 1948," 851 for "thin, with bad color" and "good for nothing," 852 for "nothing to anyone"; for the correspondence with Gide, see Roger Martin du Gard, *Oeuvres complètes*, 2 vols. (Paris: Gallimard, 1955), 1: cxxviii, RMdG to Gide, September 23, 1945; 1:cxxxi, RMdG to Gide, February 8, 1947; 1:cxxxii, RMdG to Gide, April 21, 1947; 1:cxxxiii, RMdG to Gide, August 10, 1947; 1:cxxxiv, RMdG to Gide, September 11, 1947; 1:cxxxv–cxxxvi, RMdG to Gide, April 1, 1948.

30. RMdG, *Journal*, 3:860–61, journal entry, "September 15, 1948," 860 for "seven or eight hours," 861 for "if I were to die"; 3:856, journal entry, "July 9, 1948," for "sense myself"; 3:855, RMdG to Marie-Louise Martin du Gard, June 29, 1948, for "finished"; RMdG, *Correspondance générale*, 9:267, RMdG to Henri Chaperon, August 24, 1948, for "left in unfinished."

31. RMdG, *Journal*, 3:845–50, journal entry, "June 15, 1948," 845 for "Coppet hopes," 850 for "mediocre" and "she has made a mess."

32. RMdG, *Journal*, 3:863, RMdG to Coppet, November 17, 1948, for "I shall not hide"; 3:864, RMdG to Maria van Rysselberghe, December 4, 1948, for the Rue Villar-et-de-Joyeuse apartment, the line of credit, and the Rue du Dragon apartment.

33. RMdG, *Journal*, 3:865, Christiane de Coppet to Yvonne de Coppet, December 30, 1948, for "in the eyes of the world"; 3:865, Christiane de Coppet to RMdG, December 27, 1948, for "here I am"; 3:866, RMdG to Marcel Martin du Gard, January 1, 1949, for "never before said."

34. RMdG, *Journal*, 3:856, journal entry, "July 9, 1948," for "interior monologue"; 3:857, journal entry, "July 11, 1948," for "I am waiting."

Chapter 9

1. RMdG, *Journal*, 3:872, journal entry, "January 1949," for "no desire."

2. RMdG, *Journal*, 3:877, journal entry, "April 24, 1949"; 3:881, journal entry, "July 2, 1949," for "state of unbelievable"; RMdG, *Correspondance générale*, 9:305, RMdG to Florent Margaritis, May 12, 1949.

3. RMdG, *Correspondance générale*, 9:308, RMdG to Rain, May 14, 1949, 9:323, RMdG to Mme Félix Sartiaux, July 1, 1949, and 9:327, RMdG to Suzanne Aron, July 16, 1949, for the resolution; RMdG, *Journal*, 3:884, Hélène Martin du Gard to RMdG, July 28, 1949, for "ancient drama"; 3:885, Hélène Martin du Gard to RMdG, August 17, 1949, for "embers that glow"; 3:886, RMdG to Hélène Martin du Gard, August 20, 1949, and 3:888, RMdG to Hélène Martin du Gard, August 26, 1949, for Gide.

4. RMdG, *Journal*, 3:883, journal entry, "July 21, 1949," for "his approval"; 3:886, RMdG to Hélène Martin du Gard, August 20, 1949, for Juan-les-Pins; 3:888, RMdG to Hélène Martin du Gard, August 26, 1949, for "I am attacking"; RMdG, *Oeuvres complètes*, 1:cxli, RMdG to Gide, August 24, 1949, for Roger's new work.

5. RMdG, *Journal*, 3:891–92, journal entry, "December 31, 1949," 892 for "I am completely."

6. RMdG, *Journal*, 3:893–97, journal entry, "December 31, 1949," 893 for "Hélène? What?"

7. RMdG, *Journal*, 3:897–98, journal entry, "December 31, 1949," 897 for "felt the most urgent need," 898 for Hélène's testament; RMdG, *Correspondance générale*, 9:355–56, RMdG to Schlumberger, December 10, 1949, for "her impression"; 9:362, RMdG to Chaperon, January 2, 1950.

8. RMdG, *Correspondance générale*, 9:350, RMdG to Mathilde Joyon, December 2, 1949, for "explain to him"; 9:373, RMdG to Florent Margaritis, February 9, 1950: the mistakes were remarkable for their carelessness, MDCCCVII–MCMIX, instead of the correct MDCCCLXXXVII–MCMXLIX; RMdG, *Journal*, 3:928, RMdG to Auguste Valensin, January 10, 1950, for Valensin's memento and Roger's reaction to it.

9. RMdG, *Journal*, 3:908–10, RMdG to Rougier, February 2, 1950, 909 for "when I think," 910 for "I know perfectly well"; 3:913–14, RMdG to Christiane de Coppet, February 13, 1950, 913–14 for "unbalanced and obsessed," 914 for "spend less time"; 3:916, RMdG to Christiane de Coppet, March 15, 1950, for "don't force"; 3:919, Christiane de Coppet to RMdG, June 8, 1950, for "my DISTRESS."

10. RMdG, *Correspondance générale*, 9:413, RMdG to Rougier, July 28, 1950, for "pell-mell"; 9:410, RMdG to Paul Viguier, July 14, 1950, for "a thousand little"; 9:500, note by Bernard Duchâtelet, editor, for the Masses; RMdG, *Journal*, 3:921, RMdG to

Valensin, July 22, 1950, for "gravedigger"; 3:927, RMdG to Valensin, August 23, 1950, for "purifying flames," "armfuls," and "to be burned."

11. RMdG, *Journal*, 3:933, RMdG to Christiane de Coppet, October 22, 1950, for the early copy; 3:933–34, Christiane de Coppet to RMdG, November 2, 1950, for "solemn and noble"; 3:934–35, RMdG to Christiane de Coppet, November 3, 1950, for "your reaction."

12. Gide died on February 19, 2015, at 10:30 p.m.; RMdG, *Journal*, 3:940, RMdG to Rougier, February 25, 1951, for "exemplary" and the incident during the burial; 3:966–67, Valensin to RMdG, January 5, 1952, for "objective testimony"; Le Figaro, November 27, 1951, for Mauriac; *Le Figaro littéraire*, December 29, 1951, for André Rousseaux, "La Vie posthume d'André Gide"; January 5, 1952, Roger Martin du Gard, "Sur la mort d'André Gide," for "no hint of mystical meaning."

13. RMdG, *Journal*, 3:967, Valensin to RMdG, January 5, 1951, for "your book"; 3:969, RMdG to Schlumberger, February 23, 1952, for "both terrible and true"; RMdG, *Correspondance générale*, 10:50, RMdG to Pierre Herbart, July 15, 1950, for "attributing his incapacity"; Roger Martin du Gard, *Notes sur André Gide (1913–1951)* (Paris: Gallimard, 1951), translated by John Russell as *Recollections of André Gide* (New York: Viking Press, 1953); Pierre Herbart, *A la recherche d'André Gide* (Paris: Gallimard, 1952).

14. RMdG, *Journal*, 3:949, RMdG to Marie-Louise Martin du Gard, July 20, 1951, signing himself "the Commander"; 3:953, RMdG to Valensin, October 21, 1951, for "attacking my roman-fleuve"; 9:955, journal entry, "October 1951"; 3:976, RMdG to Rougier, August 5, 1952, for the return to Le Tertre.

15. RMdG, *Journal*, 3:973–74, Christiane de Coppet to Rougier, July 23, 1952, 973 for "go back to your" and 974 for "he wants to see me as little"; 3:976–77, RMdG to Rougier, August 5, 1952, for "I have put up."

16. RMdG, *Journal*, 3:978, RMdG to Rougier, August 5, 1952, for preoccupation; 3:982, RMdG to Maria van Rysselberghe, August 14, 1952, for "sudden illumination"; RMdG, *Correspondance générale*, 10:501, RMdG to Viguier, August 21, 1952, for "the complete revision"; 10:501, RMdG to Maury, September 4, 1952, for "to demolish everything"; 10:502, RMdG to Rougier, September 16, 1952, for "I must reconstruct."

17. RMdG, *Correspondance générale*, 10:501, RMdG to Viguier, August 21, 1952, for "incoherent meditations"; 10:147, RMdG to Marcel Arland, for influenza; RMdG, *Journal*, 3:988, RMdG to Mauriac, February 18, 1953, for "you are much"; 3:991, RMdG to Rougier, May 8, 1953, for rheumatism, edema, and prostatitis; 3:993, RMdG to Rougier and Valensin, July 11, 1953, for "I would like."

18. RMdG, *Journal*, 3:995, journal entry, "September 1953," for "we spend."

19. Maurice Nadeau, *Le Roman français depuis la guerre* (Paris: Gallimard, 1963), 138–39.

20. RMdG, *Journal*, 3:996, Christiane de Coppet to RMdG, October 6, 1953, for "since this summer"; 3:997, RMdG to Christiane de Coppet, October 10, 1953, for "if I may permit myself"; 3:998–99, RMdG to Rougier, October 12, 1953, 993 for "Mama

would have" and 996 for "Hélène and I"; 3:1001, RMdG to Rougier, October 17, 1953, for "notorious misogyny"; RMdG, *Correspondance générale*, 10:510, RMdG to Viguier, October 16, 1953, for "I have never felt so miserable."

21. RMdG, *Journal*, 3:998, RMdG to Rougier, October 12, 1953, for "dispossessing Christiane" and "to ensure that my archives"; 3:1001, RMdG to Rougier, October 17, 1953, for bar Christiane; 3:1002–4, RMdG to Marie-Louise Martin du Gard, 1003 for "I no longer have the strength" and "she sleeps with him" and "you have arranged," and 1004, "two strangers."

22. RMdG, *Journal*, 3:1015, note card marked "1953," undated but from context, October 1953, which instead of destroying RMdG dated again "1954" and "1955," for "written in the midst."

23. RMdG, *Journal*, 3:1009, RMdG to Coppet, November 8, 1953, for deploring Christiane's conduct; 3:1009–10, Coppet to RMdG, November 13, 1953, 1010 for "I retain"; 3:1017, RMdG to Rougier, December 21, 1953, in reply to her letter and for "what an example!"; 3:1019, "1953: Tolerance," undated but from context December 1953, for "one can be."

24. RMdG, *Journal*, 3:1012, RMdG to Christiane de Coppet, December 1, 1953, for "certain subjects"; 3:1013–14, Christiane de Coppet to RMdG, December 3, 1953, for "I really don't understand"; 3:1021, RMdG to Christiane de Coppet, March 30, 1954, for "don't you understand" and a "tête-à-tête"; 3:1022, RMdG to Maria van Rysselberghe and Pierre Herbart, April 1954, Easter, for "I do not want" and "further offensives"; 3:1025, RMdG to Christiane de Coppet, June 2, 1954, for Ascension Sunday; RMdG, *Correspondance générale*, 10:221, RMdG to Rougier, Christmas Day 1953, for the Christmas visit as a truce.

25. RMdG, *Journal*, 3:1025, RMdG to Henri Calet, June 17, 1954, for the invitation; 3:1026, Calet to RMdG, June 19, 1954, for the acceptance; 3:1027–29, journal entry, "Notes on my meeting with Henri Calet, Monday, June 21, 1953," 1027 for "an old bourgeois," 1028 for "man of compassion," 1028 for "I am old," and 1029 for "if we can part."

26. RMdG, *Journal*, 3:1027, Christiane de Coppet to RMdG, June 19, 1954, for form and supplication; 3:1032, RMdG to Herbart, August 27, 1954, quoting Christiane's letter to Rougier, for "it's simple"; 3:1036, RMdG to Rougier, October 10, 1954, for "pure madness" and "Mama is completely crazy"; 3:1037, RMdG to Christiane de Coppet, October 11, 1954, for "if this letter is yours."

27. RMdG, *Correspondance générale*, 10:248–49, RMdG to Dorothy Bussy, July 16, 1954, for the first recurrence of phlebitis; 10:264, RMdG to Baptiste Joyon, October 19, 1954, for the second attack and for "you must accept"; RMdG, *Journal*, 3:1038, RMdG to Rougier, October 20, 1954, for the story of the chaplain, "If you've come."

28. RMdG, *Journal*, 3:1042–43, RMdG to Rougier, November 27, 1954, 1042 for "a hundred times," and 1043 for "he is gentle"; 3:1044–45, journal entry, "November 28, 1954," 1044 for "to help you finish the year," and "like a 'time bomb,'" and 1045 for "happy surprise," "things that I want," and "I congratulated myself."

29. RMdG, *Journal*, 3:1046, RMdG to Rougier, December 29, 1954, for "perhaps she was expecting"; 3:1047, RMdG to Rougier, December 30, 1954, for "I cannot accept" and "if we meet by accident."

Chapter 10

1. RMdG, *Journal*, 3:1045, RMdG to Rougier, December 1, 1954, quoting Montherlant and for "savored"; 3:1051, RMdG to Rougier, January 17, 1955, for the Pléiade edition.

2. RMdG, *Correspondance générale*, 10:292, RMdG to Jean Heber-Suffrin, May 9, 1955, for "infernal"; 10:307, RMdG to Viguier, August 6, 1955, for the revived infection; 10:302, RMdG to Frans Masereel, June 18, 1955, for "sinister obituary sound"; 10:303–4, RMdG to Rougier, July 7, 1955, for Rougier and Daniel; RMdG, *Journal*, 3:1056, RMdG to Rougier, June 9, 1955, for "alleluia."

3. RMdG, *Journal*, 3:1058, journal entry, "Le Tertre, Summer 1955," for "in the end"; 3:1058–59, RMdG to Schlumberger, September 13, 1955, 1059 for "this autobiography."

4. RMdG, *Oeuvres complètes*, "Souvenirs autobiographiques et littéraires" ("Autobiographical and Literary Memoirs") 1:xli–li, xlviii for "must rest on a solid," xlix for "private and secret nature," li for "it became impossible" and "a certain moral and intellectual."

5. RMdG, *Oeuvres complètes*, "Souvenirs autobiographiques et littéraires," 1: vii–xcii, lxxx, for "express simultaneously," lxiii for "lucid counsel," xcii for "laic successor."

6. RMdG, *Journal*, 3:1058–59, RMdG to Schlumberger, September 13, 1955, 1058, for "you will be shocked"; 3:1059, Schlumberger to RMdG, September 15, 1955; 3:1061, editorial note by Sicard, for the reading with Herbart, Léon Pierre-Quint, and Rougier and for the reaction by RMdG; RMdG, *Oeuvres complètes*, "Souvenirs autobiographiques et littéraires," 1:c–cxlii, c for "the enterprise was not."

7. RMdG, *Oeuvres complètes*, Albert Camus, "Roger Martin du Gard," 1:ix–xxxi, xii for "Jacques and Antoine" and "true hero," xxvii, for "from the moment," and xxx for "the last word"; RMdG, *Correspondance générale*, 10:321, RMdG to Camus, October 15, 1955, for "nine times," and "it enchanted"; *Nouvelle Nouvelle Revue française* 34 (October 1, 1955): 641–71; note that the *Nouvelle Revue française* was banned from 1945 to 1953 for "collaborationism," because Pierre Drieu La Rochelle had been its editor from 1940 to 1945, and took the new name after it was permitted to resume publication in 1953; RMdG, *Journal*, 3:1067, André Malraux to RMdG, February 1, 1956, for "said what ought to be said."

8. RMdG, *Journal*, 3:1064, RMdG to Rougier, October 12, 1955, quoting Christiane for "'you reproach me'" and "'pretty bibelots'"; 3:1068–69, Christiane de Coppet to RMdG, February 11, 1956 (Maria van Rysselberghe's birthday was February 9), 1069 for "you have within you"; 3:1070–71, RMdG to Rougier, April 26, 1956, 1070, for the money to Christiane; 3:1071–72, RMdG to Rougier, April 30, 1956, for Calet and Christiane.

9. RMdG, *Correspondance générale*, 10:531, RMdG to Rougier, April 7, 1956, for prostate cancer and arrangements; 10:532, RMdG to Florent Margaritis, May 15, 1956, for "not at any price"; RMdG, *Journal*, 3:1070–71, RMdG to Rougier, April 26, 1956, for the vertigo and recovery; 3:1071–72, RMdG to Rougier, for the reassurance

of no less than three physicians; 3:1074, RMdG to Roger Froment, May 20, 1956, for the ruse.

10. RMdG, *Correspondance générale*, 10:353, RMdG to Christiane de Coppet, July 14, 1956, for "profoundly distressed"; RMdG to Herbart, July 11, 1956, for "groggy"; RMdG, *Journal*, 3:1074–76, RMdG to Marcel Martin du Gard, July 17, 1956, 1075 for "what a relief" and "for several weeks"; 3:1076, Christiane de Coppet to RMdG, July 18, 1956, for "I thank you"; 3:1077, Christiane de Coppet to RMdG, July 20, 1956, for "I am nothing."

11. RMdG, *Correspondance générale*, 10:359, RMdG to Dorothy Bussy, August 16, 1956, for "fighting constantly"; 10:362–63, RMdG to Schlumberger, September 11, 1956, 362, for "calumnies" and for "shameless gangsters"; RMdG, *Journal*, 3:1077, RMdG to Froment, September 13, 1956, for "more vehement"; 3:1078, Christiane de Coppet to RMdG, October 6, 1956, for "thank you for the deposit"; 3:1078–79, journal entry, "Notes, October 7, 1956," 1078 for "thinking naively" and "she is impossible."

12. RMdG, *Journal*, 3:1079–80, Christiane de Coppet to RMdG, October 11, 1956 (RMdG noted that because the letter arrived on October 11, it must have been misdated and was probably written on October 10), 1079 quoting Christiane, for "inimical toward me" and "terrible rancor," 1080 for "you have killed," "the day when you need me," and "seems to burn"; 3:1081, RMdG to Christiane de Coppet, October 11, 1956, for "knowing how alone" and "I am certain"; 3:1081–83, RMdG to Rougier, October 16, 1956, quoting Christiane's letter, 1081 for "in three years."

13. RMdG, *Journal*, 3:1084, RMdG to Christiane de Coppet, October 16, 1956, for "'coexist' peacefully" and "maintaining prudent"; 3:1085, journal entry, "Definitive Rupture, October 18, 1956," for "letter not"; 3:1086, Daniel de Coppet to RMdG, October 18, 1956, for "my dear Dad"; 3:1087, RMdG to Rougier, October 19, 1956, for "witness"; 3:1088, RMdG to Rougier, October 24, 1956, quoting Christiane, for "so be it" and "polite neutrality."

14. Publius Flavius Vegetius Renatus, *De re militari*, translated by N. P. Milner as *Epitome of Military Science* (Liverpool, Liverpool University Press, 1993), 63, for "igitur qui"; RMdG, *Correspondance générale*, 10:365, RMdG to Herbart, for "these documents must remain."

15. RMdG, *Journal*, 3:837, journal entry, "December 28, 1947"; 3:936, RMdG to Marcel Martin du Gard, December 18, 1950; RMdG, *Correspondance générale*, 10:239, RMdG to Heber-Suffrin, May 10, 1954; 10:531, RMdG to Viguier, March 17, 1956; 10:370–72, RMdG to Rougier, November 15, 1956, 370 for "if war comes," 372 for "with which we could sustain"; 10:375, RMdG to René Agid, December 22, 1956, for "like a big Christmas present."

16. RMdG, *Journal*, 3:1089–90, journal entry, "Note for myself, February 26, 1957," 1090 for "I cannot advise you," and "if Hélène had not died"; 3:1092, RMdG to Daniel de Coppet, February 26, 1957; 3:1092, Christiane de Coppet to RMdG, March 9, 1957, telegram, for "profound nervous"; 3:1092, journal entry, "Reflections, March 9, 1957," for "what good responding"; 3:1093, RMdG to Marcel Martin du Gard, March 19, 1957, for "perhaps paralyzed."

17. RMdG, *Journal*, 3:1094, journal entry, "April 1, 1957," for the letter from Christiane, forwarded to Daniel, and Daniel's summation; 3:1094, RMdG to Christiane de Coppet, April 1, 1957, for the gift and "I embrace you"; 3:1096, RMdG to

Daniel de Coppet, April 20, 1975, quoting Christiane's letter of April 12, 1957, for "'looking after my affairs'" and "'no financial supplement'"; RMdG, *Correspondance générale*, 10:394–95, RMdG to Schlumberger, 395 for "she now appeals."

18. RMdG, *Journal*, 3:1097–98, RMdG to Daniel de Coppet, Easter (April 21) 1957, 1097 for "burglary escapade" and "I do not forget"; 3:1101–2, journal entry, "Reflections, Return to Le Tertre, Pentecost, June 8, 1957," 1101 for "nothing will ever prevent" and "Christiane, the expelled," 1101–2 for "Christiane, held apart by her mother."

19. RMdG, *Journal*, 3:1101–2, journal entry, "Reflections, return to Le Tertre, Pentecost, June 8, 1957"; 3:1102, RMdG to Christiane de Coppet, June 9, 1957, for "scope and gravity" and "you had no right"; 3:1104, RMdG to Rougier, June 14, 1957, for "Monsieur has said"; 3:1100, journal entry, "Request to my physicians, Le Tertre, June 1957," for "if I become gravely"; 3:1105, RMdG to Marcel de Coppet, June 19, 1957, for "I believe that despite"; 3:1106, Marcel de Coppet to RMdG, June 25, 1957, for "your letter brings."

20. RMdG, *Journal*, 3:1095, journal entry, "Reflections on Christiane's trip to Le Tertre, April 20, 1957," for preparing his archives; 3:1099–1100, journal entry, "Reflections and personal plans, May 15, 1957"; 3:1103, RMdG to Rougier, June 11, 1957, for "destroy the key"; 3:1114–15, journal entry, "October 16, 1957," 1114–15 for "two painful hours"; RMdG, *Correspondance générale*, 10:414, RMdG to René Palmiéry, August 28, 1957, for "archive rats."

21. RMdG, *Correspondance générale*, 10:205, RMdG to Pierre Herbart, November 6, 1953, for the trusted friends; André Daspre's introduction to RMdG, *Maumort*, x, for "if I were to disappear now."

22. RMdG, *Correspondance générale*, 10:422, RMdG to Camus, November 9, 1957, for initial congratulations, and 10:447, RMdG to Camus, February 26, 1958, for "the refusal to lie"; 10:456, RMdG to Camus, April 4, 1958, for "we will be side by side" and for the petition, which was published in *L'Express* and *L'Humanité* on April 17, in *Le Monde* on April 18; 10:550, RMdG to Schlumberger, May 22, 1958, for Roger's attitude toward the Fourth Republic and de Gaulle; RMdG, *Journal*, 3:1138, RMdG to Rougier, June 24, 1958, for the committee and Roger's declining to serve because of health; Henri Alleg, *La Question* (Paris: Editions de Minuit, 1958).

23. RMdG, *Journal*, 3:1133, RMdG to Marcel Martin du Gard, April 13, 1958, for "incredible"; 3:1134–35, Marcel Martin du Gard to RMdG, April 1958, for "Martin du Gard"; 3:1117, RMdG to Rougier, December 7, 1957, for "paternal fondness."

24. RMdG, *Journal*, 3:1117–20, RMdG to Froment, December 27, 1957, 118 for the electrocardiogram; 3:1124–25, RMdG to Froment, January 15, 1958, 1125 for "I let everything"; 3:1127–28, journal entry, "1900, 'Happy' Epoque—Nice 1958," 1128 for "people felt"; 3:1128–29, journal entry, "End of the nineteenth century: The Belle Epoque," undated but clearly an addendum to the previous entry, 1128–29 for "naturally, I hated"; 3:1126, journal entry, "State of somnolence and euphoric wakefulness," for "no man's land [written in English] of gentle"; 3:1120, journal entry, "The weariness of approaching death, 1957," for "in the evening"; 3:1121, journal entry, dated only "1957," but by context, an addendum to the previous entry, for "if I have always dreaded."

25. RMdG, *Journal*, 3:1130–32, RMdG to Coppet, March 18, 1958, 1130 for "late, past midnight," 1131 for "that was over" and "but none of that."

26. RMdG, *Journal*, 3:1130–32, RMdG to Coppet, March 18, 1958, 1132 for "having already left"; 3:1132–33, Coppet to RMdG, March 28, 1958, 1132 for "have read and reread" and "the elements of an"; 3:1142–43, RMdG to Coppet, July 31, 1958, 1143 for "before the new tomb."

27. RMdG, *Journal*, 1146–47, reprinting Roger Froment, "Sa Mort. Homage à Roger Martin du Gard," *Nouvelle Revue française* 6 (December 1958): 965–72, 1146 for "I would like," "indifference overtakes," and "I seem to have lost," 1147 for "my pain is upon me."

28. For "Eve," see Charles Péguy, *Oeuvres poétiques complètes* (Paris: Gallimard, 1957), 707–946, the specific stanza from 800; for "Clio: Dialogue de l'histoire et de l'âme païenne," see Charles Péguy, *Oeuvres en prose, 1909–1914* (Paris: Gallimard, 1957), 93–306, the specific line from 227.

29. RMdG, *Journal*, 1:391, journal entry, "Péguy catholique," January 1913, for Péguy the mystical nationalist and Catholic; 2:45–46, journal entry, "September 13, 1919"; 2:60, journal entry, "November 14, 1919," and 2:270, journal entry, "October 28, 1921," for Péguy's Clio; 3:633, RMdG to Maria van Rysselberghe, December 8, 1943, for the remark, "Péguy, for whom I have fond feelings"; 3:1147, journal entry, "Happy those who are dead"; 3:1148, reprinting Robert Kemp, "Près de Dufy, Roger Martin du Gard repose au cimetières de Cimiez," *Les Nouvelles littéraires*, September 4, 1958.

Chapter 11

1. Brébion and Crouse, Translators' Introduction to RMdG, *Maumort*, xxv–xxvi.

2. RMdG, *Maumort*, 2/xxxiii for the dedication; Brébion and Crouse, "Translators' introduction," xxvi–xxvii, for Rougier and Daspre. Citations from the novel, from its introduction, and from the scholarly apparatus are given for both the French and English versions, in that order.

3. Daspre, "Sur la genèse du roman," in RMdG, *Maumort*, xxxi–lv.

4. Brébion and Crouse, Translators' Introduction, xx, xxvi.

5. Benjamin Franklin Martin, "Unfinished Masterpiece: New Translation Brings Final Work of French Writer to American Audiences," *Baton Rouge Advocate*, January 23, 2000, *Sunday Magazine*, p. 3.

6. RMdG, *Maumort*, 1020/751, for "rough. An old soldier"; 30/26 for "reserved for the rare"; 30–31/26 for "this intuitive conviction."

7. RMdG, *Maumort*, 22/20 for "it was probably."

8. RMdG, *Maumort*, 117/90 for "it is to Guy"; 120–21/93 for "imagination was his"; 122/94 for "Old Punch"; 141/107 for "his destiny as a failure"; 152/115 for "conquer"; 209/157, 1106–14 for Saint-Léonard.

9. RMdG, *Maumort*, 235/176 for "Goethe always"; 240/180 for "taught me to bend"; 288/215 for "began taking an interest"; 100/77 for "the primordial role."

10. RMdG, *Maumort*, 294–95/221 for "I went straight"; 304/228 for "he had arrived at the"; 295/222 for "reason enough."

11. RMdG, *Maumort*, 312/234 for "talked his books"; 349/260 for "protecting his solitude"; 340/254 for "thanks, my good man."

12. RMdG, *Maumort*, 247/331 for "more essential" and "he gave me faith"; 356/266 for "Catholic faith"; 357/266 for "the dregs of the populace"; 359/267 for "had completely changed atmospheres"; 360/269 for "God the dreadful blow."

13. RMdG, *Maumort*, 365/272–73 for "that enlightened, liberal"; 368/275–76 for "that upper level"; 371/278 for "disgruntled folk."

14. RMdG, *Maumort*, 402–3/302 for "you know"; 405/304 for "enough about genius"; 417–18/312 for "criticized everything"; 419–20/314 for "diabolical ingenuity"; 490/368 for "my nights are simply"; 423–91/316–68 for the account of Xavier and the drowning.

15. RMdG, *Maumort*, 502/377 for "through veiled hints"; 504/378 for "girls of the Latin Quarter"; 504–5/378 for "to go to bed with one"; 528/394 for "silly and utterly devoid"; 530–31/396 for "what I loved."

16. RMdG, *Maumort*, 595/443 for "although one may know"; 597/445 for "to separate lovemaking"; 603/449 for "their faults and virtues"; 604/450 for "the girls."

17. RMdG, *Maumort*, 494/371 for "deep duality"; 495/371–72 for "neither an officer"; 545/407 for "a supremely discreet elegance"; 566–68/422–23 for "where there was no spare time"; 625–26/467 for "an atmosphere."

18. RMdG, *Maumort*, 626/468 for "tortured relationship"; 629/470 for "her Nordic fairness"; 630/471 for "she was always easy to live with" and "headstrong, unswerving."

19. RMdG, *Maumort*, 634/473 for "months of separation"; 634/474 for "family yoke"; 635/474 for "bloom and be happy" and "the trials"; 636/475 for "we never loved"; 642–43/479 for "I shall take to my grave."

20. RMdG, *Maumort*, 646/482 for "exceptional intimacy"; 645/482 for "those two years" and "dearest dream"; 644/481 for "deep-seated communion."

21. RMdG, *Maumort*, 650/485 for "certainly remarkable"; 659/491 for "of disappointment and perhaps of pique"; 659/492 for "tremendous joy."

22. RMdG, *Maumort*, 667/498 for "with a lighter heart"; 669/499 for "the young lady"; 671/501 for "a sort of" and "concerned with what"; 673/502 for "fruit of some" and "an act of revolt."

23. RMdG, *Maumort*, 676/504 for "beautiful clear-sightedness" and "she was no longer"; 677/504 for "grown" and "thickened"; 679/506 for "my sister had recovered."

24. RMdG, *Maumort*, 692/516 for "the brigadier general."

25. RMdG, *Maumort*, 695/517 for "bars of soap" and "to be given"; 695/518 for "an obscure desire."

26. RMdG, *Maumort*, 708/531, for "a way to live"; 707/531 for "disciplined, full of abnegation"; 708/531 for "his homeland"; 520–21 for background on Hubert Lyautey.

27. RMdG, *Maumort*, 702/527 for "he never let himself"; 703/528 for "implementer only"; 704/529 for "the aim was not."

28. RMdG, *Maumort*, 707/531 for "took part"; 713/535 for "I cultivated"; 714/535 for "fraternity of arms"; 715/537 for "part of the 'family'"; 1051, for "personally, I have" and "my rare."

29. RMdG, *Maumort*, 6–7/6 for the Great War.

30. RMdG, *Maumort*, 7/6, "he is alone"; 719/543 for "inferiority," "insufficiency," and "conventional notions."

31. RMdG, *Maumort*, 722/545, for "the wealthiest"; 724/546 for "if I were you."

32. RMdG, *Maumort*, 729/550 for "a flood of impotent"; 734/554 for "like a wounded beast."

33. RMdG, *Maumort*, 739–40/560 for "for us, liberty is not"; 742/562 for "a few injustices"; 756/570 for "is by virtue"; 762/575 for "German hegemony"; 764/577 for "all the injustices of history."

34. RMdG, *Maumort*, 774–75/584 for "the extinction of the weak"; 775/584 for "the whole effort"; 772/583 for "in France"; 776/585 for "you know the comment."

35. RMdG, *Maumort*, 734/554 for "free of its locusts"; 790–92/596–97 for "an irreparable error."

36. RMdG, *Maumort*, 1243–46 for the description of Bertrand, 1243 for "an old Punchinello"; 822–28/621–25 for the damage and repairs; 810/612 for "a mucky mess."

37. RMdG, *Maumort*, 836/631 for "mediocrity, even a certain"; 845/637 for "like it or not"; 850–51/641–42 for "what have I been"; 843–44/636 for "tomorrow no longer."

38. RMdG, *Maumort*, 647 for the Brébion and Crouse supposition; 8/7 for the outline of the novel placing Bertrand's death in 1950; 801/603 for "I have known painful griefs"; 803/605 for "he prepares his suicide."

39. RMdG, *Maumort*, 1076 for Daspre on Le Saillant; 1180 for Daspre on the Rue Saint-Guillaume, 1213 for Daspre on the Pontbrun manor; 1204–05 for Daspre on Claire Saint Gall; 1149–50, for Daspre on Xavier de Balcourt; 1193–95 for Daspre on Martin du Gard and racism; 1133 for Daspre on Desjardins; 1228–29 for Daspre on Bocca and Rose; 1222–23 for Daspre on Lt. Col. Emile Mayer (1851–1938).

40. RMdG, *Correspondance générale*, 4:406, RMdG to Sartiaux, November 27, 1928.

41. RMdG, *Maumort*, 1003/741 for "the most crucial"; 872/659 for "fundamental tendency"; 874/660 for "self-centered" and "with a minimum of inner"; 994/735 for "all agreement"; 951/708 for "the best of marriages"; 1000/739 for "I was only at ease."

42. RMdG, *Maumort*, 1038–39/763 for "one has to accept"; 1046/768 for "the contradiction."

Index